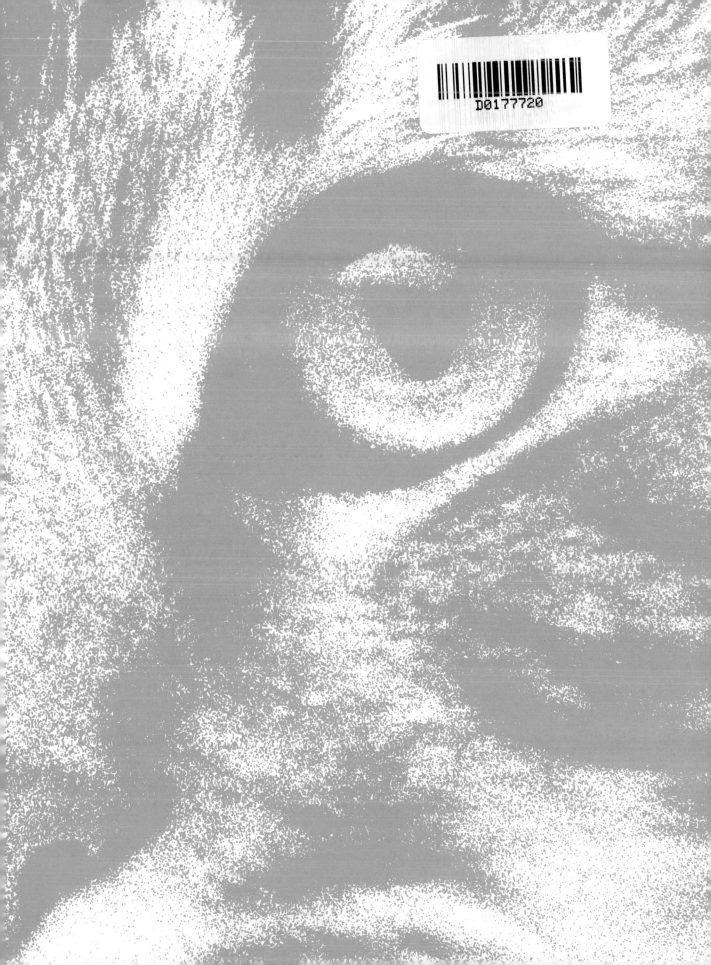

RSPCA

COMPLETE
CAT CARE
MANUAL

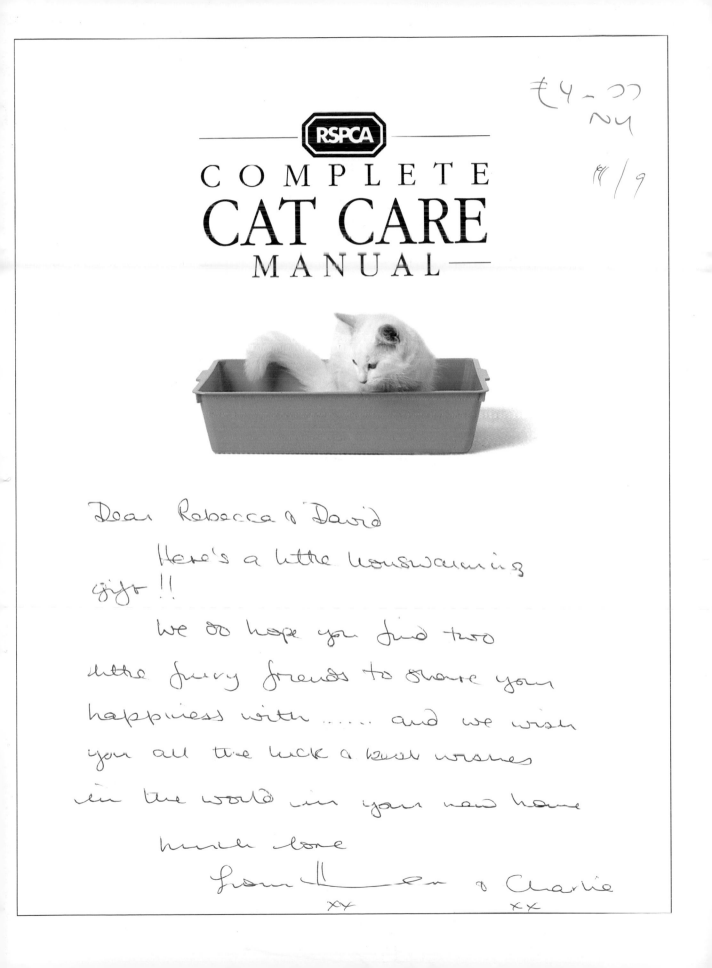

Dear Rebecca & David

Here's a little housewarming
gift !!

We so hope you find two
little furry friends to share your
happiness with ...... and we wish
you all the luck & best wishes
in the world in your new home
much love
from _____ & Charlie
xx   xx

RSPCA

COMPLETE CAT CARE MANUAL

ANDREW EDNEY
BVetMed, MRCVS

DORLING KINDERSLEY

LONDON • NEW YORK • SYDNEY • MOSCOW

http://www.dk.com

The RSPCA and Cat Care

The RSPCA is a charity, founded in 1824 to promote kindness and prevent cruelty to animals. The Society's work with pet animals is often what comes first to mind. But it is just as concerned about helping wildlife, farm animals, and those used for research purposes. In short, the RSPCA cares about all animals. The Society carries out its law enforcement work with a force of 300 uniformed inspectors stationed throughout England and Wales. It also maintains a nationwide network of animal homes, hospitals, welfare centres, and clinics. Many of these are run by voluntary workers belonging to the 207 branches that are the backbone of the Society. Education has always been an important part of the RSPCA's work, and a major focus is teaching people about the responsibilities involved in keeping an animal. Many of the problems with which it deals are caused by thoughtless or irresponsible pet owners.

This manual provides invaluable information about one of the most popular household pets – cats. It is essential reading for any existing or would-be cat owner. Cats make some of the most rewarding pets. But they are also among the most abused. The RSPCA rescues thousands of neglected cats every year. Much suffering could be prevented if people only took the trouble to find out how to look after a pet properly. Reading this manual will give you an insight into what makes your cat tick, and how to care for its needs. Understanding how to look after an animal is the key to a well-kept and contented pet.

Terence Bate
Assistant Chief Veterinary Officer, Small Animals

A DORLING KINDERSLEY BOOK

www.dk.com

Project Editor Alison Melvin
Art Editor Lee Griffiths
Managing Editor Krystyna Mayer
Managing Art Editor Derek Coombes
Photography Steve Gorton and Tim Ridley
Production Controller Antony Heller

First published in Great Britain in 1992
by Dorling Kindersley Limited,
9 Henrietta Street, London WC2E 8PS

11 13 15 17 19 20 18 16 14 12

A CIP catalogue record for this book is available from the British Library
ISBN 0-86318-856-7
Reproduced by Pica, Singapore
Printed and bound by Graphicom in Italy
D.L. TO: 1538-1997

CONTENTS

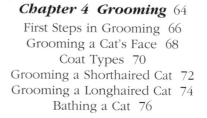

INTRODUCTION

GLORIFIED OR REVILED, feared hunter or trusted friend, the cat has shared the life of mankind in a variety of ways. The fortunes of the cat have gone up and down throughout its association with man, yet it has survived to become one of the world's most popular pets.

Cats are even beginning to overtake their greatest rival, the dog, for man's affections. In Great Britain alone there are 6.9 million cats, and in some European countries, such as Austria and Switzerland, they already outnumber dogs. What, then, is the powerful appeal of the cat? For a start, cats are quite extraordinary animals. Even people who do not really like them will concede that they are beautiful, elegant, and wondrously athletic creatures. Most people, however, feel much more than admiration or respect for them, especially if they have formed a bond with a cat of their own.

It is the companionship we share with our cats that brings such wonderful rewards, and if we are fortunate enough to observe more than one in the household, the marvellous social activity between them is a bonus. Even dogs can be included in this complex interplay, since it is quite wrong to assume that dogs and cats cannot live happily together in the same household. Provided the behavioural characteristics of each species are understood, there can be many a harmonious mixture.

Lions and Tigers in Your Home

You only have to visit a safari park or zoo to see how much big cats like lions, tigers, and leopards resemble the domestic pet that sleeps by your fireside (or, perhaps, on your bed). Apart from the obvious differences in coat markings and size, the similarities are uncanny. In addition to its body shape, your domestic cat shares similar types of behaviour with its larger relatives. At rest, all felines stretch and doze but remain constantly alert to the tiniest noise or movement. Feeding and washing are the same in all species, and the clear gaze is equally arresting in domestic cats as in wild ones. All felines spend a good deal of their time seemingly doing very little, but can be galvanized into action in a moment. They make it clear when they are angry or frightened, and purr when they are contented. This link with the wild helps to explain why so many people around the world find the domestic cat so fascinating.

It is only during the last few thousand years that the cat has become domesticated, developing from small, wild ancestors that first roamed the Earth about 12 million years ago. Even before then, the larger cats, such as lions, tigers, and leopards, were developing from a few prototypes, while other members of the cat family branched in a different direction to become specialist hunters like the cheetah, or small, forest-dwelling felines like ocelots and margay.

The Ups and Downs of Cats

As people moved around the world, so the cat went with them. The earliest signs of domestication were probably seen in the Middle East. The Ancient Egyptians were the first civilization to realize the cats's potential as a vermin hunter, who protected the corn supplies on which their lives depended. It is not surprising, then, that this reliance turned to worship. The cat became a deity in Ancient Egypt and was almost as well loved as it is today. Although it is not regarded as a deity anymore, worship has been replaced with a caring, loving relationship with present day owners.

Having enjoyed many years of great favour, it was perhaps inevitable that fortune should turn against the cat for a black period in its history. In the fifteenth and sixteenth centuries, human ignorance and bigotry were directed at anything that could be blamed for the world's ills, and just as the Ancient Egyptians looked upon the cat as an expression of divinity, religious groups in Europe encouraged a phase of fierce anti-cat feeling, resulting in the cat being seen as an agent of the devil.

This period eventually passed, however, and the elegance, grace, beauty, dazzling feats of acrobatics, engaging personality, and inestimable value of the cat as a companion were finally recognized.

Essential Care

Deciding to add a cat to your household should not be taken lightly if you and your pet are to be happy together. Therefore, it is essential that you know exactly how to care for a cat; from choosing a healthy kitten, to breeding and house training. A major section of this book covers all the varied aspects of day-to-day cat care. Becoming a cat owner is a serious business, and this chapter gives advice on what to look for when choosing your pet, as well as on basic equipment such as cat collars and containers for travelling.

Once you have chosen your cat, you must gain its confidence and learn how to handle it properly, as well as training it in acceptable household behaviour, and to respond to basic discipline. This chapter therefore gives advice on training, and also explains why your cat behaves in the ways it does.

Nutrition and Health Care

A cat is a carnivore with very specific nutritional needs, and the information in this book makes the basics of its dietary and medicinal requirements as comprehensive and as readable as possible. All cat owners need some guidance

on how to recognize problems with their pets and what action to take when something is not right. The health care section deals with everyday problems such as ear mites, worms, and fleas, as well as emergency first-aid treatments and serious illnesses. Owners are also advised how to nurse a sick cat, but in all cases, are urged to consult their local veterinary practice for help and guidance.

Breeding is extensively covered in a special section, with advice on planning a litter, helping your cat give birth, and caring for young kittens. There is even information on how different genes are passed on to give your cat certain characteristics.

Showing Off Your Cat

You may want to enter your cat in shows. Even if you do not, grooming is still an essential part of everyday feline care, especially for longhaired cats. The chapter on grooming describes how various types of feline coat should be groomed, and how to bathe your pet and care for its teeth and claws. Special grooming for a cat show is also included, along with information on how a pedigree cat is judged.

Finding Out More

If you experience difficulty with any of the feline terms used in the book, the glossary should put you straight. Lastly, there is a short section on how to find out more from the various feline organizations, as well as suggestions for further reading. Once you begin learning about your cat, you might never want to stop!

Chapter 1

INTRODUCING THE CAT

CATS ARE always enigmatic and enchanting; a source of fascination for mankind throughout history. The cat has been worshipped and persecuted in turn, but it is now in the ascendant again. Cats are perfectly suited to the urban lifestyle of twentieth-century society. Whether pedigree or ordinary moggy, they make attractive, rewarding, and relatively easy-to-care-for pets. Cats can survive and thrive in any environment. Indispensable companions to people of all ages and nationalities, they are chameleon characters; fearless hunters one moment, and purring comforters the next.

THE FIRST DOMESTIC CATS

Even though its ancestors walked the Earth over 12 million years ago, it has only been about 4,000 years since the cat was domesticated. The Ancient Egyptians first used cats to control vermin in their grain stores, but there is evidence of wild cats sharing human caves and villages long before that.

In Egypt, the cat was revered as a hunter and it became deified as an incarnation of the goddess Bastet. Other ancient civilizations later began to domesticate the cat, and Phoenician traders took tame felines to Italy, from where they spread slowly across Europe. Eventually, they even migrated to the New World with the Pilgrim Fathers. Despite a period of persecution in the Middle Ages when cats were associated with the devil, by the eighteenth century cats had become popular as household pets and had spread all over the world.

Vermin hunter
A 13th-century manuscript shows cats in their traditional role as killers of vermin. The first domestic cats had to earn their keep by destroying pests to protect stores of food.

Cat goddess
A bronze statue of the Egyptian cat goddess Bastet, from around 600 BC.

Good against evil
An Egyptian wall painting dating from around 1500 BC shows the sun god Ra as a cat slaying Apep, the serpent of darkness.

Eastern feline (above)
The domestic cat probably reached India before spreading to China or Japan. This Indian painting dates from around 1810.

ANCESTORS OF THE DOMESTIC CAT

The cats we know today, from lions and tigers to household pets, are descended from early carnivores called the miacids, which themselves evolved from the first carnivorous mammals, the creodonts. While some miacids became lions, tigers, and cheetahs, Martelli's wild cat (*Felis lunensis*) is thought to have been a direct ancestor of all modern small cats. It gave rise to the modern wild cat (*Felis sylvestris*), which developed into three main types: the European wild cat, the African wild cat, and the Asiatic desert cat. The domestic cat (*Felis catus*) is thought to have evolved from the African wild cat.

African wild cat
The African wild cat is the most likely ancestor of the domestic cat. It has tabby markings.

European wild cat
This may have added genes to the domestic cat by interbreeding.

Jungle cat (*left*)
Kept in Ancient Egypt, but probably not related to modern cats

THE SPREAD OF THE DOMESTIC CAT

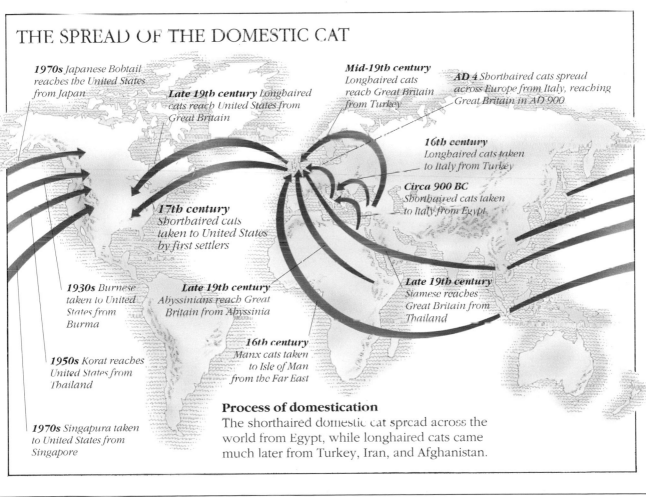

1970s *Japanese Bobtail reaches the United States from Japan*

Late 19th century *Longhaired cats reach United States from Great Britain*

Mid-19th century *Longhaired cats reach Great Britain from Turkey*

AD 4 *Shorthaired cats spread across Europe from Italy, reaching Great Britain in AD 900*

16th century *Longhaired cats taken to Italy from Turkey*

Circa 900 BC *Shorthaired cats taken to Italy from Egypt*

17th century *Shorthaired cats taken to United States by first settlers*

1930s *Burnese taken to United States from Burma*

Late 19th century *Abyssinians reach Great Britain from Abyssinia*

Late 19th century *Siamese reaches Great Britain from Thailand*

1950s *Korat reaches United States from Thailand*

16th century *Manx cats taken to Isle of Man from the Far East*

1970s *Singapura taken to United States from Singapore*

Process of domestication
The shorthaired domestic cat spread across the world from Egypt, while longhaired cats came much later from Turkey, Iran, and Afghanistan.

THE FELINE SENSES

The senses of the domestic cat, like those of its wild relatives, are designed for the purpose of stalking and killing prey. Its sense organs are those of a predator, and it can detect the slightest movement and the faintest sound. A cat's hearing, sight, touch, and smell are far more acute than in humans and most other mammals. It can see in the dimmest of lights; it can detect very high-pitched noises; and it can even taste certain smells by using the Jacobson's organ in the roof of its mouth. A cat is highly sensitive to its surroundings and will thrive under the right conditions, but it may not do so well in a home where its needs are not taken into consideration. Small children and cats do not mix, since felines dislike loud noises and sudden movements.

THE FIVE SENSES

The mouth and taste

A cat has a discriminating sense of taste. Giving a cat medicine by mixing it with its food can prove difficult, since a cat can usually detect any additions to its food bowl. Unlike dogs, cats do not have a sweet tooth, but some pampered pets do develop a liking for cake and fruit.

The ears and hearing

A cat's hearing is very acute, and it can hear high-frequency sounds up to two octaves higher than a human. A cat can usually be trained to recognize and respond to certain words, such as its name, by the tone of voice used.

The whiskers and touch

The whiskers act as antennae and help the cat to avoid objects in dim light. A cat is extremely touch-sensitive, and each individual hair on its body is responsive to the slightest vibration.

The nose and smell

All cats are territorial and mark their territory with scent to warn off other felines. A cat's sense of smell is enhanced by the Jacobson's organ, which enables a cat to analyze intriguing scents by tasting the molecules on the back of its tongue. This is called "flehming".

The eyes and sight

Although a cat has poor colour vision, its eyes are designed to make use of any available light so that it can see in extremely dim conditions. Its sight is that of a hunter, and it possesses a far wider angle of view than a human, which allows it to detect tiny movements of prey animals.

CATS AND CATNIP

The smell of catnip or catmint (*Nepeta cataria*) is irresistible to most, but not all, cats. Many cats react to the plant by sniffing it, rubbing their heads in it, rolling around in a trance-like state on their backs, and purring loudly. The effects of catnip are short-lived and it is not thought to be addictive or to cause any unpleasant after-effects. Another plant, valerian, produces similar effects.

Sniffing catnip (*left*)
A cat sniffs the scent of dried catnip for a few seconds before it takes effect. Some cats are not susceptible to the plant and may show no visible signs.

Typical behaviour
More than 50 per cent of cats respond to catnip by getting very excited and rolling around ecstatically.

MOVEMENT AND BALANCE

The cat is a hunter and predator, and needs to be quick on its feet and extremely agile. Its body is specifically designed for maximum speed from minimum effort. Most of the time a cat conserves its energy, but when it needs to, it is capable of sprinting very fast. A cat can travel at a top speed of approximately 48 km (30 miles) per hour over a short distance, enabling it to pounce on its prey before it can escape. Whereas most animals have to spend much of their lives on the ground, a cat has enviable coordination for climbing, jumping, and balancing.

FELINE COORDINATION

Jumping

All cats are superb athletes and can perform an amazing repertoire of vertical, horizontal, and twisting leaps. A cat can jump up to five times its own height in a single bound. Its strong hind-leg muscles and flexible spine enable it to thrust itself into the air and land again safely without injuring itself. A cat will always look before it leaps, carefully assessing the distance before taking off.

The tail maintains perfect balance

The cat's claws are ready to push off from the tree

Balancing

A cat is extremely well coordinated because it possesses a very efficient system for sending messages to the brain from its muscles and joints. It uses its tail as a counterbalance when walking along a narrow branch in the same way as a tightrope walker holds a long pole for balance.

The eyes are fixed straight ahead

The claws grip the branch

Climbing

From a tree or fence, a cat can patrol its territory and watch its prey without being seen. Using its strong hind-leg muscles and gripping with its front claws, going up is relatively easy, but coming down can be more difficult.

THE RIGHTING REFLEX

The eyes survey the ground

The paws are positioned on a narrow branch

The hind legs are carefully balanced

Turning over

A cat's balance and coordination are unsurpassed, and this has led to the belief that a cat is able to withstand a fall from a great height. This is not always the case (*see page 160*), but cats have survived falls of over 20 metres (65 ft). The cat's righting reflex works quickly and automatically. The cat's eyes and balance organs in the inner ear tell it where it is in space and it lands on its feet.

ASSESSING A CAT'S MOOD

Your cat lets you know when it is pleased, angry, frightened, or unhappy. Eyes, ears, tail, whiskers, and voice are all powerful indicators of your pet's mood. Although sometimes regarded as lone hunters, cats are very sociable animals that have evolved a complex body language and a range of different vocal sounds to communicate with you and with other felines. A cat's face is particularly telling, expressing a variety of different emotions ranging from contentment to fear and aggression.

BODY LANGUAGE

Happy Cat
Your cat may greet you with its tail held high and the tail tip bent slightly forward. An erect tail indicates that a cat is happy and confident. A tail flicked from side to side indicates a state of tension. A cat on the defensive fluffs up its coat and its tail fur in order to appear larger.

The tail is erect and held stiffly

Alert expression with ears pricked forward

First meeting
Cats usually establish their social order without incurring serious injury. Intense staring and emphatic body language may deter more timid cats. The engagement may break up with each cat washing itself in a very deliberate way.

Aggressive cat
A cat lying on its back is not necessarily submitting to a more dominant feline. With its teeth and claws displayed, a formidable array of weaponry is displayed.

The ears are flattened against the head

Defensive cat
A cat poised to make a strategic withdrawal may remain still for several minutes. The attention is focused, the gaze intense, and the ears pricked forward to monitor any sound.

Close companions

Cats that are part of the same household will greet each other affectionately by touching noses and rubbing their bodies together. If they are from the same litter or have grown up together they will groom each other, sleep huddled together, and play with one another.

Cat calls

The vocal reportoire of a cat is extensive, with more than 16 different sounds. Cat calls include howls of anger, yowls and growls of tom cats fighting, as well as queens on heat looking for mates. According to the intonation, a cat's miaow can be used to express many different moods.

A cat marks its territory by rubbing against objects

Making contact

Rubbing against people is an endearing habit, but your cat is not simply being affectionate. It is marking out territory with the secretions of glands around its face. The tail area and paws also carry the cat's scent.

PURRING

The purr is a low-frequency sound that is produced not by the vocal chords but from somewhere deep in a cat's chest. Purring is usually a sign of pleasure or contentment. A mother cat purrs when her kittens are born and when they begin to suckle; tiny kittens purr when they feel secure, warm, and well fed. However, a cat will also purr to comfort itself when it is nervous or in pain.

Purring for pleasure

Purring is a uniquely feline sound which usually means that a cat is relaxed and contented.

THE CAT AS A PET

Cats are becoming ever more popular household pets worldwide. There are at present about 100 million cats in the Western world (*see opposite*) and the numbers are on the increase. There are very many reasons for this feline popularity. Cats require less time and expense than many other pets and are particularly well suited to living in an urban environment. They are independent, inexpensive to purchase and to maintain, very clean, and keep mice and other vermin out of the home. Cats make affectionate and extremely devoted companions, especially for an elderly person or for someone who is living on their own.

The ideal pet
A cat is extremely adaptable and is equally happy whether living in a small apartment or in a large house.

BUILDING A GOOD RELATIONSHIP

Bonding (*left*)
Unlike a dog, a cat's affection and trust have to be earned, but once you have established a bond, it can last for life. The more you observe your cat's behaviour, the better you will understand its basic nature and its likes and dislikes.

Early lessons (*below*)
A cat makes an excellent pet for a child, once it is old enough to appreciate how an animal should be picked up and handled (*see page 41*). A child that is brought up in a household with pets will learn to appreciate the responsibilities of caring for another living creature.

Making friends (*above*)
Continue to play games with your cat from kittenhood through to adulthood (*see pages 42–43*). Most cats will pounce on a length of string or chase a bouncy ball, and some can even be taught tricks.

WHY CHOOSE A CAT?

Cats versus dogs (*left*)
Cats are by nature more independent than dogs and are easier to keep. A dog needs to be taken for a walk on a leash at least twice a day, whereas a cat is quite capable of exercising and amusing itself, although it does enjoy human company.

Dogs are more damanding pets than cats

The appeal of cats (*right*)
Stroking a cat can help to relieve stress, and the feel of a purring cat on your lap conveys a strong sense of security and comfort. Do not expect your cat to be sociable on demand – it will appreciate some privacy and peace and quiet.

Cats versus other small pets (*left*)
Cats are much easier to keep clean than other pets, such as birds and rodents, whose cages must be cleaned daily. Other small mammals make less rewarding pets because they are less intelligent and lead shorter lives.

CAT OWNERSHIP WORLDWIDE

In Great Britain and North America, there are now almost as many cats as dogs. Over 30 per cent of households in North America and 24 per cent in Europe own a cat.

| Italy 5 million | Spain 1.7 million | Belgium 1.6 million | Sweden 1.1 million | Netherlands 2.2 million | Germany 5 million | France 8.4 million | U.K. 6.9 million | North America 60 million | Japan 3.5 million | Australia 2.8 million | Denmark 0.6 million |

BASIC CAT TYPES

There are over a hundred recognized breeds of domestic cat. The main feline features that vary are body type, eye colour, coat colour, and length of coat. Although some pedigree cats are natural breeds, many others are the result of careful breeding. Most cats are of no particular breed and are crosses of different types. These are what we have come to know as "moggies". They can have long or short hair, and come in a variety of different colours, the most common of which are tabby, tortoiseshell, ginger, and black.

BODY TYPES

Cobby cat
Pedigree Longhair breeds have stocky, rounded bodies with sturdy, short legs and round faces. Their body type is described as cobby. Other characteristics of this longhaired cat include a broad head and round eyes.

Muscular cat
Most shorthaired cats have muscular builds with sturdy, short legs. This is the most common of the different feline body shapes. Some pedigree cats, such as British and Exotic Shorthairs, have more compact bodies.

Foreign longhaired cat
There are a few breeds of longhaired cat that have slim bodies which differ from the usual cobby type. This group includes oriental breeds such as the Balinese, Angora, and Somali. They are long-bodied, with slim legs, wedge-shaped heads, and almond-shaped eyes.

The coat is less woolly and full than that of Pedigree Longhairs

Foreign shorthaired cat

A foreign or oriental cat has an elegant, slim body that is very different from the muscular build of other shorthaired cats. This type of cat has long, slender legs, a wedge-shaped head, large, pointed ears, and slanting eyes. Breeds such as the Foreign Shorthair, Siamese, Abyssinian, Tonkinese, and Egyptian Mau all have this slim build.

The coat is very fine and short

TYPES OF EYES

Cats' eyes come in three basic shapes: round, slanted, and almond-shaped. Their colours are basically green, yellow to gold and, most rarely, blue. However, there is a wide range of different shades within these three basic colours. Most non-pedigree cats have green eyes.

British Smoke Shorthair

Non-pedigree Tabby

White Pedigree Longhair

British Tortoiseshell-and-White

Maine Coon

Birman

British Blue Shorthair

Egyptian Mau

Snowshoe

British Tortoiseshell Shorthair

Burmilla

Balinese

Chapter 2

BASIC CARE

WE WANT our cats to live long and happy lives – they contribute so much to our own. A cat is not a demanding pet to keep; all it needs is adequate feeding, regular grooming, and proper veterinary care. A cat thrives best with a sympathetic owner who can devote a lot of attention to it and join in with games. You can keep your cat healthy by ensuring that it is protected from diseases by yearly vaccination and that it is neutered to prevent unwanted kittens. Given time and tender loving care, you will build up trust with your cat. However, it may always regard some aspects of feline care, such as travelling in its carrier and visits to the vet, as tiresome.

BECOMING A CAT OWNER

Bringing a cat into your home will change your life. The benefits of having a feline companion bring with them obligations and, unless you are prepared to make sure that your pet will receive the care and attention that it needs, then cat owning is not for you. Having decided that you want to share your home with a cat, you need to decide what type of feline is best for you. Do you want a kitten or an adult cat? A pedigree or a non-pedigree? A longhaired or a shorthaired cat?

THE CAT FOR YOUR LIFESTYLE

Pedigree cats
The temperaments of pedigree cats can be predicted fairly reliably. Choose a breed with characteristics that you think fit in with your lifestyle.

Non-pedigree cats (left)
If you are worried about allowing a pedigree cat the freedom of your garden, choose a non-pedigree cat. "Moggies" sometimes choose their own owners by appearing on the doorstep and demanding to be fed.

Kittens (above)
Kittens demand lots of attention and need to be house trained. They adapt to a new home better than adult cats, so a kitten is a good choice if you already have other pets.

One cat or two? (right)
If you are away from home during the day, consider getting two cats. They will amuse each other and will wreak less havoc in your home.

Mother and kittens (*above*)
Think carefully about the implications of not having your cat neutered (*see pages 154–155*). A female cat with kittens needs special attention.

Longhaired cats (*above*)
The Ragdoll is an especially docile cat set apart by its reputed tendency to relax all its muscles when picked up and cradled. Longhaired cats are generally sweet natured, gentle, and enjoy a quiet life.

Show cats (*above*)
If you intend to show your cat it will require special attention and grooming. A first-class show cat represents a significant investment in terms of time and money.

Oriental cats (*left*)
Siamese, Burmese, and other oriental cats are very sociable. They are lively, inquisitive, and love people. They can also be very vocal – if you do not give them enough attention.

WHERE TO OBTAIN A CAT

It is far better to obtain a cat from a friend, neighbour, animal shelter, or recommended cat breeder than from a pet shop. Never take an animal on impulse because you have fallen for its charm. Always examine a cat very carefully before taking it home.

Friends
Friends are a reliable source of kittens since you will probably know the mother.

Animal shelters
Animal shelters often have plenty of kittens and adult cats needing good homes.

Local vets
Your vet may know of cats needing a home. Check the cat's health first.

Breeders
A breeder is a good source of pure-bred kittens. Specify whether you want a cat for showing.

ESSENTIAL EQUIPMENT

Before you bring a cat into your home, it is essential that you make preparations for the new arrival. A cat is not very expensive to keep, but it must be provided with a litter tray, a comfortable basket or bed, separate food and water bowls, a carrier, and a brush and comb. If you wish, you can also provide it with other, very useful items, such as a scratching post and a cat flap.

Brush
A brush is essential for longhaired cats. Buy the best-quality, natural bristle brush that you can afford.

Comb
A fine-toothed metal comb is useful for grooming a shorthaired cat, but a wide-toothed comb is better for a longhaired variety.

Food bowls
Every cat must have its own bowl and feeding utensils, which should always be kept clean.

Litter tray and litter scoop
A kitten or adult cat that is not allowed outside will need to be provided with a plastic litter tray. This needs to be cleaned daily; a plastic scoop allows the used litter to be removed without soiling the hands.

Cat basket (*below*)
A basket should be comfortable, warm, and easy to clean.

Cat carrier (*right*)
There is a wide range of different carriers available (*see page 48*).

Water bowls
Fresh water that is replenished daily should always be available for a cat, even if it is also given milk.

Cat bed (*right*)
Beds come in many different varieties, including bean-bag beds and sheepskin hammocks.

CHOOSING A KITTEN

You can share your life with your cat for 14 years or more, so it is crucial that you choose a kitten that will grow up to be a healthy and happy adult. Do not be tempted to buy a kitten that is weak and sickly just because you feel sorry for it, or to ensure that it gets veterinary treatments; you will probably be letting yourself in for large veterinary fees and a lot of heartbreak.

If you buy a pedigree kitten and it falls ill or does not settle within a week or two, you may be able to take it back to the breeder if you have discussed the possibility beforehand.

When choosing a kitten, you should take into consideration the type of home it comes from and its mother's state of health. If possible, you should watch the kitten playing so that you can check for lameness. Ideally, kittens should not be separated from their mother until they are ten to twelve weeks of age.

The nose is velvety and slightly damp

The eyes are bright and clear

The mouth and gums are pink in colour

The fur is soft and smooth to the touch

Nine-week-old kitten (actual size)
A healthy kitten has a firm, muscular body and feels much heavier than it looks when you pick it up.

The limbs show no signs of lameness

The tail has no kink or other deformity

WHAT TO LOOK FOR WHEN CHOOSING A KITTEN

The ears should be clean with no discharge. Constant scratching may be a sign of mites.

The eyes should be clear, bright, and free from discharge. The third eyelid should not be showing.

The nose should be cool and damp, without any nasal discharge or crusting around the nostrils.

The mouth and gums should be pale pink in colour and the breath odour-free.

The abdomen should be slightly rounded but not pot bellied, which may be a sign of roundworms.

The coat is a good pointer to how healthy the kitten is; it should be glossy with no signs of fleas.

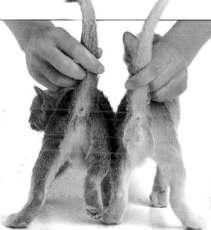

The rear should be clean, with no signs of diarrhoea or any discharge from the genitals.

SEXING A KITTEN
The female kitten's anus and vulva are very close together; the anus and penis are further apart in the male.

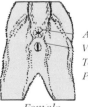 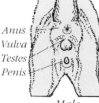

Anus
Vulva
Testes
Penis

Female   *Male*

FIRST INTRODUCTIONS

If you already have pets, introducing a new cat into your household has to be managed carefully. An adult cat, in particular, will resent the presence of another feline and will defend its territory very fiercely. The pets in residence have to be slowly accustomed to the newcomer and this will take time and a lot of patience. Feed the animals separately and supervise all meetings for the first few weeks.

A kitten pen
In the security of a pen, two kittens get used to their new home.

ADDING A CAT TO YOUR HOME

INTRODUCING A CAT TO A DOG

Do not let the dog get too close

1 Control the dog (keep it on a lead if necessary) so that it does not bark or become excited and scare the cat. Wait until the dog and cat are accustomed to each other before allowing the dog to get too close or to lick the cat.

2 After a couple of weeks of careful supervision, the cat and dog should have accepted each other's presence, and should be able to sit in the same room. Eventually, the cat may become the dominant partner in the relationship.

INTRODUCING A KITTEN TO AN ADULT CAT

1 Trim both cats' claws beforehand. Allow the cat to sniff the kitten – initially, there will probably be some hissing. Separate the animals if the cat attacks the kitten, but otherwise do not interfere more than is necessary.

The cat will be wary of the kitten at first

2 It may take up to a month for the cats to settle down. It is usually easier to bring a young kitten, rather than an adult cat, into a house that already has another feline.

INTRODUCING A KITTEN TO SMALL PETS

Rabbits
A kitten can frighten a rabbit by clambering all over it. An adult cat should not be left unsupervised with a pet rabbit.

Guinea pigs
A guinea pig will be a source of fascination to a kitten. Never let rodents out of their cages when an adult cat is on the prowl.

Happy pets
Provided all your pets have their own separate living areas, peaceful co-existence between different species can be achieved.

BASIC ROUTINES

You cannot train a cat in the same way as a dog to obey specific commands, but it does need to be house trained in order to live in a human household. Because a cat is by nature a remarkably clean and fastidious animal, it usually learns very quickly how to use a litter tray. A cat is a fairly undemanding pet to keep. All it really needs is regular feeding, grooming, toilet facilities, health care, and a corner for its bed or basket where it can enjoy a quiet cat-nap. However, it is important to maintain a daily routine in caring for your cat, since it will be unhappy if it is ignored or if you forget to feed it. Plan well ahead before introducing a cat into your home. It will be easier for your pet to adjust to its surroundings if essential items (*see pages 28–29*), such as a litter tray, food bowl, and basket, are installed before it arrives.

LITTER TRAINING

House training
Cats are quick to learn how to use a litter tray. Keep the tray near the door so that your pet can easily make the transition to going outside.

TYPES OF LITTER TRAY

Covered tray
A timid cat will appreciate the privacy of an enclosed litter tray.

Ordinary tray
Place the tray in a quiet corner.

TYPES OF LITTER

Reusable Washable, non-absorbent litter.

Fuller's earth Based on natural clay.

Lightweight Very convenient to carry.

Wood-based Good for absorbing liquid waste.

ESTABLISHING ROUTINES

Playtime
Play is vital for a cat's development and an activity that should be encouraged and shared by every owner. Try to spend a little time, say 10 to 15 minutes each day, playing with your cat, and continue the games into adulthood to keep your pet fit (*see pages 42–43*).

Feeding time
Nourishing meals must be provided for your cat. Prepared foods from reliable manufacturers are the safest and most convenient option. They can be supplemented with the occasional fresh food treat.

Bedtime
Cats like to sleep for up to 16 hours a day, and every cat should have a quite spot for its bed. Do not let your cat stay outside at night since this is when most road accidents happen.

Regular grooming
Whether your cat is a pedigree or a moggy it needs to be groomed regularly. Grooming should be started as young as possible (*see page 67*).

TRAINING A CAT

A cat will not do anything that it does not want to, so training has to concentrate on gently persuading your pet to modify its natural behaviour. You must keep in mind that a cat is not behaving badly when it scratches a favourite chair – in fact, it is keeping its claws in trim by stripping away their outer layers, as well as marking its territory with scent. If you want to protect your best furniture, provide your cat with a scratching post. The younger your cat is the easier it will be to train it to use a post. Give your cat the freedom to come and go by providing it with a cat flap. This simple device is easy to fit and most cats quickly learn to use it.

USING A SCRATCHING POST

Perch from which the cat can survey its surroundings

The rope is impregnated with catnip

Toy balls make the post more interesting

HOME-MADE POSTS

A log complete with bark makes an ideal, natural scratching post for the garden. For indoor use, you can make your cat its own scratching pad using an old piece of carpet attached to a wooden plank.

Training

Whenever your cat looks as if it is going to claw the furniture, reprimand it and gently put its paws on the scratching post. The post can be made more attractive by rubbing a little catnip on it. Manufactured posts come in a range of designs; this one has a perch for the cat to sit on and balls for it to play with.

USING A CAT FLAP

The clear plastic door allows the cats to see outside

1 The cat flap should be positioned at the right height for the cat to step through, about 15 cm (6 in) from the base of the door. Begin training the cat to use the flap by propping it partly open, and then tempting the cat through with a little food on the other side.

The locking device keeps unwanted visitors out

2 The cat will quickly learn to push open the door itself when it wants to go outside. An electro-magnetic cat flap is useful for preventing strange cats from entering the house. This type of door can only be activated by a magnet. The latter should be worn on an elasticated collar.

The magnet worn on the cat's collar opens the flap

15 cm (6 in)

TYPES OF CAT FLAP

Most cat flaps swing in two directions and have a magnetic strip along the sides to keep out draughts. Whatever the type of flap, it should be easy to open, so that the cat can push it with its head without the risk of getting its neck or paws stuck.

Standard cat flap
A standard cat flap like this one is inexpensive and easy to install, but does not have a locking device.

Lockable cat flap
A locking device is useful if you want to prevent your cat from going outdoors at night and for keeping other cats out.

COLLARS AND LEADS

A cat does not need much in the way of accessories, but a collar with a name tag is essential if you are going to let your pet outside. A cat should be trained to wear a collar from an early age. Start by putting the collar on for a short period each day until the cat is used to wearing it. A collar with an identity disc giving the cat's name and your address and telephone number is useful in case of accidents, and will help prevent your cat from being mistaken for a stray should it wander or get lost. If you live in a city or near a busy road, you may want to train your cat to walk on a harness and lead. This will take a lot of gentle coaxing, and even then you may not get your cat to go where you want.

A collar must fit properly

Elasticated collar
A collar must have an elasticated section so that a cat can slip out of it should it get caught.

TYPES OF COLLAR AND LEAD

Flea collars are not suitable for young kittens and must be used as directed

There is a collar to suit every budget, ranging from the simple type to diamond-studded ones

A tartan collar is ideal for a fashion-conscious cat that needs a different collar for every day of the week

A collar should have an elasticated safety section and felt backing, and should be easily adjustable

You can cut down a collar intended for an adult cat to fit a kitten

Select a light leather or cord lead that is suitable for a cat

Collars
There is a wide range of different collar designs. Always take the collar off when grooming to check for skin irritation.

A harness is essential for lead training because a cat can slip out of a collar

NAME TAGS AND BELLS

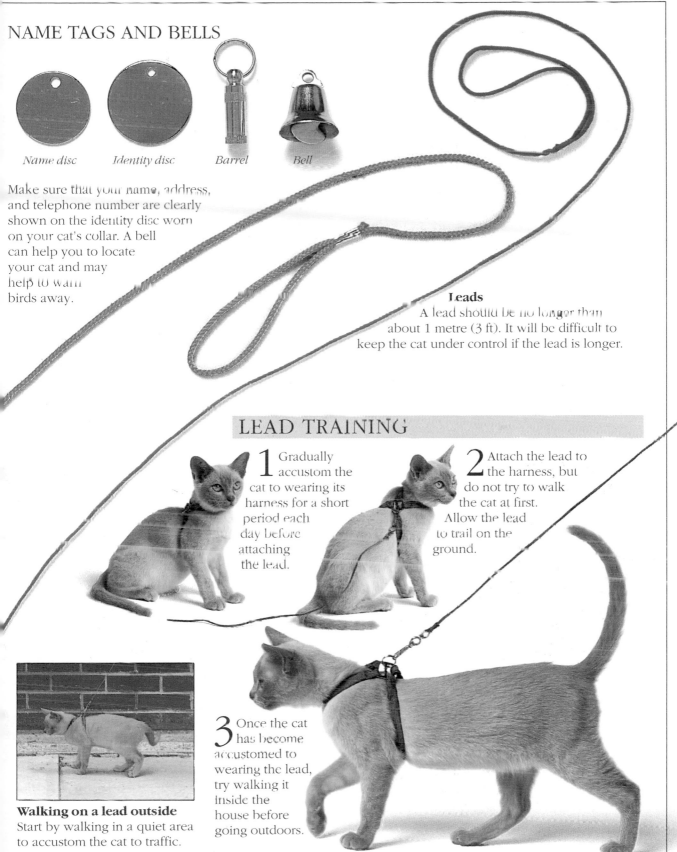

Name disc   *Identity disc*   *Barrel*   *Bell*

Make sure that your name, address, and telephone number are clearly shown on the identity disc worn on your cat's collar. A bell can help you to locate your cat and may help to warn birds away.

Leads
A lead should be no longer than about 1 metre (3 ft). It will be difficult to keep the cat under control if the lead is longer.

LEAD TRAINING

1 Gradually accustom the cat to wearing its harness for a short period each day before attaching the lead.

2 Attach the lead to the harness, but do not try to walk the cat at first. Allow the lead to trail on the ground.

3 Once the cat has become accustomed to wearing the lead, try walking it inside the house before going outdoors.

Walking on a lead outside
Start by walking in a quiet area to accustom the cat to traffic.

HANDLING A CAT

Physical contact is very important for establishing a close relationship with your pet. When holding or carrying a cat, you should allow it to adopt the position in which it feels most comfortable and talk to it in a reassuring way. A cat will soon let you know when it has had enough and wants to be left alone; a determined, protesting cat can be quite a handful. You should also learn where your cat likes to be stroked and which areas of its body are particularly sensitive. When handling a cat, take it in its own time and never use force or sudden movements, which will frighten it.

PICKING UP A CAT

1 First, gain the cat's confidence. Once the cat is relaxed, gently lift it, supporting its hindquarters.

2 Lift the cat in as natural a position as possible. Talk to the cat to reassure it.

Support the rear and hind legs

Holding a cat
Cats enjoy being held for brief periods, but they do like to be in control of their own movements and will usually only feel at ease in the arms of a human who they know and trust. Some individuals can be trained to sit on their owners' shoulders.

3 Use one arm to support the cat's hindquarters, and the other for support and for gentle stroking.

CHILDREN AND CATS

Best of friends
Some cats can be frightened by children, who need to be taught how to stroke and play with their pet. This cat has complete confidence in its young companion.

Holding a kitten
Children find kittens irresistible and should be discouraged from picking them up and cuddling them.

First introductions
Introduce a cat to a child very gradually; initial contact should be confined to gentle stroking.

Correct handling
Physical contact should not be forced or prolonged if a cat wants to be put down.

Do not try to hold on to a struggling cat

STROKING ZONES

Chest and ears
Most cats enjoy being stroked or rubbed around the ears and chest.

Neck and back
A relaxed cat appreciates being stroked on its neck and back.

Abdomen
Do not stroke a cat's abdomen and back legs unless you know it well.

PLAYING WITH A CAT

One of the many joys of owning a cat is watching it play. Learning to play is essential for the development of kittens because it teaches them important skills that they will need as adults. After the age of about six months, a cat loses some of its playfulness. It prefers to save its energies for the more serious business of hunting and may need to be encouraged to play games.

You can make any game more appealing for your cat by joining in, but the best way to keep a cat playful is to provide it with a companion. A couple of cats brought up in the same household will continue to play together in adulthood.

Catnip mice

Small balls

Toys
Some favourite toys include catnip mice, sacks filled with dried catnip, bouncy balls, and feathers.

Catnip sack

Fluffy feather

Feather and string

SOLITARY GAMES

Ping-pong ball
A small, bouncy ball is an ideal toy for your cat to pat and push around with its paws. Be prepared to retrieve it from behind doors and underneath armchairs.

Catnip mouse
If your cat likes catnip, this toy will have it purring in ecstasy. Catnip toys do lose their scent after a while and need to be replaced.

Cat's cradle (*left*)
A ball of wool makes an irresistible toy. A cat will enjoy trailing it around chairs and table legs. Never allow your cat to play with cotton or wool unsupervised since it may swallow it.

GAMES FOR SHARING

Hide-and-seek
A cardboard box is ideal for playing games of hide-and-seek. After sniffing every corner of a box, a cat likes to hide itself away, but once inside it will probably be ambushed by its feline companion.

Mouse on a string (*above*)
A cat is fascinated by any object that is dangled in front of its nose. A piece of string tried to a short pole will keep your cat amused.

A cat tries to paw a feather held just out of its reach

Fun with feathers
A feather is a good toy for tickling and playing with your cat, but watch out for its claws. If you do not move your hand away very quickly, you are likely to get scratched.

Feline fishing (*above*)
Trail a feather on a piece of string or cord for your cat to chase. Drag the feather slowly in front of the cat's paws and wait for it to pounce, then slowly reel it in.

Pouncing practice
A cat will be fascinated by a cardboard tube and will wait hopefully for something interesting to emerge. Reward its patience by giving it a catnip toy to play with or a tasty cat treat.

THE OUTDOOR CAT

Where it is possible, a cat will enjoy being allowed outside, and will set up its own territory to patrol and defend, even if this consists of only a small town garden. An entire tom will have a larger area to defend than a neutered male or a queen. A cat marks its home ground with scent by scratching trees and rubbing itself against fence posts. Urine spraying also acts as a warning to other cats to keep away, especially when it is carried out by tom cats. All these feline signals have to be reinforced regularly, since they act as signposts to other cats. The more recent the scent, the more other cats take notice.

EXERCISE AND TERRITORY

Tree climber
While all cats enjoy climbing trees for exercise or to survey their territory, kittens can sometimes become frightened by the height and need to be helped down. On the whole, however, mature cats have no difficulty in retracing their steps to the ground when they are ready to do so.

Vantage point (*left*)
A roof, fence, or wall makes a good vantage point from which a cat can watch over its territory and make sure that no inruders trespass on its patch. From such a high point, the cat can also see the best hunting and resting places. All cats will have favourite areas for sleeping or just watching.

An erect tail signifies alertness to everything that is going on

Cat patrol
A cat will need to patrol its territory regularlyto defend it against other cats that might want to muscle in. It will also have to sniff out the scent of its rivals, so that it does not get into trouble by straying into another feline's territory.

The cat's sensitive nose investigates every scent

COMMON DANGERS IN THE GARDEN

Practically every garden has some hazards in it, since a large number of plants are toxic to animals (*see pages 167*). Even though a cat will not normally eat garden plants, it is wise to keep poisonous ones to a minimum when laying out your garden. A high fence, preferably with the top sloping inwards, may be needed if there is a busy road nearby, both to keep your pet in and to keep out other cats.

All toxic materials should be kept out of a garden where there are animals, or securely locked up out of harm's way. Substances that are poisonous to cats include slug pellets (especially metaldehyde), rodent poison, creosote, wood preservatives, insecticides, and pesticides. If a cat can get into a garage or garden shed, it may also be at risk from paint, oil, petrol, and carbon monoxide fumes.

Garden dangers
Poisonous plants, garden chemicals, dogs, and rival cats are among the common hazards for a cat in even the most innocent-looking garden. A kitten may fall into a pond or swimming pool and be unable to get out.

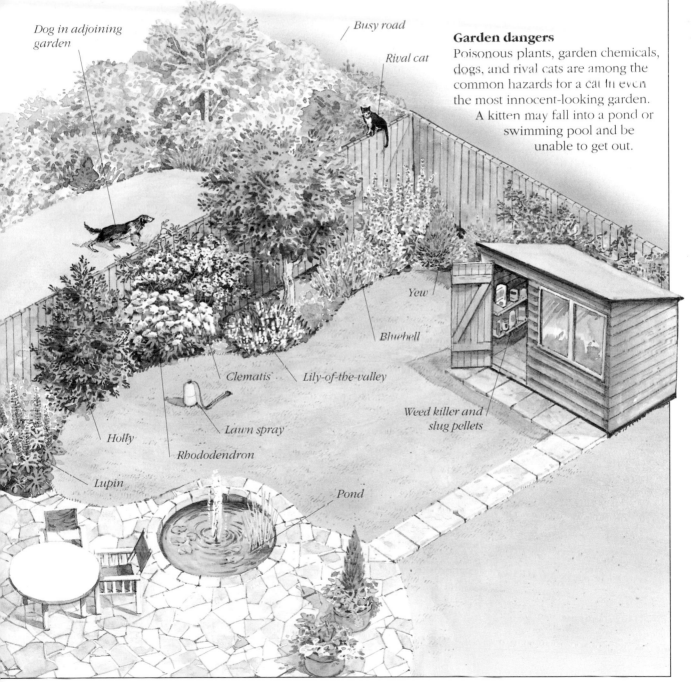

Dog in adjoining garden

Busy road

Rival cat

Yew

Bluebell

Clematis

Lily-of-the-valley

Weed killer and slug pellets

Holly

Lawn spray

Rhododendron

Lupin

Pond

THE INDOOR CAT

A cat is by its nature a very independent creature that likes to be able to come and go as it pleases. However, some cat owners living in large cities or high-rise apartments may find it impossible to let their pet outside and prefer to keep it safely confined to the home. Most cats can live quite happily indoors, provided that all their needs for amusement, exercise, and safety are catered for. It is best to accustom a cat to being inside when it is still a kitten. Its litter tray must be cleaned daily, and it should be provided with plenty of toys and games or, better still, a feline companion. You may want to try training your cat to walk on a lead for short trips outside the home (*see page 39*).

Best friends
A feline companion will ensure that an indoor cat never becomes bored when it is left alone.

OUTDOOR RUNS FOR CATS

Outdoor pens
If you wish to allow your cat access to the outside world while still keeping it safe, an outdoor run is the answer. It should be constructed of stout posts and wire netting, and provided with a covered shelter in case of bad weather. A cat may also appreciate a tree or post for climbing and scratching.

INDOOR LAWN
Most cats enjoy chewing on grass, from which they may get certain extra vitamins. If your cat is kept indoors, you should provide it with a pot of fresh greenery such as lawn grass, catnip, thyme, sage, or parsley.

Grass in pots
Sow some seeds in a pot for a regular supply of fresh grass.

COMMON DANGERS IN THE HOME

A home can be full of hazards for a cat, especially a kitten or a new arrival. Cats are naturally curious, so washing machines, tumble driers, refrigerators, and ovens should never be left open. Hot irons, kettles, and saucepans full of boiling liquids should not be left unattended. Kittens may chew electrical flex, and some cats may chew plants and cut flowers out of boredom. Some houseplants such as ivies, philodendrons, and poinsettias, can be toxic (*see page 167*). Fragile ornaments such as china vases can be knocked off shelves by exploring cats. Open fires should always be protected by a guard, even when unlit. Other dangers include detergents and chemicals, threaded needles, pins, and plastic bags. An open window on an upper floor can lead to a cat falling out injuring itself.

Indoor hazards
Any home can be full of potential dangers for a cat, especially a kitten or a newcomer. They range from open fires and poisonous houseplants to electrical equipment and cooking utensils.

Open window
Food left out
Boiling saucepan
Sharp knife
Boiling kettle
Poisonous houseplant
Breakable ornaments
Hot iron
Household detergent
Rubbish bin
Washing machine door open
Plastic bags
Open fire
Pins and needles
Electrical flex

TRAVELLING AND MOVING HOUSE

Cats do not adjust to travel as readily as dogs, and should be confined to carriers for the duration of any trip. You should get your cat used to its carrier before undertaking any journeys and, if possible, introduce it to travelling in a car while it is still young. You will need a secure carrier, ideally one made out of plastic, wire, or wicker. A warm blanket will provide good insulation in cold weather; in exceptionally hot weather you may need to cover the carrier with a damp cloth.

Never leave a cat unattended in a car on a hot day since it may get over-heated. Do not allow a cat to travel loose in a car because it may become agitated or get in the driver's way and cause an accident.

TRANSPORTING A CAT

Wire carrier
Well ventilated, secure, and easily cleaned, a plastic-coated wire carrier is ideal for moving a cat. Line it with a towel or newspapers in case of accidents.

TYPES OF CARRIER

Wicker carrier (*left*)
Traditional wicker carriers give a cat some privacy, while allowing it to see out. The disadvantages of this type of carrier are that it is difficult to keep clean and may not be entirely "catsafe".

Cardboard carrier
A cardboard carrier is only suitable for emergencies or when taking a calm cat on a short journey.

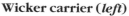

Plastic carrier (*right*)
Like wire carriers, lightweight plastic carriers are easy to disinfect and clean. Larger carriers will accommodate two cats if they are used to travelling together.

PUTTING A CAT INTO A CARRIER

1 First close all the doors and windows. Allow the cat to use its litter tray before being put into the carrier. Pick up the cat in a purposeful but gentle way. The cat may start to struggle when it sees the carrier.

CAR SICKNESS

Tranquillization is possible for cats that are very bad travellers or when undertaking a long journey. Tranquillizers must only be obtained from a vet.

2 Lift the cat into the carrier, supporting its hind legs. The carrier should always be lined with newspapers or a towel, even if you are only going on a short trip.

The carrier should be lined in case of accidents

Make sure the carrier is fastened

3 Keep your grip on the cat until just before you secure the door. Given the chance, a cat will jump out and will become agitated if you have to chase it around the house.

MOVING HOME

Confine your cat to a quiet room of the house while the furniture is being moved to prevent it from becoming scared and running off. Do not feed the cat before the journey since this may make it sick if it is a bad traveller. When the furniture van has gone, put the cat in its carrier and transport it to your new home. On arrival, allow the cat time to settle down and get used to its surroundings. Provide it with food, water, and a litter tray and keep it confined to the house for at least five days. After this time, you can allow the cat outside for short periods, ideally under close supervision.

Car travel
A cat must be confined for car travel.

TRAVELLING ABROAD AND CATTERIES

Holidays and travel abroad require careful planning by the cat owner. For all travel, whether by air, road, rail, or sea, a cat will have to be in a container approved by the carrying company. For long journeys it will need food, water, and access to a litter tray.

Although it is not advisable to sedate a cat for travelling, a vet can prescribe a tranquillizer if you have a nervous animal. A pregnant or nursing queen and young kittens should not be taken on long journeys.

If you are going abroad or cannot take your cat with you, make sure that it will be cared for properly in your absence. whether by friends, neighbours, at an approved cattery, or by a "cat-sitting" agency.

AIR TRAVEL

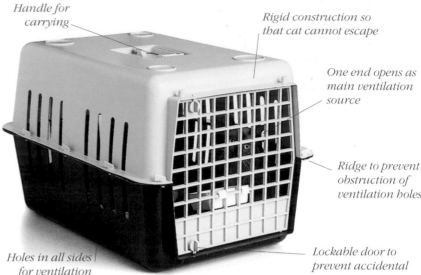

Handle for carrying

Rigid construction so that cat cannot escape

One end opens as main ventilation source

Ridge to prevent obstruction of ventilation holes

Holes in all sides for ventilation

Lockable door to prevent accidental opening

Feline freight
Cats being transported by air must be contained in a carrier like the one above. Such a container must be strong and light, and allow plenty of ventilation, especially for long journeys. Instructions for feeding and watering and the owner's name and address should be clearly marked.

QUARANTINE
When a cat enters Great Britain it must be quarantined in an approved cattery for six months to ensure that it is free from rabies (*see page 124*). The penalties for smuggling cats are severe, since they represent a potential health risk to humans. In the United States, travelling between States with an animal is forbidden unless you have the required vaccination and health documents. If you take your cat abroad, you will need to comply with the regulations issued by the transportation company. A vet will be able to advise you on regulations and which authorities to contact.

Confinement
A cat taken abroad may have to spend time in quarantine either upon arrival or on return to its home country to prevent the spread of rabies.

BOARDING YOUR CAT

You should select a cattery well in advance of your holiday. Inspect the premises and make all the arrangements in good time, since many establishments are booked for months ahead. The cattery should be spotlessly clean and tidy, and the cats well cared for. The cats should be able to look out and see each other, but should be kept apart to prevent the spread of infection. All feeding and drinking bowls must be kept clean and sterile, and cat beds should be disposable, or of a material that can be thoroughly disinfected for each new occupant. You should inform the staff if your cat has special dietary needs, and you must ensure that your pet's vaccinations are up-to-date. The cattery should allow you to leave your cat several items to remind it of home such as a favourite toy. There must be effective security at the cattery, with at least two barriers to the outside world to prevent the escape of boarders or the entrance of strange cats

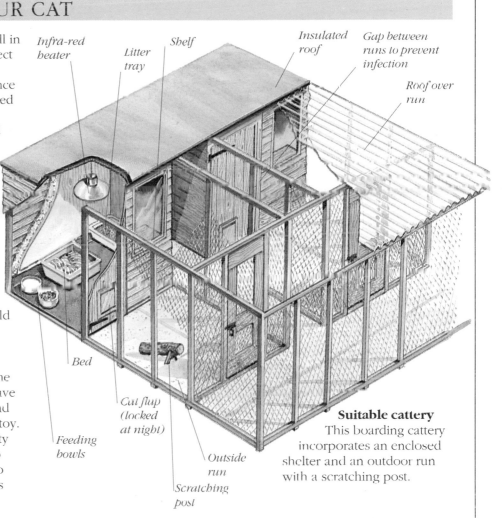

Infra-red heater

Litter tray

Shelf

Insulated roof

Gap between runs to prevent infection

Roof over run

Bed

Cat flap (locked at night)

Feeding bowls

Outside run

Scratching post

Suitable cattery
This boarding cattery incorporates an enclosed shelter and an outdoor run with a scratching post.

Communal cattery
Some boarding catteries have larger chalets for a nursing queen and her kittens, or for several adult cats from one household (cats from different households should not share the same accommodation). Many catteries have long-stay facilities for cats that have to be boarded for long periods, for example if an owner is abroad. Fees vary according to the facilities provided and are usually payable when a cat is collected.

KEEPING A CAT HEALTHY

One of the responsibilities of caring for your cat involves taking it to the vet for regular check-ups, vaccinations, and boosters. This essential part of feline maintenance should commence from the very first day that you bring your kitten home and continue through to its old age. Choose a veterinary practice in your neighbourhood that specializes in treating small animals. If the cost of veterinary care is a problem, there are a number of animal charities that provide subsidized treatment.

CHOOSING A VET

How to find a vet
Ask cat-owning friends to recommend a veterinary practice in your area. Find out what services are available, the fees charged, the consulting hours, and what the arrangements are in the event of an emergency.

USING A VET

Register your cat with a vet as soon as you bring it home and arrange for it to have a complete medical check-up to make sure that it is healthy. If you suspect that your pet is unwell, it is advisable to take it to a vet as soon as possible. Never try and treat your cat at home without obtaining veterinary advice. It will usually be impossible for you to make a diagnosis yourself, and the cat's condition is likely to worsen if you delay seeking professional treatment.

HEALTH INSURANCE

You may wish to take out a health insurance policy in case your cat falls ill. In return for paying a yearly premium, the pet insurance will cover most of the vet's fees for any course of treatment. It will not cover routine treatments such as vaccinations or neutering operations. Many pet insurance companies will also pay out a lump sum if a cat is killed in an accident, lost, or stolen.

You and your vet
A vet will advise you on keeping your cat healthy.

BASIC HEALTH CARE

Regular check-ups ensure that teeth and gums are healthy

Regular check-ups
Keep a watch on your kitten's health by looking out for unusual behaviour and by taking it for regular check-ups.

HEALTH CHECKLIST
When you contact your local vet, it is helpful to be able to supply some details of its history. This is a list of questions that you may be asked about your cat:
- Is it alert and active?
- Is it eating and drinking?
- Is it vomiting or retching?
- Is it passing urine and faeces normally?
- Is it coughing or sneezing?
- Is it pawing at its eyes or ears?
- Is it showing any signs of pain?

Vaccinations
A kitten should be vaccinated at about eight or nine weeks of age.

Protection from diseases
A kitten must be vaccinated to protect it against infections such as Feline Infectious Enteritis

TRACING A CAT
If your cat is missing, start by searching your home and garden, since it may simply be locked in a cupboard. Once you have looked in all the obvious places, ask your neighbours for help. Put notices with a description and photograph of your cat in local shop windows, and offer a reward for its return.

You can contact the animal welfare organizations in your area to find out if your pet has been picked up, and local vets in case it has been involved in an accident. Do not give up hope. Cats have a great ability to survive and there are cases of pets returning home after periods of several months.

A cat that goes outside must wear a collar with an identity disc giving your name and telephone number. Alternatively a tiny identity microchip can be injected under the skin in your cat's neck. Consult your vet for advice.

Chapter 3

FEEDING

FELINE NUTRITION is an exacting science since cats are carnivores with very special nutritional requirements. All cats require regular meals of wholesome, high-protein food and a constant supply of fresh water. Cats are by their nature very careful eaters, preferring their food to be fresh and served in a clean bowl. They will turn their noses up at stale food or any that is served direct from the refrigerator. The nutritional state of a healthy cat is reflected in its appearance; it will have a shiny coat, bright eyes, an alert demeanour, and supple muscle tone. A good-looking, healthy cat is your reward for feeding your pet a well-balanced diet.

CORRECT FEEDING

A cat's unique nutritional needs make it a very demanding animal to feed (*see pages 58–59*). It is also a very careful eater that quickly rejects its food if it does not have the right smell or if it is served at the wrong temperature. Its keen senses of smell and taste allow it to detect if a food is less than fresh. Try to make sure that your cat is fed at the same time each day and always in the same place.

Sometimes a cat supplements its diet by catching and eating small prey animals, but this does not mean that it is hungry or that you can prevent it from hunting by feeding it more. A cat hunts through instinct, and even a well-fed pet may catch mice given the opportunity.

Protein is essential for the growth and repair of tissues and for the regulation of metabolic processes

Essential fatty acids help give a sheen to a cat's coat

Vitamin A is essential for healthy eyes

Calcium and vitamin D are needed to build healthy bones and teeth

Carbohydrates add fibre to a cat's diet and provide additional energy

Optimum health
A well-fed cat is active and alert; its eyes are bright and its coat is glossy.

FEEDING EQUIPMENT

Even if you have more than one cat, each animal should have its own food and water bowls. You will also need to set aside a can opener, fork, spoon, and knife specially for serving your cat's food. All equipment must be washed after each meal. You can store your pet's cutlery in a plastic box so that it does not get mixed up with the household crockery. Plastic lids are useful for resealing opened cans. An automatic feeder has a timing device that allows it to open at preset times. It is only suitable if you are leaving your cat for no longer than 24 hours.

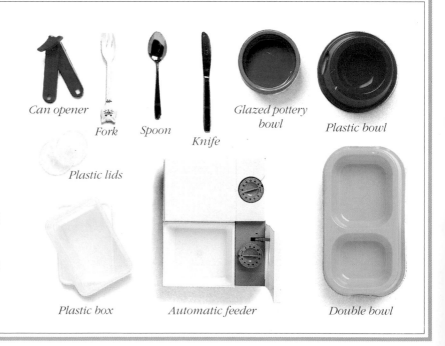

Can opener

Fork

Spoon

Knife

Glazed pottery bowl

Plastic bowl

Plastic lids

Plastic box

Automatic feeder

Double bowl

GUIDELINES FOR FEEDING

Ten basic rules

1 Feed prepared foods only from a reputable manufacturer.
2 Do not feed a cat food intended for a dog or other pets.
3 Always keep food bowls and feeding utensils clean.
4 Do not give a cat any food that is even slightly spoiled.
5 Carefully remove any small bones from fish and chicken.
6 Serve food at room temperature.
7 Dispose of uneaten food once the cat has finished.
8 Keep a watch on your cat's weight and do not let it overeat.
9 Do not put reheated food back in the refrigerator.
10 Consult a vet if your cat has refused food for 24 hours.

Do not give a cat too many scraps

Overfeeding
Feed your cat two to three small meals a day, following the manufacturer's recommendations. Do not give many snacks between meals.

Competition for food
A little competition makes for healthy appetites. You will not find a fussy eater in a household where there is more than one cat.

WATER AND MILK

A cat gets most of the moisture that it requires from its food and many felines seem to drink little. However, you should make sure that fresh water is available at all times. If a cat is fed dry or semi-moist types of food it will need to increase its water intake because these foods contain very little moisture. For this reason it is advisable to restrict the amount of dry food given. Although milk contains a lot of valuable nutrients, it is not essential for a healthy feline diet. As an alternative to cow's milk, try giving one of the lactose-reduced brands available.

Some cats are unable to digest milk

Milk ration
Do not give cow's milk to a cat prone to stomach upsets, since it is likely to have difficulty in digesting it.

A Cat's Dietary Needs

Cats require certain dietary components and animal-derived nutrients. They are not vegetarians, and although they can digest some vegetable matter, they are unable to live long on a completely meat-free diet. Even though a cat does not have a strict dietary need for greenery, you should make sure it has access to grass. Most cats seem to enjoy chewing on grass, and it may provide them with extra vitamins such as folic acid. A cat may vomit after eating grass, since this helps it to clean out its system and to regurgitate unwanted matter, such as hairballs. You should make sure that any chemicals or fertilizer used on your lawn are non-toxic to animals.

Eating grass
Although a cat may sometimes chew grass, it cannot digest much vegetable matter.

YOUR CAT'S WEIGHT

An average adult cat should weigh about 4–5 kg (9–11 lb). Although cats do not vary in size as much as dogs, a cat's weight does vary according to the type of breed. A small cat may weigh only 2.5 kg (5½ lb), and a large cat as much as 5.5 kg (12 lb). The following is a list of average weights:

Feline obesity is usually due to a combination of overfeeding and lack of exercise. Neutered and elderly cats are most commonly affected. The occasional cat may have a hormonal problem, but a cat usually becomes fat because it is eating more food than it requires. A very overweight cat will have a large abdomen that hangs down. Its breathing is laboured, and it soon becomes less active. Carrying the excess weight puts a strain on the cat's heart and makes it more susceptible to arthritis and other disorders in old age. If your cat is overweight, you should establish how much it is eating. It may be supplementing its diet by hunting or it may be being fed elsewhere.

KITTENS

Age	Weight
One day	70–135 g (2½–5 oz)
One week	110–250 g (4–9 oz)
Three weeks	215–420 g (8–15 oz)
Four weeks	250–500 g (9–18 oz)
Five weeks	290–620 g (10–22 oz)
Six weeks	315–700 g (11–25 oz)
Seven weeks	400–900 g (14–31 oz)

ADULTS

Average	2.5–5.5 g (5½–12 lb)
Pregnant	3.5–5.5 kg (8–12 lb)
Lactating	3.5–5.5 kg (9–12 lb)

REDUCING WEIGHT

Consult a vet to make sure that your cat's excess weight is not due to a medical problem. Cut down the cat's calorie intake by reducing the amount of food given under veterinary guidance. You can obtain a prescription, low-calorie diet from your vet that is especially formulated for feline weight loss.

Obesity
A very overweight cat has a shorter life expectancy compared with other cats.

THE NUTRITIONAL REQUIREMENTS OF AN ADULT CAT*

Component	Requirement	Source	Comments
Protein	A cat's diet should be made up of 28 per cent protein. Kittens require double this,	Complete cat food, meat, fish, eggs, milk and cheese.	Needs 20 per cent more protein than a dog.
Fat	A cat's diet should be not less than 9 per cent fat.	Animal and vegetable fats and oils.	Must have certain animal fats only found in meat and fish.
Carbohydrate	Should not be more than 40 per cent of the cat's diet.	Cereals, rice, pasta, potatoes, and dry cat food.	A useful source of energy and extra fibre.
Calcium Phosphorus Sodium Potassium Magnesium Iron Copper Manganese Zinc Iodine	1 g per day 0.8 g per day 0.2 g per day 0.4 g per day 0.05 g per day 10 mg per day 0.5 mg per day 1.0 mg per day 4.0 mg per day 0.1 mg per day	All essential minerals are found in a healthy, balanced diet. Two of the most important dietary minerals, calcium and phosphorus, are found in animal products such as milk.	A cat is unlikely to suffer from a mineral deficiency if it is fed a balanced diet. An excess of minerals can be dangerous.
Vitamin A Vitamin B$_1$ (Thiamin) Vitamin B$_2$ (Riboflavin) Vitamin B$_6$ Pantothenic acid Niacin Folic acid Vitamin B$_{12}$ Choline Taurine Vitamin C Vitamin D Vitamin E Vitamin K	550 international units per day 0.5 mg per day 0.5 mg per day 0.4 mg per day 1.0 mg per day 4.5 mg per day 0.1 mg per day 0.02 mg per day 200 mg per day 100 mg per day No dietary requirement 100 international units per day 8.0 mg per day No dietary requirement	All essential vitamins are found in a healthy, balanced diet. Vitamin A is found in liver, egg yolk, and butter. Vitamin B$_1$ is found in eggs, liver, cereals, and milk. Vitamin C is not needed in a cat's diet, since it can be manufactured in the body. Fish liver oils and animal fats are good sources of vitamin D. The action of sunlight on the cat's skin produces vitamin D.	Vitamins are essential for regulating all bodily processes. Any deficiency or excess may cause disease. Vitamin A poisoning is usually caused by a cat eating too much liver. A diet based on oily fish, such as tuna, can cause a deficiency of vitamin E.
Water	50–70 ml per kg of the cat's body weight.	Water is supplied in a balanced diet.	Water must always be available.

* Source: NRC National Academy of Sciences (1986), Washington, DC.

VITAMIN AND MINERAL SUPPLEMENTS

A variety of vitamins and minerals is essential to your cat's health and to the maintenance of its bodily functions. If you feed your cat a well-balanced, varied diet, extra vitamins should not be necessary since it will get all the nutrients it requires from its food. Giving vitamin and mineral supplements can be potentially harmful. An excess of vitamins A, D, or E, or of calcium and phosphorus, can cause serious health disorders, while an excess of cod liver oil can cause bone disease. Always seek the advice of a vet before giving supplements – they may be helpful if a cat has some metabolic problem, or for a pregnant queen or young kittens that require extra vitamins for growth.

Yeast tablets are a source of B vitamins.

Vitamin powder for adding to food.

Cat sweets containing added vitamins.

PREPARED CAT FOODS

Cats are nutritionally very demanding animals, requiring a high level of protein and fat. It is unwise to feed a cat on fresh foods alone and far safer to rely on a reputable manufacturer to supply a balanced diet. Most canned cat foods are "complete", in other words they contain all the necessary dietary constituents in the right proportion (*see page 59*). Note the feeding recommendations given, and spend a little time reading the labels to check on the nutritional content of the ingredients. Do not overfeed your cat, since it may become overweight and lazy.

TYPES OF CAT FOOD

Canned white fish, flaked and with the bones removed

Canned foods
These contain meat, fish, gelling agents, fat, water, vitamins, and cereals.

Canned tuna chunks

Canned chicken and turkey with herbs

Canned, medium-textured lamb chunks

Salmon-flavoured dry food

Chicken-flavoured dry food

Beef-flavoured dry food

Seafood-flavoured dry food

Chicken-and-fish-flavoured dry food

Dry foods
Usually fed as part of the diet. Fresh water must always be available.

DAILY FEEDING REQUIREMENTS

Life stage	Type of complete food	Energy	Amount	Number of meals
Weaning to 8 weeks	*See page 153*	–	–	–
2–4 months	Canned kitten food	250–425 calories	300–500 g (10.5–18 oz)	3–4
4–5 months	Canned kitten food	425–500 calories	500–700 g (18–25 oz)	3–4
5–6 months	Canned kitten food	500–600 calories	700–800 g (25–28 oz)	2–3
6–12 months	Canned kitten food	600–700 calories	700–800 g (25–28 oz)	1–2
Adulthood*	Canned food	300–550 calories	400–800 g (13–28 oz)	1–2
	Semi-moist food	300–550 calories	400–750 g (13–26 oz)	1–2
	Dry snack food	Feed only as an occasional meal or mixed with a canned cat food.		–
Late pregnancy (last third)	Canned food	Feed at least a third more than normal, especially in the late stages of pregnancy (*see page 146*).		2–4
Lactation	Canned food	Feed at least three times more than normal to satisfy the mother and kittens' increased requirements.		2–4
Old age**	Canned food	Feed more where absorption is poor but less if the cat is inactive (*see page 139*). Take veterinary advice.		1–2

* Cats vary in activity and may need less or more food overall. ** Cats with special dietary needs should be fed under veterinary supervision.

Semi-moist foods
Semi-moist foods can be alternated with canned or fresh foods.

Chicken-and-liver-flavoured dry food

Beef-flavoured semi-moist food

Liver-flavoured semi-moist food

Chicken flavoured semi-moist food

Tuna-flavoured dry food

Cat treats
Milk-flavoured drops can be fed as a treat.

Liver-flavoured dry food

Cat chews
Cat chews provide exercise for a cat's teeth and gums.

FRESH FOODS

The easiest way to ensure that your cat enjoys a balanced diet is to feed it on a canned cat food produced by a reliable pet food manufacturer. However, you can feed your cat a meal of fresh food once or twice a week to add variety and interest to its diet.

PREPARING FRESH FOODS

Fresh food treat
Your cat will like the taste and texture of fresh food and, if it is fed mainly on canned cat food, it will enjoy the change from its usual diet.

Cooked meat
Give your cat an occasional treat by cooking it some fresh beef, lamb, pork, or offal. Meat can be baked, grilled, or boiled, and should be cooled and chopped into small chunks before serving.

Cooked meat with vegetables
Cooked carrots, peas, or greens can be added to meat for extra vitamins.

Cooked meat with pasta
Add a little cooked rice, pasta, or potato to your cat's food bowl to make the meat or fish go further. Vegetables and carbohydrates should only make up a very small proportion of your cat's diet.

Minced meat
Your cat will enjoy the occasional meal of cooked minced beef.

Cooked fish
White fish such as coley, cod, or haddock is good for tempting a cat that is unwell or has a poor appetite. Fish should never be served raw; gently poach or steam it and remove bones.

Cooked poultry
Feed your cat all the leftover parts of a chicken, including the skin and giblets. Chop the chicken into small pieces, taking care to remove bones.

Canned sardines
Sardines, mackerel, or herring make a very nutritious treat.

Canned tuna
Canned tuna or salmon make a quick and convenient meal. Bones should be removed before serving.

Scrambled egg
A lightly scrambled egg makes an excellent light meal. Never feed a cat raw egg whites.

Porridge
Porridge or baby cereal made with warm milk is appreciated by growing kittens. Do not add any sugar.

A satisfied cat
When a cat has finished eating a tasty meal, it will sit and wash its face with its paw.

Chapter 4
GROOMING

Cats are meticulous about keeping themselves neat and tidy. It is rare to see a healthy cat looking bedraggled. Cats only fail to groom themselves when they are unwell or when they become old and frail. Owners of longhaired cats do need to give their pets daily help with grooming. Fortunately, Pedigree Longhairs are generally placid, good-natured characters, which enjoy the prolonged attention. If you accustom your cat to a grooming routine when it is young, it will be much easier when it gets older. A well-groomed cat, fed on a balanced diet, is a happy and active individual.

FIRST STEPS IN GROOMING

Grooming needs to be regular and frequent, but it does not have to take up much of your time unless you are preparing a cat for showing. If you accustom your pet to being groomed from a young age, it will be much easier to handle when it is an adult. Do not encourage a kitten to play with combs or brushes, since if it coninues to do this in later life, it is likely to scratch you and make grooming difficult.

If your cat is kept indoors it should have its claws trimmed regularly, so that they do not become overgrown. Declawing (the surgical removal of a cat's claws) deprives the cat of its natural means of defence and may result in behavioural problems from stress. This practice is actively discouraged in most countries.

TRIMMING THE CLAWS

1 Light pressure on the cat's foot will expose the claws. A badly overgrown claw can grow into the paw pad and become infected, requiring veterinary treatment.

2 Using sharp clippers, cut off the white tip. Take care not to cut the sensitive quick.

GROOMING EQUIPMENT

Clippers   Comb   Brush   Toothbrush

You will need sharp nail or guillotine clippers for trimming your cat's claws, a bristle brush and comb for removing tangles in the coat, and a small, soft toothbrush for cleaning the teeth. All items should be used on only one cat.

WHERE TO TRIM THE CLAWS
It is safer to err on the cautious side and cut less claw rather than more. Cutting into the pink quick is painful and will result in bleeding. If you are unsure, ask a vet to show you how to trim your cat's claws correctly.

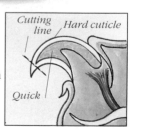

Cutting line   Hard cuticle   Quick

GROOMING A KITTEN

*Use a comb to
remove tangles*

*Hold the kitten
still while gently
stroking it*

1 To calm the kitten and
get it used to being
groomed, stroke it gently
before starting to use the
brush and comb.

2 Comb through the kitten's
coat from head to tail,
looking for signs of fleas or
other parasites at the same time
(*see page 103*).

3 Brush the fur to remove any
dead hair. Pay particular
attention to the legs and to the
area between the toes, which
can become soiled.

4 Gently brush the teeth and
gums to accustom the kitten
to a routine of dental hygiene
from an early age (*see page 69*).

Contented kitten
Grooming from
kittenhood will
strengthen
the bond
between you
and your cat,
and ensure
that it develops
into a pet that
loves attention.

GROOMING A CAT'S FACE

Before grooming your cat, you should examine its eyes, ears, and teeth for signs of health problems and clean them if necessary. In most cases, the eyes and ears will only require a quick wipe with cotton wool. Discoloration of the fur around the eyes may occur in Pedigree Longhair breeds as the result of blockage of the tear ducts, and should be cleaned off. Consult a vet if the problem is recurrent. Your cat's teeth should ideally be brushed once a week.

The corners of the cat's eyes should be free from discharge

The ear flaps should be kept clean with no signs of dirt or dark wax

The teeth should be brushed weekly

Facial grooming
A cat's eyes, ear, and teeth need regular attention. Examine your cat once a week before grooming.

CLEANING THE EYES

1 A healthy cat's eyes rarely need much attention. Consult a vet if there is any sign of a discharge. Dampen a piece of cotton wool with water.

2 Wipe gently around each eye with a separate piece of cotton wool. Be careful not to touch the eyeball itself.

Remove staining from the corners of the eyes

GROOMING EQUIPMENT

Cotton wool Baby oil   Small bowl

Use cotton wool dampened with warm water or baby oil.

3 Dry the fur around the eyes with cotton wool or a tissue. Owners of longhaired cats may need to remove any staining in the corners of the cat's eyes.

CLEANING THE EARS

1 Inspect the cat's ears for signs of inflammation. Dark-coloured wax may be caused by ear mites and require veterinary attention (*see page 107*).

2 Moisten a piece of cotton wool with a little baby oil and wipe away any dirt on the insides of the cat's ears.

3 Use a circular motion to gently clean the cat's ears but do not probe inside. Never poke cotton-wool buds in a cat's ears.

FELINE EARS

A cat's ear is a very delicate structure and should be treated with caution. Do not poke anything into the ear.

CLEANING THE TEETH

DENTAL EQUIPMENT

Toothbrush

Toothpaste *Cotton buds*

You need cotton-wool buds, a small toothbrush, and a tube of toothpaste.

Examine the gums and teeth

1 Gently open the cat's mouth to check that its gums and teeth are healthy. The gums should be firm and pink and there should be no broken teeth.

2 Accustom the cat to having its teeth brushed by lightly touching its gums with a cotton-wool bud. Put a little pet toothpaste on the cat's lips so that it can get used to the taste.

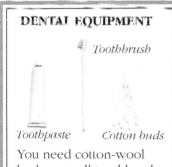

3 After a couple of weeks, try brushing the cat's teeth using a small, soft toothbrush. Use either a pet toothpaste or salt and water.

COAT TYPES

Types of feline coat can be divided into the following basic categories: longhaired, shorthaired, curly, wirehaired, and hairless. A cat's coat has a topcoat of "guard" hairs that are thick and weather-proof. The undercoat consists of soft "down" hairs and bristly "awn" hairs. Different cat breeds have different grooming requirements.

Sphynx
The virtually hairless Sphynx has fine fur on its face, ears, paws, and tail. The skin should be regularly washed with a sponge.

COAT COLOURS AND MARKINGS

The basic domestic cat has a tabby coat; all other coat markings are the result of selective breeding. There is an enormous variety of coat colours, including black, white, chocolate, blue, smoke, lilac, red, cream, and tortoiseshell. Coat patterns and shades also vary.

Red Tabby British Tabby Shorthair

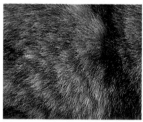
Silver Spotted British Spotted Shorthair

Tortoiseshell British Tortoiseshell Shorthair

Grey British Blue Shorthair

Grey and white British Bicolour Shorthair

Tortoiseshell British Tortoiseshell Shorthair

White Pedigree Longhair

Classic tabby Non-pedigree Shorthair

Chocolate tortoiseshell Cornish Rex

Pale grey Foreign Lilac Shorthair

Black British Black Shorthair

Brown Abyssinian

GROOMING DIFFERENT COAT TYPES

Shorthaired coat
A shorthaired cat requires little help with its appearance. However, grooming once a week will keep your cat's coat looking glossy and smooth.

Longhaired coat
Longhaired cats need the most attention and require daily grooming. Check for knotted fur on the abdomen and legs.

Angora (*right*)
An Angora's fur is fine and silky, with a tendency to wave. Grooming is particularly important in the spring, when this type of cat sheds its thick winter coat.

Rex (*right*)
A Rex's curly coat is very easy to groom. The fur is short, very silky to the touch, and particularly curly on the back and tail. Use a chamois leather to polish the coat.

Exotic Shorthair
An Exotic Shorthair's coat is very dense and slightly longer than that of other shorthaired cats. This cat should be combed or brushed daily.

Maine Coon
The fur of a Maine Coon is thick, but the undercoat is slight, which makes grooming easy. Gentle brushing every few days is all that is needed.

GROOMING A SHORTHAIRED CAT

Grooming your cat is a task that requires some patience, but your efforts will be rewarded if you make time for regular sessions. Cats are fastidious animals that wash themselves daily with immense care, but most appreciate and enjoy a little human help.

Start grooming your cat from as early an age as possible (*see page 67*). An older cat that is set in its ways will not be so willing to submit itself to being brushed and handled. Establish a routine by setting aside a time for grooming, preferably when the cat is relaxed, perhaps after feeding. One or two sessions a week should be sufficient for most shorthaired cats.

As cats approach old age, or if they are ill, they become less competent and not so inclined to groom themselves properly, and may need more help in keeping neat and tidy.

GROOMING METHOD

1 With a metal comb, work through the cat's fur from head to tail to remove any dirt. Look for signs of fleas at the same time (*see page 103*).

4 Every few weeks, apply a few drops of coat conditioner to help remove grease from the coat.

GROOMING EQUIPMENT

Metal comb *Bristle brush* *Rubber brush* *Chamois leather*

You will need a metal comb, bristle and rubber brushes, and a chamois leather. Keep all equipment as clean as possible.

5 Using a chamois leather or cloth, rub the conditioner into the coat to bring out the natural gleam.

2 Using a bristle brush, work along the lie of the coat. Brush all over the cat's body, including the chest and abdomen.

3 A rubber brush is excellent for removing dead hair and is particularly good for oriental-type cats with fine, short fur.

FLEAS AND PARASITES

While grooming your cat, examine its coat. You are unlikely to see many fleas, but you may be able to see flea droppings as black specks.

6 Stroking is enjoyable for your cat and will also help to remove dead hair and keep the coat smooth.

British Blue
If your pet is fed a balanced diet and given plenty of daily care and attention this will show in its glossy, healthy coat.

GROOMING A LONGHAIRED CAT

In the wild, a longhaired cat would only moult in the spring, but because domestic cats are kept in artificially lit and heated surroundings, they tend to moult all the year round. Longhaired pedigree cats, in particular, need daily grooming sessions to keep their fur free from tangles. As well as keeping the coat clean, neat, and glossy, grooming serves to remove loose hairs and dead skin, and tones up the circulation and muscles.

It is important to accustom a longhaired kitten to being groomed from an early age (*see page 67*). Neglect by an owner can have serious consequences, leading to a deterioration of the cat's coat, painful, matted hair, and even swallowed balls of fur forming inside the stomach.

If your cat dislikes being groomed, brush it very gently, a little at a time, until it becomes used to the process.

GROOMING METHOD

1 Start by combing the fur on the abdomen and legs to untangle knots.

2 Gently comb the fur upwards towards the cat's head one section at a time to pull out all the dead hairs.

5 Comb the fur around the neck in an upward direction so that it forms a ruff.

6 Vigorously brush the fur the "wrong way", working from head to tail. Remove all talcum powder from the cat's coat before showing.

GROOMING EQUIPMENT

Wide-toothed comb   *Talcum powder*   *Bristle brush*

You will need a wide-toothed comb, talcum powder, and a natural bristle brush.

3 To help remove grease and dirt, sprinkle a little talcum powder on to the coat once a week.

4 To remove tangles, first sprinkle with talcum powder and then gently tease the knots out by hand.

MATTED FUR

Any knots must be teased out by hand or with a knitting needle. If the coat is neglected, it may need to be disentangled by a vet.

Do not forget to brush the cat's tail

7 Finally, make a parting down the middle of the tail and gentle brush the fur out on either side.

Smoke Longhair
A longhaired cat's fur should be luxuriant and silky to the touch.

BATHING A CAT

Some people may be surprised at the idea of bathing a cat, but there may be times when this is essential, for instance if your cat's coat becomes contaminated with oil or grease. Show cats are bathed regularly, usually a few days before a show (*see page 182*). Make sure you get everything ready beforehand, with the shampoo, towels, comb, brush, and jug for rinsing all within easy reach. You may need to enlist the aid of an assistant who can help you to keep the cat calm while you bathe it.

Use a safe cat shampoo or a baby shampoo, and be careful not to get any soap into the cat's eyes or ears. If you have a shorthaired cat, you may prefer to give it a dry shampoo – rub warm bran into the coat and then vigorously brush it out.

BATHING METHOD

1 Fill a bath or large bowl with about 10 cm (4 in) of warm water. Test the temperature of the water and lift the cat firmly into the bath.

4 Rinse the cat, using plenty of warm water, until all traces of soap have been removed.

5 Lift the cat out of the bath and wrap it in a large, warm towel. Dry it off.

BATHING EQUIPMENT

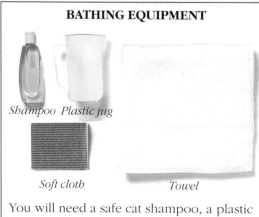

Shampoo *Plastic jug*

Soft cloth *Towel*

You will need a safe cat shampoo, a plastic jug or shower attachment, a soft cloth, and a large towel for drying the cat off so that it does not catch a chill.

2 Wet the cat with a little shampoo mixed with warm water from the neck downwards, using a jug or shower attachment.

3 Gently massage the shampoo well into the cat's coat. Take care not to get any soap into the cat's eyes or ears.

Do not put undiluted shampoo on a cat's coat

HANDLING DURING BATHING

Handle the cat firmly but gently. A cat does not like getting its fur wet and may try to scratch or bite. Talk to the cat to reassure it.

7 If the cat is not frightened, dry it thoroughly with a hairdrier. Hold the drier at a safe distance, gently brushing the fur at the same time.

6 Carefully wipe around the cat's eyes, ears, and nose, using a soft, damp cloth *(see page 68)*.

Chapter 5

THE PROBLEM CAT

BADLY BEHAVED cats are a nuisance. Some normal feline behaviour may be difficult for a human owner to understand and even more difficult to curb. On the other hand, abnormal cat behaviour, such as soiling and spraying inside the house, and aggression, may be stress-related problems that can be tackled if the cause of the upset can be identified. Alternatively, you may find that your cat is extrovert or introvert by character. Understanding and patience are essential if you are living with a "problem cat".

RECOGNIZING SIGNS OF STRESS

A life in the wild would certainly be more stressful for a feline than living within a human household. However, a pet may suffer from stress if it is exposed to certain stimuli or if its needs are not attended to properly. Anxiety can cause a cat to react in bizarre ways that include soiling and spraying indoors, chewing wool, biting and scratching, and nervous grooming. There are different causes of stress. They usually involve illness, pain, fear, or a change in the household routine caused by the arrival of a new baby or pet. A cat may also suffer from stress following the loss of an owner.

ANXIOUS FELINE BEHAVIOUR

The anxious cat
An anxious cat may appear nervous, crouching low down on the ground. Other feline responses to stress include panting and shedding fur.

The body is tense

The pupils are dilated

Aggression (*left*)
A normally placid, affectionate cat may suddenly start to behave in an aggressive way, biting and scratching its owner. There is usually a good reason for this type of behaviour. It may be a sign that the cat is unwell, in which case it should be examined by a vet. A cat may also become aggressive or destructive through boredom (*see page 86*).

The tail is held upright as the cat sprays the chair leg

Territory marking indoors (*right*)
A cat may spray inside the house if it is suffering from stress due to a change in its routine, or if another cat has been introduced into the home. The area must be washed with a dilute disinfectant to remove the odour and discourage the cat from repeating the behaviour.

Soiling indoors

A cat that soils floors or furniture may be suffering from a urinary problem that requires veterinary treatment. If the cat is otherwise healthy, it may be a sign of stress. Do not scold or smack the cat. Provide it with a clean litter tray until the problem is resolved. Deter the cat from soiling in the same place again by covering the spot with tin foil or plastic sheeting.

An anxious cat may lick and chew its fur

Nervous grooming (*above*)

There are cases of cats responding to stressful situations by over-grooming. The cat may continually lick and chew one particular area of it body for no apparent reason. This can lead to skin conditions such as dermatitis, eczema, and even baldness. A vet may treat the cat by prescribing tranquillizers.

IDENTIFYING PROBLEMS

If there is no obvious reason for your cat's problem, consult a vet who may refer your pet to an animal behaviourist for treatment.

Chewing wool

Certain breeds of oriental cat, especially Siamese and Burmese, may sometimes obsessively chew wool and other types of fabric. Such cats may be reverting to infant behaviour as a result of stress.

DEALING WITH UNWANTED BEHAVIOUR

We need to recognize the difference between normal but unwanted feline behaviour and more serious problems, such as phobias and obsessive behaviour. There are aspects of normal cat behaviour that can put a strain on your relationship with your pet. Try to understand that your cat is merely following its natural instincts when it chooses a favourite plant for its toilet or scratches your best armchair. If your pet is taught discipline from kittenhood, it is less likely to behave in an undesirable way as an adult.

Never shout at or smack a cat; a firm "No" will usually stop it in its tracks. As a last resort, a quick squirt of water with a water pistol will prevent a cat from persisting with any unwanted behaviour.

UNWANTED FELINE BEHAVIOUR

Digging up plants

A cat's habit of digging up the soil around plants (both indoors and out) when selecting a site for its toilet is a nuisance to many gardeners. If your cat selects a nearby garden for its toilet, you and your pet will soon become very unpopular with neighbours.

The cat dislikes the feel of the gravel

Remedy (*right*)

Garden plants can be surrounded with wire mesh or netting to discourage a cat from using a particular spot. Various odours, such as buried moth balls, may also act as deterrents. Probably the most effective way to stop a cat's gardening activities is to place sharp gravel around precious plants.

Fighting with other cats

An unneutered tom cat is likely to fight with other rival cats. An entire male cat's natural instinct is to defend its territory against other males and to seek out females to mate with. If you own such a cat and allow it to roam free outdoors, you can expect it to often come home battle-scarred from brawling.

Remedy (*above*)

Neutering a male cat makes it less aggressive towards other cats. It is likely to have a smaller territory to protect, stray less, and make a more affectionate pet (*see page 154*).

Eating houseplants

Cats often like to nibble at the leaves of houseplants. A cat that is confined indoors may eat plants as a substitute for grass, which all cats like to chew on. Do not keep any plants that are toxic to cats in your home (*see page 167*).

A cat may eat houseplants if it has no access to grass

Remedy (*right*)

Houseplants can be protected by putting dilute lemon juice on the leaves. If this does not work, try spraying the cat with a plant spray or water pistol (using only clean water) every time it misbehaves.

Scratching furnishings

A cat scratches furnishings not merely as a way of manicuring its claws, but also to mark the extent of its territory as a signal to other felines. The more confined or threatened a cat feels, the more likely it is to mark its home.

Remedy (*right*)

Think carefully when choosing curtains, carpets, and chairs. Some textured fabrics or hessian-type wallpaper will be irresistible to a cat. Train your cat to use a scratching post (*see page 36*).

A post is good for sharpening claws

CARING FOR AN INTROVERT CAT

Cats are well known for their independent nature, but some individuals may be rather timid and withdrawn. The root of the problem usually lies in the way a cat was raised. A kitten should be brought up in a stimulating environment, in which it feels secure. It should be encouraged to investigate any new object and to interact with other cats. A kitten that is not used to being handled and is deprived of human attention will grow up into a cat that is wary and timid with humans.

THE TIMID CAT

Wary of humans
A timid or nervous cat may have been mistreated or undersocialized when it was young. A sudden noise or the appearance of a stranger in the house is enough to make it hide away in a corner.

The eyes are wary

The tail is held between the legs

Gentle reassurance (*below*)
Never reach for a timid cat, but let it come to you in its own time. A cat perceives any unwanted advance as aggression. Reassure the cat by speaking to it softly and, if it will allow it, gently stroking it at the same time. The cat may feel safer if it is on a table or raised surface above floor level – it will feel intimidated if you are standing over it. Avoid making sudden movements or loud noises. Keep visitors away until the cat has gained confidence.

A secure refuge (*above*)
A timid cat needs a quiet refuge where it can retreat to in times of stress. An enclosed cat bed may help it to overcome its nervousness.

THE DEPENDENT CAT

The ears are forward and alert

The mouth is open; this cat is very vocal

Demanding attention

Another type of introvert cat is completely reliant on its human owner and will probably follow you around looking for reassurance. A dependent cat will seek constant love and attention. It will probably cry when it wants to be picked up or when it wants to be fed, or sometimes simply because it wants attention.

The body is held upright, demanding attention

Making friends (*right*)

A dependent cat is likely to suffer from loneliness whenever it is separated from its owner. Provide it with a feline companion and encourage it to be more independent by giving it plenty of opportunity to explore outside and meet other cats.

Companionship (*above*)

A kitten may help encourage a dependent cat to be more outgoing and less reliant on its owners for amusement. The kitten will make an ideal companion for the older cat to play with if it is to be left alone for long periods, and will prevent it from getting bored or lonely. The younger the kitten, the more likely it is to be accepted by the adult cat (*see page 33*).

CARING FOR AN EXTROVERT CAT

A boisterous or extrovert cat can be quite a handful. It will require costant attention to keep it out of mischief. Most felines grow out of kittenish behaviour, but an extrovert cat will stay lively and playful into adulthood. It is neither possible nor practical to train a cat in the same way as a dog. However, a kitten or young cat should be taught some basic discipline to prevent it from developing bad habits in later life.

THE AGGRESSIVE CAT

Biting and scratching
A cat may bite or scratch during play, or when it is being stroked. There is usually a reason for aggressive behaviour. The cat may be unwell or in pain.

The ears are held back

The claws are out

The back legs are used to kick

Tap the cat's nose gently with two fingers

Discipline (*left*)
Never smack or strike out at a cat. This will only make it nervous and cause it to run off and hide. However, you should scold a cat every time it misbehaves, using a firm, sharp tone of voice. A gentle tap on the cat's nose with two fingers may also be effective.

An extrovert cat needs toys for stimulation

Attention seeking
Most cats get all the stimulation they need by exploring their outside environment. A cat that is confined indoors and not given enough attention may become aggressive and destructive. An indoor cat needs plenty of human contact and stimulation in the form of games and toys (*see pages 46–47*) to keep it amused. A feline companion may help, especially if the cat is left alone for long periods.

THE STRAYING CAT

Leaving home

An unneutered cat or one that is not getting the care and attention that it needs (for example, if it is left alone or fed at irregular times) may stray or desert the home altogether. A cat can survive very well without humans, or, if it wants, find a new home. However, it may be picked up as a stray, or become wary of humans and revert to a semi-feral state.

The eyes and ears are alert

The tail is held high

The stride is confident and purposeful

Keeping a cat confined

A cat that has a tendency to stray may need to be confined indoors for a short period. To prevent your cat from wandering too far from home, train it to come when you call it at feeding times. A cat should not be allowed to stay outdoors all night since this is when most traffic accidents tend to happen.

A cat relies on its owner to provide it with food

Feeding times (*right*)

If a cat is fed at regular times in the morning and evening, this will ensure that it is not far from home at feeding times. Your relationship with your cat is based on the principle that you provide it with food. If this supply is withdrawn, a cat is likely to go off in search of a new home.

Chapter 6

YOUR CAT'S HEALTH

WHEN YOU take a cat into your home, its health becomes your responsibility. Your vet will provide vaccinations against infectious diseases, regular check-ups, and treatment for your cat if it should become unwell. You should learn to keep a careful watch on your cat's health at home, so that you can recognize the first signs of illness. Disorders that affect a cat's eyes, ears, and coat are usually fairly obvious. If you notice any abnormalities in the appearance of your cat or any changes in its behaviour, contact a vet immediately.

THE HEALTHY CAT

A healthy cat is a glorious sight. It is confident, alert, and interested in and aware of everything that is going on around it, even when it appears to be taking a quiet cat-nap. Assessing your cat's state of health by regularly examining it (*see page 96–97*) and carefully observing its behaviour is not difficult, but does need to be done in a routine way so as not to miss any vital sign. A cat that is unwell often does not show any symptoms, and you may not notice that there is something wrong until it is too late, and your pet is very sick.

It is best to look over your cat when it is fairly relaxed and, if possible, without it realizing what you are doing. If you know what to look for, a quick survey of your cat when you are grooming it or when it is sitting on your lap should tell you much about its condition.

A cat's behaviour is usually the best indicator of whether it is healthy. If you notice any small changes, such as a loss of appetite, a marked decrease in levels of activity, or listlessness, do not hesitate to consult a vet immediately. If you are worried about any aspect of your cat's health or notice any type of unusual behaviour, you can telephone the surgery first and ask the advice of the trained staff before you make an appointment for a consultation.

Skin and coat
A cat's coat should look sleek and glossy, and be springy to the touch. The skin should be free of scratches or fight wounds, and there should be no signs of fleas or baldness.

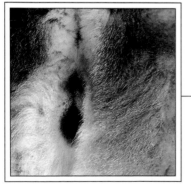

Rear
A cat will keep the area under its tail very clean. There should be no evidence of soreness or diarrhoea.

Feline fitness
A healthy cat should have a good appetite and, when it wants, can be very active, moving with grace and agility. It should groom itself regularly and enjoy being petted and handled.

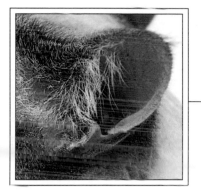

Ears
The outer part if a cat's ears tend to become dirty and should be gently cleaned once a week (*see page 69*). The ears should be a healthy pink colour inside, and there should be no signs of discharge or accumulation of dark-coloured wax. Never poke anything into the ear canal.

Eyes
A cat's eyes should be clear and bright, and free of any discharge. If the third eyelid is showing, this is a sign that a cat is unwell.

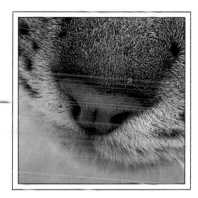

Nose
A cat's nose should feel soft and velvety, and damp to the touch. The nostrils should be free of discharge and have no crusting on the surface. Consult a vet if a cat is sneezing continually since this may be a sign of a respiratory virus.

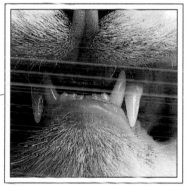

Mouth and teeth
Regular brushing will keep a cat's teeth clean and its breath free of smell. There should be no broken teeth and the gums should be pale pink and free of inflammation.

SIGNS OF ILL HEALTH

The signs described below and opposite may be accompanied by changes in your cat's general behaviour, and these can often be the first indication that something is wrong. Your cat may spend more time sleeping, drink more than normal, be reluctant to go outside, or lose its appetite. It is difficult to tell if your cat is in pain and which part of its body is affected; it may be restless, cry out, or just want to hide itself away. If you can say when your cat first showed signs of ill health, this will help the vet make a diagnosis.

EYE DISORDERS
(*see page 105*)
• Discharge from the eye
• Inflammation of the eyelid
• Change in the eye colour
• Abnormal sensitivity to light
• Visible third eyelid
• Problems with vision

EAR DISORDERS
(*see page 107*)
• Discharge from the ear
• Dark brown wax in the ear
• Persistent scratching or rubbing of the ears
• Head shaking or holding head to one side
• Swelling of the ear flap
• Hearing problems

RESPIRATORY DISORDERS
(*see page 109*)
• Laboured breathing
• Persistent sneezing
• Persistent coughing
• Discharge from the eyes and nose
• High temperature

MOUTH AND TOOTH DISORDERS
(*see page 115*)
• Drooling and pawing at the mouth
• Inflamed gums
• Missing, loose, or broken teeth
• Bad breath
• Difficulty in eating
• Loss of appetite

When to call a vet
Contact a vet immediately if your cat appears to be in pain or if it is obviously injured. Keep the telephone number of the surgery in a prominent position, so that you can find it easily in case of an emergency.

SKIN PARASITES
(*see page 103*)
• Persistent scratching
• Loss of hair
• Excessive grooming
• Biting at the skin and coat
• Signs of parasites in the coat

DIGESTIVE DISORDERS
(*see page 111*)
• Repeated vomiting
• Persistent diarrhoea
• Loss of appetite
• Blood in the faeces or vomit
• Persistent constipation

SKIN AND COAT DISORDERS
(*see page 101*)
- Persistent scratching
- Excessive licking and grooming
- Biting at the skin and coat
- Swelling under the skin
- Bald patches in the coat
- Increased shedding of the hair

NERVOUS DISORDERS
(*see page 121*)
- Convulsions and fits
- Muscle spasms and tremors
- Partial or complete paralysis
- Staggering gait
- Acute skin irritation

BLOOD AND HEART DISORDERS
(*see page 123*)
- Collapse or fainting
- Bluish discoloration of the gums
- Breathing difficulties
- Unwillingness to exercise
- Coughing while exercising

REPRODUCTIVE DISORDERS
(*see page 117*)
- Failure to breed
- Bleeding from the genitals
- Abnormal discharge from the vulva
- Swelling of the mammary glands
- Swelling of the testes

INTERNAL PARASITES
(*see page 113*)
- Worms passed in the faeces
- Persistent diarrhoea
- White "grains" visible on the rear
- Licking and rubbing of the behind
- Pot-bellied appearance
- Loss of weight

URINARY DISORDERS
(*see page 119*)
- Straining to pass urine
- Abnormal urination or incontinence
- Blood or excessive cloudiness in the urine
- Excessive thirst
- Persistent licking of the genitals

BONE, MUSCLE, AND JOINT DISORDERS
(*see page 99*)
- Lameness and limping
- Swelling around the affected area
- Tenderness when area is touched
- Reluctance to walk or jump
- Abnormal gait

DIAGNOSIS CHART

This flow chart is intended to be a rough guide for you to find out what is wrong with your cat. If your pet is showing any of these clinical signs, it may be the first sign of a health problem. Always contact a vet if you are in the slightest doubt about your cat's health.

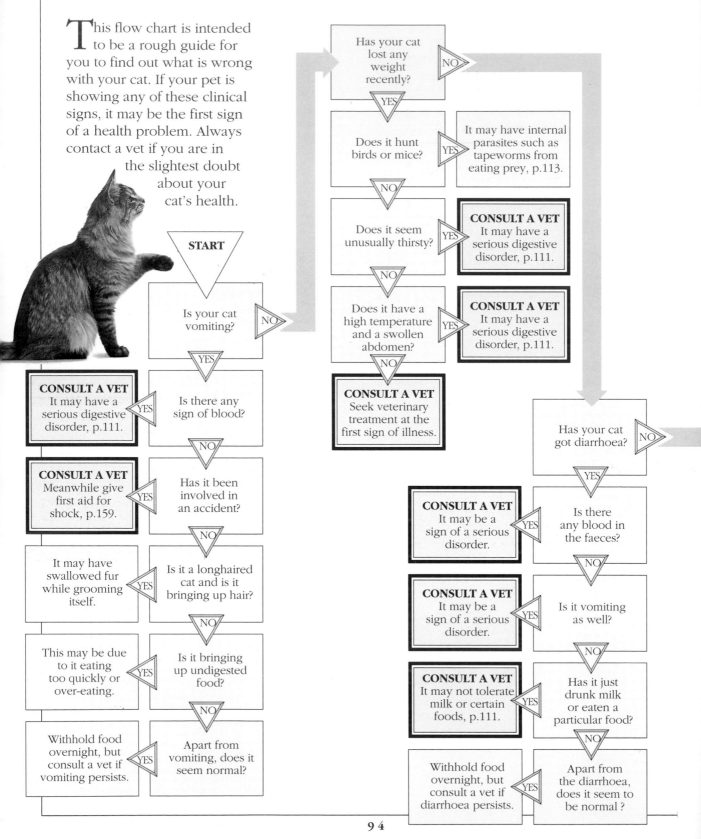

START

Is your cat vomiting? — NO

Has your cat lost any weight recently? — NO

YES

Is there any sign of blood? — YES → **CONSULT A VET** It may have a serious digestive disorder, p.111.

Does it hunt birds or mice? — YES → It may have internal parasites such as tapeworms from eating prey, p.113.

NO

Has it been involved in an accident? — YES → **CONSULT A VET** Meanwhile give first aid for shock, p.159.

Does it seem unusually thirsty? — YES → **CONSULT A VET** It may have a serious digestive disorder, p.111.

NO

Is it a longhaired cat and is it bringing up hair? — YES → It may have swallowed fur while grooming itself.

Does it have a high temperature and a swollen abdomen? — YES → **CONSULT A VET** It may have a serious digestive disorder, p.111.

NO

CONSULT A VET Seek veterinary treatment at the first sign of illness.

Is it bringing up undigested food? — YES → This may be due to it eating too quickly or over-eating.

NO

Apart from vomiting, does it seem normal? — YES → Withhold food overnight, but consult a vet if vomiting persists.

Has your cat got diarrhoea? — NO

YES

Is there any blood in the faeces? — YES → **CONSULT A VET** It may be a sign of a serious disorder.

NO

Is it vomiting as well? — YES → **CONSULT A VET** It may be a sign of a serious disorder.

NO

Has it just drunk milk or eaten a particular food? — YES → **CONSULT A VET** It may not tolerate milk or certain foods, p.111.

NO

Apart from the diarrhoea, does it seem to be normal? — YES → Withhold food overnight, but consult a vet if diarrhoea persists.

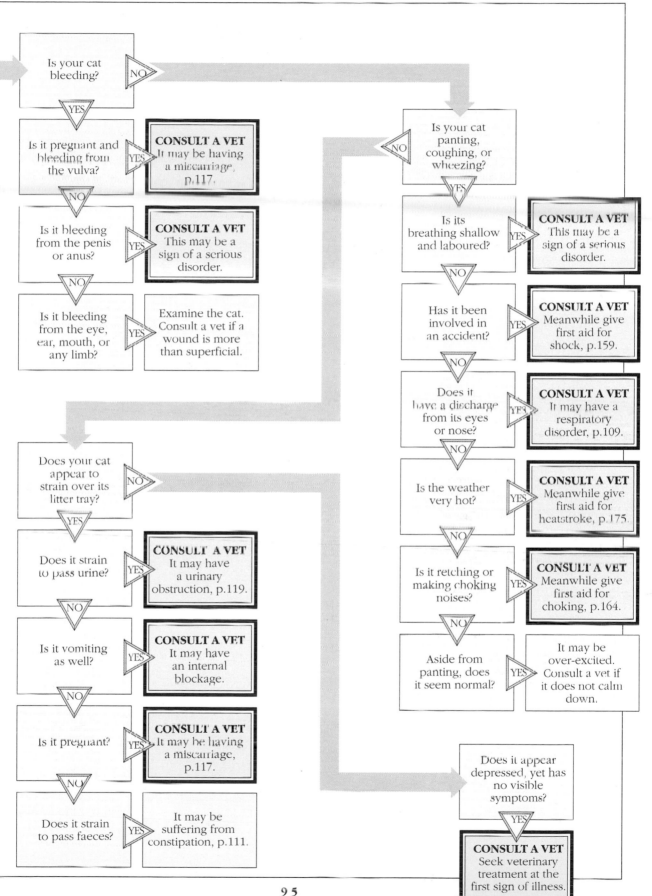

Is your cat bleeding? **NO**

Is your cat bleeding? **YES**

Is it pregnant and bleeding from the vulva? **YES**
CONSULT A VET It may be having a miscarriage, p.117.

Is it pregnant and bleeding from the vulva? **NO**

Is it bleeding from the penis or anus? **YES**
CONSULT A VET This may be a sign of a serious disorder.

Is it bleeding from the penis or anus? **NO**

Is it bleeding from the eye, ear, mouth, or any limb? **YES**
Examine the cat. Consult a vet if a wound is more than superficial.

Does your cat appear to strain over its litter tray? **NO**

Does your cat appear to strain over its litter tray? **YES**

Does it strain to pass urine? **YES**
CONSULT A VET It may have a urinary obstruction, p.119.

Does it strain to pass urine? **NO**

Is it vomiting as well? **YES**
CONSULT A VET It may have an internal blockage.

Is it vomiting as well? **NO**

Is it pregnant? **YES**
CONSULT A VET It may be having a miscarriage, p.117.

Is it pregnant? **NO**

Does it strain to pass faeces? **YES**
It may be suffering from constipation, p.111.

Is your cat panting, coughing, or wheezing? **NO**

Is your cat panting, coughing, or wheezing? **YES**

Is its breathing shallow and laboured? **YES**
CONSULT A VET This may be a sign of a serious disorder.

Is its breathing shallow and laboured? **NO**

Has it been involved in an accident? **YES**
CONSULT A VET Meanwhile give first aid for shock, p.159.

Has it been involved in an accident? **NO**

Does it have a discharge from its eyes or nose? **YES**
CONSULT A VET It may have a respiratory disorder, p.109.

Does it have a discharge from its eyes or nose? **NO**

Is the weather very hot? **YES**
CONSULT A VET Meanwhile give first aid for heatstroke, p.175.

Is the weather very hot? **NO**

Is it retching or making choking noises? **YES**
CONSULT A VET Meanwhile give first aid for choking, p.164.

Is it retching or making choking noises? **NO**

Aside from panting, does it seem normal? **YES**
It may be over-excited. Consult a vet if it does not calm down.

Does it appear depressed, yet has no visible symptoms? **YES**
CONSULT A VET Seek veterinary treatment at the first sign of illness.

EXAMINING A CAT

If you suspect that your cat is unwell, a basic check on its bodily functions will be useful in assessing its condition. You can make such health checks part of a regular routine, beginning from an early age. Regular examination has a number of benefits. It allows you to detect early changes in your cat's state of health, and makes it possible for you to give the vet a full report on any unusual signs that you have observed. Most important of all, it helps to reinforce the bond between you and your cat.

When subjecting your cat to examination, always be firm but gentle, and talk to it in a reassuring way. None of the techniques shown on these pages is difficult. They just require a little understanding of feline behaviour and practice.

TAKING THE PULSE

1 Place the cat on a table or other raised surface. Make sure that the cat is as calm and relaxed as possible by talking to it in a soothing way.

2 The cat's pulse is best felt high up on the inside of the hind leg. You should always count the pulse beats for at least two separate minutes.

TAKING THE TEMPERATURE

1 First, shake the thermometer and lubricate it with petroleum jelly. Lift the cat's tail and insert the thermometer.

READING A THERMOMETER

38–39°C

A healthy cat's temperature is between 38 and 39°C (100 and 102°F).

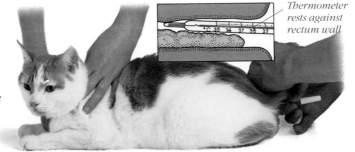

2 Carefully hold the thermometer in the cat's rectum for at least one minute. Remove and wipe it before reading.

Thermometer rests against rectum wall

VITAL SIGNS

Normal pulse, temperature, and respiration rates are: Pulse: 160–240 per minute; Temperature: 38–39°C/ 100–102°F; Respiration: 20–30 per minute.

CHECKING BODY FUNCTIONS

Breathing
Listen to either the breaths out or the breaths in. Here the cat's breathing is being checked by a vet, with a stethoscope.

Abdomen
With the cat at ease, gently palpate the abdomen for any signs of swelling or tenderness. Use a gentle touch since the cat may react if it is in pain.

Ears
Look into the ears but do not put things in them. Note any scratches to the outer ear, inflammation, or dark-coloured wax, which may be a sign of ear mites.

Eyes
Look for discharges, inflammation, or signs of injury. Do not put any drops in a cat's eyes without consulting a vet and never touch the eyeball itself.

Mouth
Open the cat's mouth and look for broken teeth, inflamed gums, or a build-up of dental deposits that may require scaling by a vet.

Claws
Gentle pressure on the cat's foot will unsheathe the claws. Note any broken or missing claws, and any injuries to the soft web of skin between the cat's paw pads.

BONE, MUSCLE, AND JOINT DISORDERS

A cat's agility and elegance are made possible by its highly refined skeleton and the joints and muscles that make it work. Cats are seldom victims of muscle or joint disorders, although an elderly feline may suffer from inflammation of the joints and lameness, which require treatment by a vet. The most serious problems are bone fractures, joint sprains, and injuries from fighting. Always consult a vet for treatment of any serious injury since the cat is likely to be suffering from severe shock.

Fractures
Although a cat's skeleton is very strong, fractures do occur as a result of accidents.

THE FELINE SKELETON

Muscles
A cat's muscles are joined to the bones by tendons. These serve as levers to move the bones together or apart so that the cat can move.

Caudal vertebrae

Sacral vertebrae

Lumbar vertebrae

Thoracic vertebrae

Cervical vertebrae

Cranium (brain box)

Mandible (lower jaw)

Pelvis

Scapula (shoulder)

Ribs

Bones
A cat's skeleton is light, strong, and flexible, with about ten per cent more bones than the human body.

Sternum (breastbone)

Humerus

Femur (thigh)

Tibia (shin)

Carpus (wrist)

Radius

Ulna

Phalange (finger and toe)

Tarsus (ankle or hock)

Metatarsus (hind paw)

Metacarpus (forepaw)

BONE, MUSCLE, AND JOINT DISORDERS

Disorder	Description and signs	Action
Bone fractures	Most fractures are caused by traffic accidents or awkward falls. Broken bones are classified according to their severity. A simple fracture does not break through the skin, whereas in a compound fracture the bone is exposed. Fractures are associated with shock, blood loss, and internal injuries.	Consult a vet immediately for fixation of the broken limb. Do not attempt to treat a fracture yourself by splinting the limb (*see page 161*).
Dislocation	A dislocated joint can be the result of a fall or other accident. The hip is the joint most commonly affected. Signs are a sudden pain with an inability to put weight on the limb.	Urgent veterinary treatment is needed. The vet will replace the joint in its socket under an anaesthetic.
Bone infection	A deep fight wound may worsen and the infection spread to the bone. Signs of a bone infection include lameness, fever, swelling, and perhaps a discharge.	All serious bite wounds must be treated by a vet. Antibiotics may be prescribed to prevent infection.
Undermineralization	Kittens fed a diet of all muscle meat do not get enough minerals. This leads to poor bone development and stunted growth. The condition can also affect adult cats.	A vet can advise on the necessary corrections to the diet. Treatment may involve giving a mineral supplement.
Vitamin excess	Feeding a cat an excessive amount of foods high in vitamin A or D, or overdosing with a vitamin supplement can result in deformities of the spine.	The diet must be corrected at once. Do not give vitamin supplements unless recommended by a vet.
Cleft palate	A birth defect caused by a failure of the bones of the hard palate to develop fully (*see page 115*).	Surgery to correct the defect may sometimes be possible.
Arthritis	This condition sometimes occurs following a joint infection, dislocation, or trauma. It is most often due to a degeneration of the cartilage in joints as a result of old age. Signs include painful, stiff joints and lameness.	Consult a vet immediately if your cat shows any signs of lameness. Anti-inflammatory drugs may be prescribed to relieve the condition.
Sprains	Although muscle problems are rare, a sprain may sometimes occur when a tendon or ligament is stretched beyond its limits. The signs are swelling and a temporary lameness.	If there is any swelling of the limb, consult a vet immediately. Treat with cold compresses.

BONE FRACTURES

When bones break as the result of an accident, the surrounding tissues are likely to be damaged as well. The cat will probably be in severe shock and the fractured limb will be swollen and painful due to internal bleeding and bruising. The bones must be immobilized for as long as it takes for them to heal properly. Cats make good subjects for treatment, since they take to cage rest and can cope with plasters and pins. Even if a limb has to be amputated, a three-legged cat quickly learns to get around without difficulty.

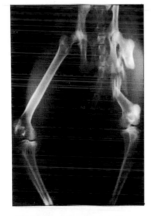

Before treatment
A radiograph shows the extent of injuries to a thigh bone. Although the femur is shattered into several pieces, it is not beyond repair.

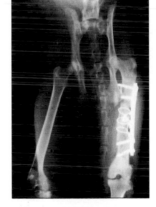

After treatment
Following surgery, the broken bone fragments have been realigned and immobilized. Healing usually takes several weeks.

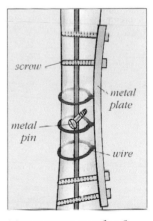

Treatment method
The bone fragments are carefully pieced together. They are immobilized using a combination of encircling wires, a steel plate, and some screws.

screw
metal plate
metal pin
wire

SKIN AND COAT DISORDERS

There are two types of skin disorder: parasitic and non-parasitic. External parasites such as fleas, lice, and ticks are very common in cats (*see pages 102–103*). Other non-parasitic conditions that can affect the skin and coat are dermatitis, ringworm, stud tail, feline acne, tumours, and abscesses due to fight wounds. Most problems are not contagious and respond well to treatment. Ringworm, however, can be transmitted to other cats, and even to humans.

The main signs of skin disorders are irritation, inflammation and changes in the surrounding skin, and hair loss. They are not specific to any one ailment. Changes in the skin and coat can sometimes be an indication of a serious illness, and if a cat stops grooming itself this may be an early sign that it is unwell.

Self grooming
Meticulous grooming keeps skin and coat problems to a minimum.

ANATOMY OF THE SKIN

Layered protection
The skin helps to control a cat's temperature and to minimize water loss. The coat is made up of heavy guard hairs and finer secondary hairs, all joined to a system of muscle fibres that allow the hair to be erected, especially along the back and over the tail.

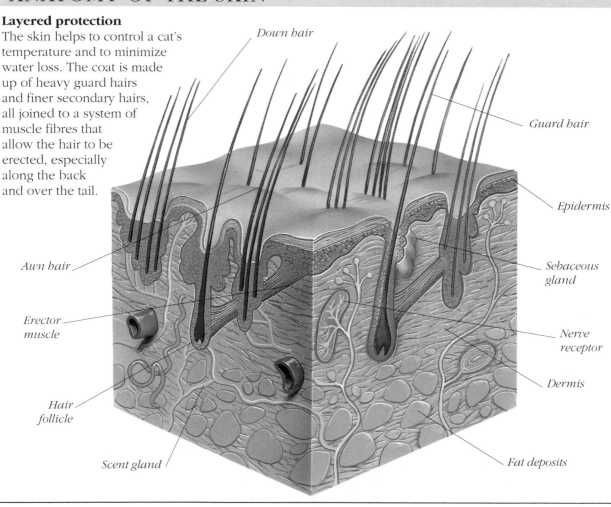

Down hair

Guard hair

Epidermis

Sebaceous gland

Awn hair

Erector muscle

Nerve receptor

Dermis

Hair follicle

Scent gland

Fat deposits

SKIN AND COAT DISORDERS

Disorder	Description and signs	Action
Abscess	This is a painful swelling that becomes infected and filled with pus. It is usually caused as a result of a fight wound (*see page 169*). The most common sites of abscesses are on the face and around the base of the tail.	Consult a vet if your cat has been bitten. The wound may become septic and require veterinary attention.
Dermatitis	Dermatitis is a term for several skin problems (commonly called eczema) which can cause inflammation and dry, scaly skin. Allergic dermatitis is caused by an allergy to certain foods (such as fish) or to flea dirt, and may result in hair loss. Flea collar dermatitis is the result of a reaction to the insecticide in the collar and causes itching and redness. Solar dermatitis may affect the skin on the ears of white cats in hot countries (*see page 107*).	Consult a vet. Treatment for dermatitis may involve giving the cat antibiotics, and using anti-inflammatory or hormonal agents. Solar dermatitis may be controlled by applying protective suntan cream to the cat's ears. Flea collars should be removed at the first sign of irritation.
Ringworm	A skin infection caused by a parasitic fungus and not a worm. Signs of infection can be difficult to spot and vary from a few broken hairs on the face and ears to small, round patches of scaly skin on the cat's head, ears, paws, and back. A cat may carry the disease without showing any symptoms.	Ringworm can be treated with a variety of antiseptic creams and, in severe cases, anti-fungal drugs. Disinfection of all bedding is important because it is transmissible to humans (*see page 125*).
Tumour	A skin tumour is a swelling on or beneath the cat's skin and can be either benign or malignant – the latter means that it is cancerous. Cancerous growths usually grow very rapidly and cause bleeding and ulceration.	Examine any lump or growth that appears on your cat's skin. Consult a vet immediately if you are concerned.
Nervous grooming	Nervous licking or grooming of the coat may result in partial hair loss and sometimes dermatitis. This behaviour may be caused by boredom or anxiety (*see page 81*).	Treatment involves identifying the reason for the stress. Tranquillizers or sedatives may be prescribed.
Feline acne	Acne on a cat's chin and lower lip is caused by blocked ducts leading to blackheads, pimples, and small abscesses forming on the skin.	Consult a vet if you notice any skin abnormality. Antibiotic treatment is sometimes needed.
Stud tail	This is an excessive secretion of oil from the sebaceous glands at the base of the tail. It commonly affects unneutered male cats and may cause staining on pale-coloured cats.	Wash the coat with a safe shampoo, but consult a vet if it becomes infected or if there is irritation.
Hair loss	A neutered cat may suffer from hair loss on its hindquarters and abdomen. This may be due to a hormonal imbalance.	Consult a vet to identify the reason for the baldness.

RINGWORM

This skin infection is caused by a parasitic fungus not a worm. It lives on the surface layers of the skin, causing inflammation and scratching. Signs of ringworm infection are usually seen as bald patches of scaly skin on the head, ears, paws, and back.

Some cats show no symptoms of the disease other than a few broken hairs. Diagnosis can be made using an ultra-violet lamp and by examining affected hairs under a microscope. Ringworm is highly contagious among cats living in a household and can be transmitted to other animals, even including humans. Disinfection of baskets, bedding, and bowls during an outbreak is essential.

Treating ringworm (*above*)
The fur around the affected area may be clipped before treatment.

DERMATITIS

This is an inflammation of the skin and can be associated with many different factors. It is commonly caused by an allergic response such as a reaction to flea dirt or certain foods. This results in an inflamed, itchy rash developing on the cat's skin. The condition can be aggravated by self-mutilation and infection. All skin conditions require careful investigation by a vet so that a proper diagnosis can be made. Procedures include various skin tests in which small samples of skin are removed and examined under a microscope.

SKIN PARASITES

A variety of parasites can inhabit a cat's coat. Fleas are the most common cause of feline skin problems. Specks of "flea dirt" are easily seen in the coat, looking like large soot particles. Irritation can result from the fleas themselves, or from sensitivity to their saliva or droppings. Fleas are involved in the life cycle of tapeworms, and can lead to anaemia.

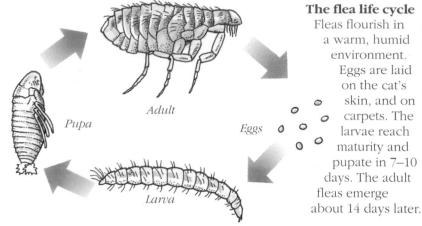

Pupa   *Adult*   *Eggs*   *Larva*

The flea life cycle
Fleas flourish in a warm, humid environment. Eggs are laid on the cat's skin, and on carpets. The larvae reach maturity and pupate in 7–10 days. The adult fleas emerge about 14 days later.

COMMON FELINE PARASITES

Flea Visible as pinhead-size, red-brown insects. Found around the neck and at the base of the tail.

Signs of infestation
Continuous or persistent scratching may be the first sign of infestation by parasites. Check the irritated area, then take appropriate action.

Ear mite The most common feline health problem, producing reddish-brown wax.

Fur mite Highly contagious. Visible as dry scales (dandruff) on the cat's back.

Tick Round, blood-sucking parasite. Must be removed carefully from skin.

Harvest mite Visible as tiny red dots on the cat's feet in autumn. Can be very irritating. Also known as "chiggers".

HUMAN INFECTION
Most parasites prefer not to live on humans. When they do get into clothing or on to skin, they are fairly easy to remove with sensible hygiene.

Louse Pinhead-size insect that feeds on the skin. Its white eggs (nits) may be visible on the cat's fur.

SKIN PARASITES

Parasite	Description and signs	Action
Fleas	The most common skin parasite. Fleas can carry tapeworm larvae (*see page 112*). The presence of fleas is shown by persistent scratching and small black specks ("flea dirt") in the cat's coat. Some cats are allergic to flea bites due to a sensitivity to the flea's saliva.	Ask your vet to recommend a suitable insecticide spray or powder. Do not use a flea collar on a kitten or sick cat. Always follow the manufacturer's instructions very carefully.
Ticks	Sheep ticks are sometimes found on cats in country areas. They resemble small, blue-grey swellings and suck the cat's blood. A heavy infestation can sometimes cause anaemia. There are some ticks in Australia that secrete a toxin which can result in paralysis (tick poisoning).	Dab the tick with alcohol and then remove it with tweezers. If the mouthparts remain in the skin, this can cause an abscess. Ask your vet to advise you on a suitable insecticide.
Lice	Lice are uncommon in healthy cats. They are found on the head and along the back and can be seen as white eggs (nits) attached to the cat's fur.	Consult a vet. In severe cases, the fur may need to be clipped, and the cat bathed in a suitable insecticide.
Mange mites	These minute skin parasites burrow into the cat's skin and cause a range of skin conditions, including inflammation and hair loss. The head mange mite affects the cat's head and neck. Other mites that can cause skin irritations are fur mites (also known as "walking dandruff"), harvest mites, and ear mites (*see page 107*).	If you suspect that your cat has mites, consult a vet for identification and treatment of the skin parasites with a safe insecticide.
Fly strike	This condition especially affects longhaired cats with neglected or matted fur. Blow flies lay their eggs in the cat's fur and the larvae burrow under the skin, causing skin damage and bacterial infections.	Consult a vet. The matted hair and damaged skin need to be cleaned with a safe antiseptic and treated with a suitable insecticide.
Bot flies	This type of fly is found mainly in parts of the United States. The bot fly grubs penetrate the cat's skin and may be seen as swellings on its neck, back, sides, and abdomen.	Veterinary treatment is needed if a cat has multiple swellings.

FLEA COLLARS

Collars are a useful aid to flea control, supplying continuous anti-flea medication. They should complement, rather than replace, normal household hygiene. Over-exposure to the medication in flea collars can sometimes cause skin irritation.

Safety (*right*)
Regularly remove flea collars to check for irritation.

TREATING PARASITES

The first rule in controlling fleas and other parasites is to maintain a high standard of hygiene in the cat's environment. No amount of dressings, powders, or sprays will be completely effective if this rule is not followed, since many parasites live or lay their eggs away from the cat and thrive in well-heated, modern homes. As well as treating the cat, you should also disinfect its bedding and all surrounding furnishings with a house spray to prevent parasites recurring. Cats are highly sensitive to a variety of insecticides, so you should ensure that preparations are always used as directed. A flea collar (*see page 38*) should have an elasticated section and should be replaced every few months to ensure its effectiveness. Do not put a flea collar on a cat unnecessarily, if you have already managed to eliminate fleas from the house.

Sprays (*left*)
Keep any sprays away from the eyes. A cat may be frightened of the noise.

EYE DISORDERS

Changes in the appearance of a cat's eyes, whether due to infection or injury, are usually very noticeable. The most common eye conditions affect the cat's outer eye and the conjunctiva (the membrane covering the eyeball). The third eyelid is an extra protection that is not normally visible in a healthy animal, but which may come across the eye if a cat is unwell. Signs of problems to watch out for are discharge or watering, closure of the eye, and any cloudiness or change in colour. Consult a vet if you notice any abnormality – if left untreated, many eye conditions can lead to impaired sight or even blindness. Most common eye disorders can be treated with antibiotic drops or ointments prescribed by a vet (*see page 132*).

Inspecting the eyes
A vet can examine the deeper parts of a cat's eyes using an ophthalmoscope.

HOW THE EYE WORKS

Pupil dilation
The cat's vertical pupil protects the retina from bright light and can adjust to different light levels.

Pupil in bright light

Pupil in darkness

The structure of the eye
Light passes through the cornea and the lens to the light-sensitive cells of the retina, where impulses are sent to the brain via the optic nerve. A cat's eyes are specially designed to collect the maximum amount of light.

Optic nerve

Vitreous humour

Retina

Lens

Upper eyelid

Aqueous humour

Cornea

Pupil

Lower eyelid

Iris

Conjunctiva

Suspensory ligaments

EYE DISORDERS

Disorder	Description and signs	Action
Conjunctivitis	This common disorder is an inflammation of the outer layer of the eye (conjunctiva). The eyes will look red and swollen, and there will be a discharge. One or both eyes may be affected. Conjunctivitis can be a symptom of a viral infection such as Feline respiratory disease (*see page 109*).	Consult the vet for an examination of the cat's eyes. Treatment will usually be in the form of antibiotic drops or ointment. Never use medicines intended for humans.
Corneal damage and ulceration	Injuries to the eyes and eyelids during fights are common and normally heal quickly. If the wound becomes infected, there may be ulceration and even penetration of the cornea.	Consult a vet immediately. Urgent treatment of corneal ulcers is essential to avoid complications.
Protrusion of the third eyelids	The inner eyelid in the corner of the eye is not normally visible, but it may come across to protect an injured eye. If both eyes are affected, this is a sign that the cat may be out of condition or suffering from a viral infection.	Urgent treatment is needed where there is any injury to a cat's eyes. A cat should always be examined by a vet if it is out of condition.
Keratitis	An inflammation of the cornea results in the eye becoming cloudy. Signs include watering and sensitivity.	Urgent treatment is needed to prevent the condition from deteriorating.
Cataracts	An opacity of the lens of the eye is sometimes a congenital condition, but it is more often associated with elderly or diabetic cats.	Careful veterinary assessment is needed. Surgery may be possible to restore vision if both eyes are affected.
Glaucoma	This serious condition occurs when there is an increase in pressure within the eyeball. As a result, the cornea becomes cloudy and the eyeball enlarges.	Any apparent enlargement or change in the eyes should receive prompt veterinary treatment.
Bulging eye	Severe bulging or even dislocation of the eyeball may occur following an accident or as the result of an eye tumour.	Emergency veterinary treatment is needed as soon as possible.
Retinal diseases	Degeneration of the light-sensitive cells at the back of the eye (retina) may be inherited or due to a dietary deficiency. This eye disorder results in sight loss and may eventually lead to blindness.	Urgent veterinary treatment is required for diagnosis and to prevent the condition from deteriorating.
Watery eyes	An overproduction of tears or blocked tear ducts may cause facial staining.	Usually an inherited defect associated with Pedigree Longhairs (*see page 133*).

THE THIRD EYELIDS

Gentle pressure on a cat's eyeball will expose the tiny shutter at the corner. If these eyelids are visible, this can be a sign that a cat is out of condition, or is suffering from diarrhoea or worms. Exposure of the third eyelid on one side only may be due to an injury, fight wound, or object in the eye.

Eyelids (*left*)
A cat must be examined by a vet if the third eyelid is visible.

BLINDNESS

Severe eye conditions such as retinal diseases or cataracts can result in a loss of sight. Cats cope surprisingly well with failing sight brought on by old age or even with the loss of an eye following an accident or trauma. In familiar surroundings, they soon learn to adjust their behaviour by using their other senses to compensate. Consult a vet immediately if you notice any sudden loss of vision. This may not be apparent if you look at the cat's eyes, but you may notice it misjudging heights or bumping into furniture.

Eye test (*left*)
To test sight, cover one eye and move your finger towards the other eye, making the cat blink. A torch shone into the eye will show the pupil reflex.

EAR DISORDERS

A cat's ears control its sense of balance and hearing. Infections of the middle and inner ear can therefore cause problems with mobility, as well as affecting a cat's hearing. The commonest causes of infection are micro-organisms, foreign bodies, or ear mites. Signs of ear disorders to watch out for are persistent scratching, head shaking, twitching of the ears, discharge, and the presence of dark wax. Deafness can occur following an infection, but it is more often a congenital defect associated with cats with white coats. Old age usually results in some loss of hearing.

Examining the ears
A vet can inspect the lower part of the ear canal using an auriscope. Do not poke anything into a cat's ears.

HOW THE EAR WORKS

The outer ear
Sound waves are gathered by the sensitive outer ear and channelled to the ear drum.

Ear flap

Semi-circular canals

The inner ear
The ear drum vibrates, moving the ossicles in the middle ear, which pass on the movement to the inner ear. The sound waves are translated into electrical impulses and conveyed to the brain.

Auditory nerve

Cochlea

Ossicles (hammer, anvil, and stirrup)

Outer ear

Oval window

Ear drum

Middle ear

Eustachian tube

EAR DISORDERS

Disorder	Description and signs	Action
Ear mites	Mite infestation is very common in cats (especially in kittens). Tiny mites live in the ear canal and can cause irritation if they are present in large numbers. Signs of ear mites include persistent scratching and the accumulation of dark brown, pungent wax in the ears.	An examination of the cat's ears with an auriscope can confirm the presence of ear mites. All cats and dogs in the household will need to be treated with ear drops (*see page 133*).
Ear infection	An inflammation of the ear canal can be caused by the presence of a foreign body, fungus, or bacteria in the ear. The cat will scratch the inflamed ear, leading to infection and sometimes a discharge.	Consult a vet for examination of the cat's ears. Treatment will usually involve administering ear drops (*see page 133*).
Middle and inner ear infections	If an infection spreads to the middle or inner ear, it can result in damage to a cat's hearing. Signs of this disorder include loss of hearing and sense of balance. An affected cat may tilt its head to one side.	Prompt veterinary treatment with a course of antibiotics is usually needed. Delay may result in permanent damage to the cat's hearing.
Blood blister (haematoma)	Fighting or constant scratching may rupture blood vessels in the ear flap, producing a large blood blister. This is not painful, but it will cause irritation and the cat may continue to scratch and worry at it.	Consult a vet, who will drain the fluid from the ear. If the blood blister is left untreated, this may lead to scarring and a "cauliflower ear".
Sunburn	Pale-coloured cats living in hot countries, such as Australia, are prone to sunburn on their ear tips because of the lack of protective pigment in the skin (*see page 173*). In time, skin damage may lead to cancerous growth and to the cat's ear becoming thickened and inflamed.	The cat should be kept indoors during the hottest part of the day. A sunblock cream may provide some protection. Amputation of the ear tips is the only treatment for cancer.
Deafness	Loss of hearing may be the result of old age, middle ear infections, head injuries, or the ear canal becoming blocked with wax. Some cats are deaf from birth, especially some white cats with blue eyes (*see page 133*).	A thorough veterinary examination is required where deafness is suspected.
Foreign bodies	Foreign bodies, such as grass seeds, can sometimes get caught in a cat's ears and may cause irritation and eventually lead to infection (*see above*).	Consult a vet if the foreign body is not visible and cannot be easily removed (*see page 165*).

EAR MITES

Most cats harbour some ear mites, but they usually only cause health problems if they are present in large numbers. The tiny mites feed on the delicate lining of the ear canal, causing irritation and the production of brown wax. This makes the cat scratch or shake its ears, thereby causing inflammation. Early veterinary attention is vital to make sure that any ear infection does not spread to the inner ear and affect the cat's centres of hearing and balance. It is important to keep your cat's ears clean and check regularly for signs of irritation or infection.

Ear mites are very contagious, so always treat both ears and dose all animals in the household.

Signs of mites (*above*)
Persistent scratching and head shaking are signs of mites.

EAR INJURIES

Because of their exposed position, a cat's ears are very prone to being bitten, torn, or scratched during fights. Such injuries can become infected if the wound is deep and may require veterinary treatment. Violent or persistent scratching may sometimes rupture blood vessels on the ear flap, producing a blood blister. Although this is not painful, it will irritate the cat who will continue to scratch it. A vet can drain the fluid from the ear and support it, so it can heal in its correct shape. The ears of white cats are prone to damage from both frostbite (*see page 173*) and sunburn – the latter can lead to cancerous growth.

RESPIRATORY DISORDERS

Most respiratory illnesses that affect cats are due to infections by bacteria or viruses and the upper respiratory tract is usually affected. Although the majority of conditions are mild and respond to careful nursing, they can become serious if neglected. Like human beings, cats can sometimes suffer from colds and occasional sneezing, coughing, and wheezing. Signs of respiratory disorders include breathing difficulties and discharge from the eyes and nose. A sick cat's breathing may be deep and laboured, or shallow and rapid. Coughs may be fluid and chesty, or dry and harsh. It is important to get prompt veterinary help if your cat is showing any sign of illness, in order to prevent the condition from becoming chronic or life-threatening.

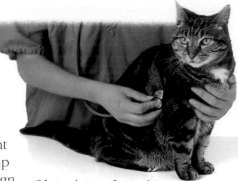

Listening to breathing
A vet can listen to a cat's breathing with a stethoscope. Radiographs may also help with the diagnosis.

THE RESPIRATORY SYSTEM

Breathing
Air is drawn into the cat's lungs through the nasal passage, which filters and warms it. The air passes down the trachea into the bronchi and the lungs, where the oxygen is absorbed by the blood and taken around the body.

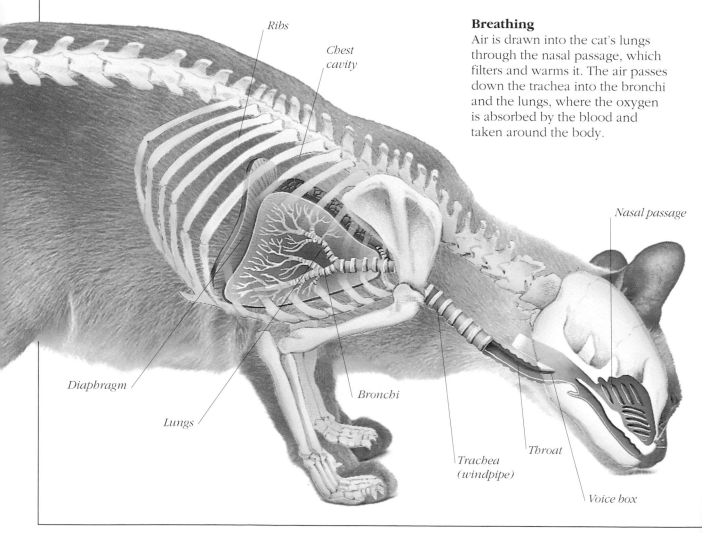

Ribs

Chest cavity

Nasal passage

Diaphragm

Lungs

Bronchi

Trachea (windpipe)

Throat

Voice box

RESPIRATORY DISORDERS

Disorder	Description and signs	Action
Feline respiratory disease ("cat flu")	The two most common respiratory viruses are Feline Viral Rhinotracheitis (FVR) and Feline Calici Virus (FCV). FVR is usually the more serious disease. The main sign of FVR is a watery discharge from the eyes and nose which becomes thicker as the disease progresses. A cat with FCV may also have a runny nose and eyes, and it will typically have ulcers on its tongue and mouth.	Prevention of FVR and FCV by vaccination is essential. Antibiotics may reduce the severity of the disease's effects but much depends on the cat's immune system being able to fight off the virus. Recovery is often due to careful home nursing.
Pneumonia	A lung infection may follow severe respiratory diseases. Fever, difficulty in breathing, nasal discharge, and a cough are often associated with pneumonia.	Urgent veterinary treatment is needed. Careful nursing and cage rest are both an important part of the treatment.
Bronchitis	This condition usually accompanies other respiratory diseases. It is caused by an inflammation of the air tubes (bronchi) that link the windpipe to the lungs. Persistent coughing is the main symptom.	Urgent veterinary treatment is needed. Careful nursing and cage rest are both an important part of the treatment.
Pleurisy	A bacterial infection may lead to an inflammation of the layer covering the lungs (pleura). This causes a build-up of fluid in the chest cavity which makes breathing difficult.	Urgent veterinary treatment is needed. The fluid in the chest cavity may need to be drained.
Asthma	An allergic sensitivity can sometimes bring on an asthma attack. It is characterized by a sudden difficulty in breathing and wheezing and coughing.	Urgent veterinary treatment is needed to ease breathing and prevent repeated asthma attacks.
Chlamydial disease	This is caused by bacteria which produce signs similar to Feline respiratory disease (see above).	A vaccine may give some protection against the disease.
Nasal discharge	A watery discharge from the nose and eyes is a sign of several infections. If the discharge is accompanied by sneezing and snuffling, the irritation may be due to an infection of the nasal cavities.	Consult a vet for examination and diagnosis of the infection.
Lungworm	This tiny parasite may be found in the lungs of cats in rural areas. Severely affected animals may have a dry cough.	A vet can prescribe drugs to treat the lungworm parasite.

LUNGWORM

The most common lung parasite that can infect cats is the lungworm. The signs of infection are usually mild, and most cats show no symptoms at all. A few, however, may develop a persistent dry cough. The lungworm life cycle is complicated, since it involves a snail or slug, as well as a rodent or bird, before it matures into an adult in a cat. An infected cat can often cough up parasites and get rid of them, but drugs are also available. In parts of the United States tiny lung flukes can also infest cats.

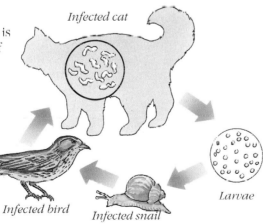

Infected cat

Infected bird   *Infected snail*   *Larvae*

Lungworm life cycle (*above*)
Larvae are eaten by a snail or slug, which, in turn, is swallowed by a bird or rodent. When this host is eaten by a cat the cycle is completed.

CAT FLU

The term "cat flu" is misleading, since there are several different viruses known by this name. Cats should be vaccinated against the main two feline respiratory viruses, Feline Calici Virus and Feline Viral Rhinotracheitis. However, other viruses exist for which there is no vaccine. The signs of all these infections are similar. An infected cat will have a runny nose and eyes, and may be sneezing or coughing. Cat flu can be serious, so it is best to consult a vet if your cat is showing any signs of illness. Telephone the surgery first, so that any necessary precautions can be taken to prevent the infection from spreading to other cats.

DIGESTIVE DISORDERS

Nutrients are broken down and used in a variety of ways to make a cat function properly. The digestive system is the centre of this mechanism, converting food eaten by a cat to energy. The most common problems affecting the digestive system are vomiting, diarrhoea, constipation, and appetite and weight loss. A cat may stop eating because it feels ill or has difficulty swallowing. Or it may eat too much, for a variety of reasons. Food may be vomited immediately after eating or only partly digested. A cat may show signs of excessive thirst, or of constipation or diarrhoea. Watch the symptoms carefully, since such health problems may require immediate medical attention.

Careful feeding
This is a cat's best protection against major diseases.

THE DIGESTIVE SYSTEM

Mouth

Oesophagus

Liver

Stomach

Large intestine

Pancreas

Small intestine

Anus

Feline food processor
Food mixed with saliva first passes through the oesophagus into the stomach, where digestive juices begin to break it down. It then travels to the cat's intestines, which digest nutrients and send them to the liver, where they are converted for use. Undigested material travels to the large intestine, and is excreted through the anus.

DIGESTIVE DISORDERS

Disorder	Description and signs	Action
Feline Infectious Enteritis (FIE), also known as Feline Panleukopenia	This widespread viral disease is highly contagious. It is spread by direct or indirect contact with an infected cat. FIE develops rapidly, so that in severe cases young kittens may die before a diagnosis can be made. The virus attacks the gut and the white blood cells. The main signs are depression, loss of appetite, and persistent vomiting and diarrhoea.	Vaccination is effective in protecting a cat against FIE infection (*see page 53*). Early diagnosis and isolation of an infected cat is important to stop the disease from spreading. Careful nursing is essential to prevent dehydration.
Feline Infectious Peritonitis (FIP)	This virus primarily causes an infection of the abdominal cavity but it also affects the liver, kidneys, nervous system, and brain. FIP mainly attacks cats under three years of age as older cats are more resistant. The main signs are loss of appetite, fever, weight loss, and a swollen abdomen.	There is no protective vaccine against this disease. An infected cat must be isolated to prevent the disease from spreading to other cats. Treatment is not usually effective.
Vomiting	It is normal for a healthy cat to vomit occasionally, for example after eating grass or when getting rid of hairballs. Severe vomiting, abdominal pain, and excessive thirst indicate a serious digestive disorder that may be caused by a cat ingesting an irritant or contaminated food.	Vomiting or regurgitation of food may be due to several reasons. Consult a vet if the vomiting is severe or if it persists for more than 24 hours.
Diarrhoea	Mild diarrhoea may be caused by stress or a change in diet, but if the symptoms persist it may suggest a bacterial or viral infection. Diarrhoea accompanied by vomiting or blood in the faeces is a sign of a serious disorder.	Consult a vet if the diarrhoea persists for longer than 24 hours or if there is any blood in the faeces. Do not allow the cat to become dehydrated.
Liver disease	The liver may be damaged as a result of a viral disease or a cat ingesting a poison. Signs of liver malfunction may include vomiting, diarrhoea, excessive thirst, and abdominal pain.	Consult a vet immediately. Diagnosis can be aided by analysis of blood, urine, and faecal samples.
Diabetes	This condition is due to the inadequate production of insulin by the pancreas. Early signs are frequent urination, excessive thirst, increased appetite, and unexplained weight loss.	Treatment involves careful dietary control and, in some cases, daily injections of insulin.
Dietary sensitivity	Some oriental cats are unable to digest the sugar in milk, and this may cause diarrhoea and vomiting. Other foods that may cause allergic reactions include fish and eggs.	A full veterinary examination is required to determine the cause of the sensitivity where it is not known.
Constipation	A cat should have a bowel movement at least once a day. Elderly cats, particularly longhaired types, are the most likely to suffer from a blockage in the bowel due to constipation.	Dose the cat with liquid paraffin by mouth. If there is no movement after two days, seek veterinary treatment.

DIARRHOEA AND VOMITING

Cats vomit fairly readily as a means of protecting themselves against harmful substances. Anything more than occasional vomiting should be investigated by a vet, since it may indicate a serious problem. Diarrhoea can be very debilitating and requires prompt veterinary attention, especially if the cat is vomiting or if blood is present. If not treated, severe diarrhoea and vomiting can lead to collapse and even death through rapid dehydration. Such symptoms may be due to poisoning or Feline Infectious Enteritis, both of which need immediate veterinary treatment.

Examination (*above*)
A vet gently feels the abdomen for signs of swelling.

REFUSING TO EAT

Tempting a sick cat to eat is a delicate task. Try warming small amounts of a favourite food to blood temperature and feeding several times daily.

Appetite loss (*above*)
Always consult a vet if a cat refuses food for more than 24 hours.

INTERNAL PARASITES

Parasites do not cause a cat much discomfort except when they are present in large numbers, but your cat is better off without them. The most common feline parasites are the worms that infest the intestinal tract, but there are also flukes, lungworms, heartworms, and protozoan organisms such as Toxoplasma (*see page 125*).

Many parasites spend their immature stages in another host, such as a rodent, flea, or bird, which must be eaten by a cat in order for the parasite to complete its life cycle.

Young cats are most at risk from parasitic infections, so it is essential to worm kittens from as early as four weeks old.

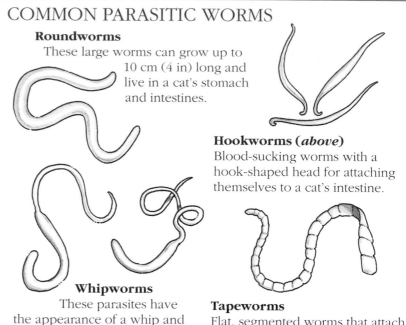

COMMON PARASITIC WORMS

Roundworms
These large worms can grow up to 10 cm (4 in) long and live in a cat's stomach and intestines.

Hookworms (*above*)
Blood-sucking worms with a hook-shaped head for attaching themselves to a cat's intestine.

Whipworms
These parasites have the appearance of a whip and live in the large intestine.

Tapeworms
Flat, segmented worms that attach themselves to a cat's intestine.

LIFE CYCLES OF COMMON PARASITES

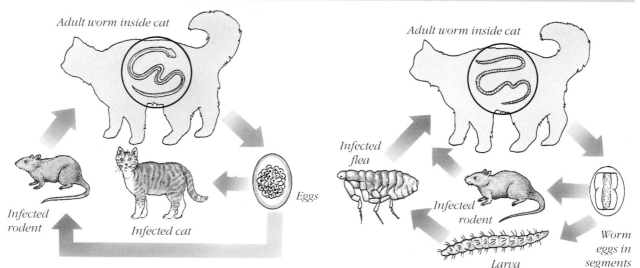

Adult worm inside cat

Infected rodent

Infected cat

Eggs

Adult worm inside cat

Infected flea

Infected rodent

Larva

Worm eggs in segments

The roundworm life cycle
The adult worm lives in the cat's intestinal canal. It lays eggs that pass out in the faeces and these are then eaten by a rodent. When another cat eats the secondary host, the cycle begins again. A cat may also accidentally ingest eggs while grooming.

The tapeworm life cycle
The adult tapeworm sheds segments full of eggs, which pass out in the faeces. The eggs are then eaten by a rodent or bird, and develop into larvae. The life cycle is completed when this host is eaten by a cat. Larvae can also be passed on by fleas.

INTERNAL PARASITES

Parasite	Description and signs	Action
Roundworms	Roundworms live in the stomach and intestines and feed on digested food in a cat's gut. An adult cat may show no signs of having worms, but occasionally mature worms may be passed, or eggs may be detectable in the faeces. Kittens can be infected via their mother's milk and become seriously weakened. Symptoms of a severe roundworm infestation include diarrhoea, constipation, anaemia, a pot-bellied appearance, and a loss of weight and condition.	Consult a vet, who can advise you on a suitable roundworm treatment. It is important that kittens and pregnant queens should be dosed with worming tablets. Cats that hunt should be treated routinely two or three times a year.
Tapeworms	Tapeworms are most often found in adult cats. The worm has a long, segmented body and attaches itself to the intestine wall. The segments containing eggs are passed with the cat's faeces, sometimes becoming stuck to the fur under the tail and drying out to resemble grains of rice. The shedding of segments may cause irritation and the cat will lick its behind.	A vet can prescribe an appropriate tapeworm treatment. Flea control is also essential to prevent re-infection since fleas can be intermediate hosts for certain species of tapeworm.
Hookworms	Blood-sucking hookworms are found in parts of Australia and the United States. They live in the small intestine and can be passed to unborn kittens. Signs are diarrhoea and weight loss.	A vet can prescribe an appropriate hookworm treatment. Strict hygiene measures are also recommended.
Threadworms and whipworms	Tiny threadworms and whipworms live in the gut and can infect cats in parts of Australia and the United States. Signs may include diarrhoea, but these worms rarely cause illness.	A vet can prescribe an appropriate worming treatment.
Flukes	Flukes are rarely found in cats, but these flatworms can sometimes infest the small intestine and liver in the United States and Asia. They are caused by a cat eating infected raw fish. Signs include digestive upsets, and sometimes anaemia.	A diagnosis by a vet is required to confirm a fluke infestation. Treatment is not always effective and preventive measures are very important.
Lungworms	These tiny parasites sometimes infest a cat's lungs and can cause respiratory disease (*see page 109*).	Consult a vet for treatment with a safe deworming drug.
Heartworms	Cats in some countries are infected by worms that live in the heart (*see page 123*).	Consult a vet for treatment with a safe deworming drug.

PREVENTING INFESTATION

Discuss a worming programme with a vet as soon as you get your cat. Maintaining hygiene standards around the home and keeping your cat free of external parasites, such as fleas, will also reduce the numbers of internal ones. Kittens

Worming (*left*)
Try concealing a worming tablet in a small piece of food.

should be dosed from about four weeks old, and if worms and eggs are found in the faeces, a course of treatment should be prescribed. Adult cats, particularly those that hunt prey and are allowed to roam freely, should be checked for worms at least twice a year.

Even though it may not be possible to prevent your cat from eating prey, you can reduce the risks of infestation by keeping its indoor environment unhospitable to parasite carriers such as mice and fleas. When you spray or dust your cat with insecticide, treat its bedding as well. Do not use any rodent poisons in the house, since they can be extremely toxic to cats (*see page 167*).

TREATMENT

There are many different worming preparations. It is important to obtain the correct remedy for the type of parasite infesting your cat. Worming medicine may be given in the form of a paste, which can be added to food or given directly by mouth. When giving tablets, make sure that your pet swallows them and does not spit them out. Some tablets may be only for roundworms, while others may kill a variety of parasites.

Tablets for roundworm.

Tablets for tapeworm.

MOUTH AND TOOTH DISORDERS

The cat's mouth and teeth are adapted to their role of hunting and catching prey, while the tongue is equipped with hooked, abrasive papillae used for grooming. Damage or inflammation to a cat's mouth, teeth, gums, palate, or tongue can make it difficult for it to eat, and it may be unable to groom itself. Eventually, the animal's life is endangered if action is not taken in good time.

Cats do not often get cavities in their teeth, but bacteria and debris may sometimes build up on the tooth surface to form plaque, and when mixed with minerals in the saliva, this hardens into tartar or "calculus". If not treated, gingivitis may result, followed by recession of the gums and the loss of teeth. A number of micro-organisms, especially those associated with Feline respiratory disease or "cat flu" (*see page 109*), can cause ulceration of the mouth. Occasionally, objects such as fish bones can become lodged in the mouth and need to be removed (*see page 164*).

Carnivore
Although a cat's teeth are not very prone to decay, they benefit from regular cleaning. This is especially the case with older cats.

THE CAT'S TEETH

Feline fangs
Adult cats have 30 teeth, shaped for cutting and tearing meat, rather than for grinding or chewing. The carnassial teeth are adapted for slicing through flesh. A kitten gets its milk teeth at about 14 days old, and loses these to adult teeth at four to six months old.

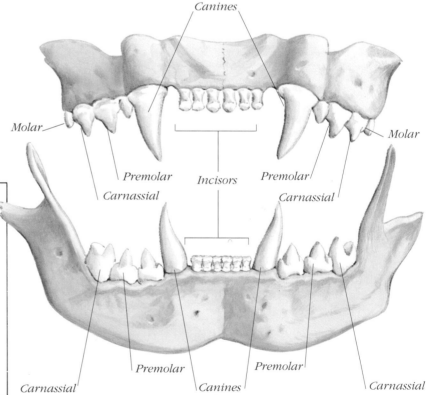

Canines

Molar

Molar

Premolar

Incisors

Premolar

Carnassial

Carnassial

Premolar

Premolar

Carnassial

Canines

Carnassial

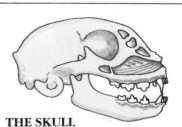

THE SKULL
A cat has an immobile upper jaw, the maxilla bone, and a hinged lower jaw called the mandible, which consists of a vertical and a horizontal part.

MOUTH AND TOOTH DISORDERS

Disorder	Description and signs	Action
Cleft palate	Kittens are sometimes born with the two sides of the hard palate at the roof of the mouth not properly joined. Affected kittens will not be able to suckle milk properly.	Surgery to repair the hard palate may sometimes be possible.
Dental problems	Dental problems are common in older cats. The deposition of plaque on the tooth surface leads to brownish-yellow tartar ("calculus") forming on the teeth. This results in food being trapped, which causes inflammation of the gums (gingivitis). If the infection invades the tooth socket (periodontitis), the tooth will become loose or an abscess may form. A cat with dental problems may have bad breath and it may experience difficulty in eating and paw at its mouth.	Regular brushing of your cat's teeth with a toothbrush helps prevent the build-up of plaque. If there is extensive tartar or a cat is very uncooperative, a vet can descale the teeth using an ultrasonic scaler under an anaesthetic.
Gingivitis	An inflammation of a cat's gums is the first sign of dental problems and is usually associated with a build-up of tartar on the teeth. Gingivitis may start as a dark red line bordering the teeth, but if it is left untreated the gums will become sore and ulceration may occur. A cat with gum disease may have bad breath, drool, and experience difficulty in chewing food.	Consult a vet if you notice any redness around a cat's mouth and gums. Regular brushing of a cat's teeth will help to keep the gums healthy.
Mouth infection	Stomatitis is an inflammation of the mouth lining. It may result from a foreign body in the mouth, a viral disease, or dental problems. An affected cat will have difficulty in eating and the inside of the mouth will appear reddened.	Treatment depends on the cause of the infection. A vet will be able to identify the underlying cause.
"Rodent ulcer"	A "rodent ulcer" is a slowly enlarging sore or swelling on a cat's upper lip. Its cause is not known but it may be the result of constant licking.	Consult a vet for treatment. "Rodent ulcers" tend to recur if the treatment is stopped too soon.
Salivary cyst	If the salivary glands or ducts that carry the saliva to the mouth become blocked, this can result in the formation of a salivary cyst (ranula) under the tongue.	Prompt veterinary treatment to drain the cyst is required since the cat will be unable to eat.
Mouth ulcers	Ulcers on a cat's tongue and gums are sometimes caused by Feline respiratory disease (*see page 109*) or kidney disease.	Consult a vet for an examination to determine the underlying cause.

GUM DISEASE

An inflammation of the gums is known as gingivitis. This is most commonly associated with an accumulation of tartar or "calculus" on the teeth, but can also indicate an internal disease if it is very severe. Feline Immuno Deficiency Virus (*see page 123*) and kidney disease (*see page 119*) are often associated with inflammation of the gums. When an infection becomes established, the gums will recede and in time the teeth will become loose in their sockets.

Gingivitis (*above*)
A dark red line along the gums is a sign of infection.

Occasionally, a cat may have bad breath without any apparent visible changes in its mouth. All clinical signs must be investigated by a vet, since they can lead to your cat losing its teeth or being unable to eat. Gum disease may be prevented by feeding your cat a sensible diet. A cat fed on soft food alone is especially prone to dental problems. The inclusion of chunks of meat or dry food in the diet will provide a cat with something to chew on and help remove debris.

CLEANING TEETH

Tartar build-up can be retarded by cleaning a cat's teeth regularly. You may need someone to hold the cat steady while you brush its teeth using a special toothpaste or a weak saline solution (*see page 69*).

Brushing (*above*)
While the upper lip is held back, the back teeth can be brushed.

REPRODUCTIVE DISORDERS

Since a large number of male and female cats are neutered (*see pages 154–155*), problems with the reproductive system are fairly uncommon. Most entire cats are very fertile and experience no difficulty in producing offspring, but there are disorders that can prevent queens from conceiving, or males from producing sperm.

There is no equivalent of the human menopause in cats. Reproductive activity does slow down as they grow older, but they can still reproduce and give birth at an advanced age.

Tumours of the testes are rare, but mammary tumours are fairly common. They usually occur after the cat is ten years old and need urgent attention. There is no evidence that having a litter of kittens before being neutered is good for a queen. Neutering may help tumours to regress, or even prevent their development if carried out early. Males with one or both testicles undescended are best castrated, since the condition is inherited.

Ultrasound scans
Ultrasound scans can be used to help monitor pregnancy in cats, as they are in humans.

THE REPRODUCTIVE ORGANS

The male
The testes produce sperm that travel down the spermatic cord to the urethra. The penis is equipped with spines that trigger ovulation.

The female *(below)*
The female cat comes into heat, or "oestrus", when the brain signals the pituitary gland to release a hormone that causes the ovaries to produce eggs. Another hormone causes behavioural changes, such as "calling" (*see page 144*).

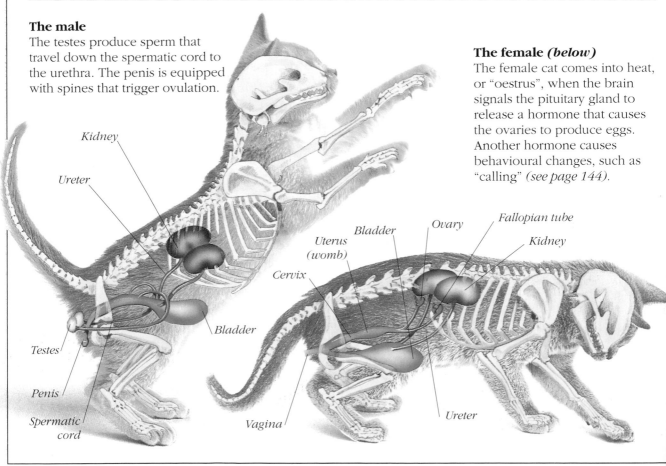

Kidney

Ureter

Testes

Penis

Spermatic cord

Bladder

Uterus (womb)

Cervix

Bladder

Ovary

Fallopian tube

Kidney

Vagina

Ureter

REPRODUCTIVE DISORDERS

Disorder	Description and signs	Action
Female infertility	If a female cat fails to conceive after mating, this may be due to a number of factors. The queen may be suffering from a nutritional deficiency (such as lack of vitamin A) or she may have been mated at the wrong time.	A proper diagnosis of the cause of infertility can only be made after a thorough veterinary examination.
Male infertility	Infertility is very rare in male cats, but it may be due to an infection of the male reproductive organs or an inherited problem. Although a male cat with one undescended testicle (monorchid) can still be fertile, a cat with both testicles undescended (cryptorchid) will probably be sterile.	A proper diagnosis of the cause of infertility can only be made after a thorough veterinary examination. Do not breed from a monorchid cat, since the condition is inherited.
Ovarian cysts	A queen that is not mated may develop ovarian cysts. These cysts produce large quantities of the female sex hormone, which causes frequent or continuous heat periods.	Consult a vet if a queen has abnormal heat cycles.
Abortion and resorption	Miscarriage may be brought on by stress, trauma, an infection, or a foetal abnormality. Signs of miscarriage include bleeding and discharge from the vulva, and the onset of premature labour. Developing kittens less than seven weeks old may sometimes be absorbed back into a mother cat's body.	If you notice any unusual signs that may indicate a premature birth, you should contact a vet immediately.
Kittening problems	Most cats have no difficulty in giving birth, but occasionally a queen may require assistance (*see pages 174–175*).	Consult a vet immediately if a cat appears distressed during kittening.
Metritis	The uterus can become infected following a difficult birth, particularly if a queen is elderly. Signs may include abdominal pain and a bloody discharge from the vulva.	Consult a vet immediately if there are any abnormal signs following kittening.
Pyometra	An accumulation of fluid in the uterus is most common in ageing queens. Signs include loss of appetite, high fever, depression, and a vulval discharge.	Consult a vet immediately. An affected cat will need to be spayed.
Mastitis	Mastitis is an inflammation of the mammary glands. The glands appear reddened and swollen, and the kittens are unable to suckle and may show signs of hunger or weakness.	Consult a vet immediately. In severe cases, the kittens may need to be reared by a foster mother or by hand.

FEMALE REPRODUCTIVE PROBLEMS

While a spayed cat will not be affected, an unneutered female cat may suffer from several disorders of the reproductive tract. Pyometra is due to a degeneration of the uterus, occurring as the queen gets older. Cysts develop in the uterus, causing inflammation and the womb to fill up with fluid. The condition can result in toxaemia and death if not treated. Immediately after giving birth, a queen may suffer a prolapse of the uterus, when the womb is pushed outside the body. If this happens, contact a vet immediately, since the condition can lead to severe shock and death. Other health problems associated with the female reproductive system include ovarian cysts, infertility, miscarriage, and problems with kittening (*see pages 174–175*).

Birth problems (*left*)
Seeking veterinary help sooner rather than later is the rule for kittening.

NURSING PROBLEMS

Several disorders can prevent a queen from producing milk. Mastitis causes a swelling of the mammary glands. Lactational tetany ("milk fever") results from a fall in the calcium in the blood.

Perfect mother (*above*)
Most queens are excellent mothers and will suckle orphan kittens.

URINARY DISORDERS

Problems that affect a cat's urinary system warrant urgent veterinary investigation, since such disorders can be serious and life-threatening. If your cat strains when passing urine, or cannot pass any at all, contact a vet immediately. A cat's urine is fairly clear or pale yellow, and if it becomes cloudy or coloured, this may indicate a bladder infection or even the start of kidney disease. Excessive thirst and frequent urination can sometimes be a sign of diabetes or liver disease, while incontinence may often be associated with a hormonal imbalance, or a spinal injury. To prevent urinary problems, make sure water is always available, and do not feed a cat only on dry food, since too little fluid can lead to a urinary obstruction.

Drinking too much
If your cat is drinking to excess or passing more urine than usual it must be examined by a vet without delay, since this may be a sign of kidney disease.

THE URINARY SYSTEM

Urination
The urinary system is responsible for keeping optimum levels of useful chemicals in the blood and eliminating toxic ones. Waste material is filtered through the kidneys and released as urine down the ureters to the bladder. The urine then passes through the urethra and out of the body.

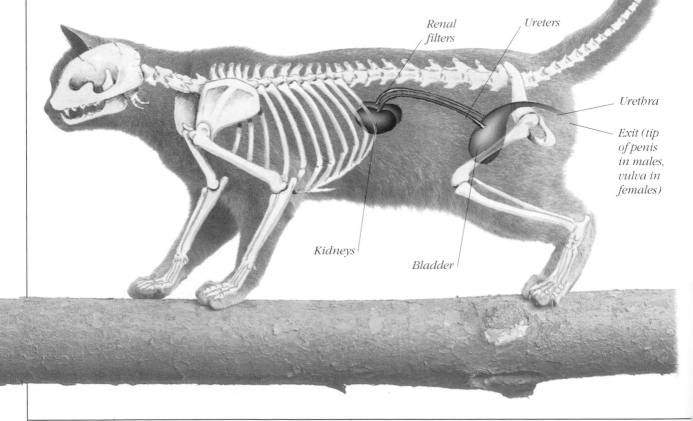

Renal filters

Ureters

Urethra

Exit (tip of penis in males, vulva in females)

Kidneys

Bladder

URINARY DISORDERS

Disorder	Description and signs	Action
Chronic kidney disease	This is the most common disorder that affects elderly cats. The gradual deterioration of the functioning of the kidneys makes it difficult for a cat to eliminate waste products from its body. An affected cat may start to urinate more frequently and will have an increased thirst. Other common signs of kidney disease are weight loss, bad breath, and mouth ulcers.	Consult a vet, who will be able to make a proper diagnosis after taking a sample of blood. Careful dietary management is essential in order to compensate for kidney damage.
Acute kidney disease	Acute kidney disease is not as common as the chronic form and usually affects younger cats. It may be caused by bacterial or viral infection, or as the result of a cat swallowing a toxic substance. The signs are vomiting and loss of appetite, severe depression, and dehydration.	Consult a vet immediately – he will try to combat the toxin if the disease is caused by poisoning. Fluids need to be given to combat dehydration.
Urinary obstruction or Feline Urological Syndrome (FUS)	Minute crystals or a sandy sludge can sometimes cause a blockage of the bladder if they build up to plug the urethra. This particularly affects neutered male cats because the urethra of the female cat is relatively wide. A cat with urinary problems will strain to pass a little bloodstained urine and, in severe cases, it may not be able to pass any water at all. The bladder may be distended and the abdomen tense and painful to the touch. This condition causes an affected cat a great deal of pain and disease.	Urgent veterinary treatment is required to relieve a bladder obstruction. Careful dietary control is needed to ensure that a cat has a high water intake.
Cystitis	An inflammation of the bladder is most commonly caused by a bacterial infection or may be associated with FUS (*see above*). In Australia, cystitis can be caused by a bladder worm. Signs include frequent urination accompanied by straining and an increased thirst. The urine may be blood-strained and the cat may persistently lick its rear end.	Consult a vet immediately in order to ensure that the condition does not worsen – if this happens, the bladder may become blocked.
Incontinence	Frequent or constant urination due to a loss of voluntary control may be due to old age, injury, or an infection of the bladder. This is not the same as urine marking or spraying, which is territorial behaviour.	If there are any other signs, such as straining, consult a vet immediately. Do not limit the cat's water intake.

URINARY INFECTIONS

An inflammation of the bladder, known as cystitis, may be due to a bacterial infection and can be treated successfully if it is detected early. The symptoms of infection are frequent urination with some discomfort, straining, and constant licking under the tail. Cystitis can affect both sexes, but it is mainly toms and young neutered males that suffer from the more serious Feline Urological Syndrome. If a cat does not drink enough water, or is fed only dry food, the urine may become too concentrated and the salts in it form a sandy deposit or stones, which block the urethra, the narrow passage to the outside.

The cat then experiences difficulty and pain when urinating. FUS is not usually found in females. It is a condition that requires emergency veterinary treatment.

Straining (*below*)
A cat should show no signs of discomfort when passing urine.

KIDNEY PROBLEMS

The kidneys are often the first organs to show signs of ageing, deteriorating gradually (*see page 138*). Without treatment the cat's condition may worsen, until the kidneys produce little urine, resulting in a build-up of toxic material inside the cat, which can be fatal. Urgent medical treatment is needed before the condition becomes irreversible. However, if the symptoms are recognized early enough, the cat may be treated successfully and go on to enjoy a long and normal life. Apart from deterioration through old age, kidney failure can also occur as the result of an injury, or following a serious disease, such as Feline Infectious Peritonitis (*see page 111*).

NERVOUS DISORDERS

The grace, coordination, and agility of cats require a highly sophisticated system of nervous control. The intricate network of nerves runs without mishap for most of the time, but if a problem does occur, it tends to be of a serious nature. Although relatively rare, cats are occasionally subject to fits and seizures. These may be due to several causes, including brain tumour, poisoning, or an inherited epileptic condition. However, the most common cause of nervous problems is physical damage as a result of road traffic accidents. An inflammation of the brain or spinal cord can be associated with some infectious diseases. Paralysis of a limb can result if the spinal cord or the nerves supplying that part of the body are damaged in an accident. If the nerves do not heal, the paralysis may be permanent.

Poisoning
If a feline eats a rat or mouse killed with poison, it may become very ill, since the substance often attacks the nervous system.

THE CENTRAL NERVOUS SYSTEM

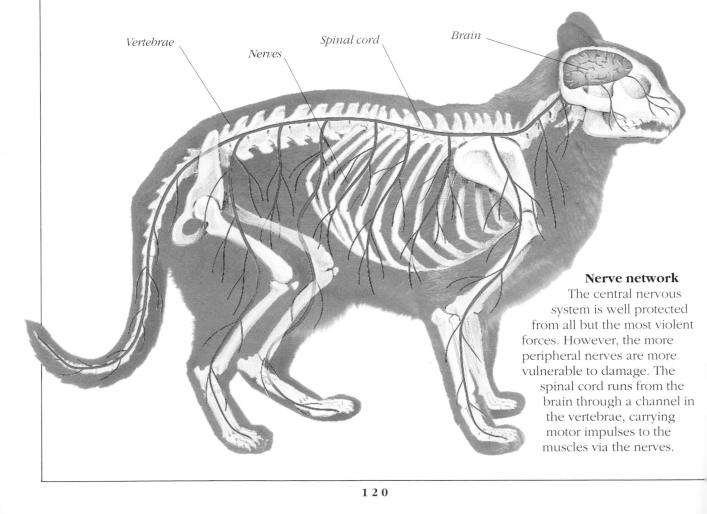

Vertebrae

Nerves

Spinal cord

Brain

Nerve network
The central nervous system is well protected from all but the most violent forces. However, the more peripheral nerves are more vulnerable to damage. The spinal cord runs from the brain through a channel in the vertebrae, carrying motor impulses to the muscles via the nerves.

NERVOUS DISORDERS

Disorder	Description and signs	Action
Brain damage	Severe trauma to the brain is most often due to a road traffic accident or fall and is usually fatal. Strokes are very rare in cats. They are due to a blood clot forming on the brain and often result in a loss of functioning of one part of the body. Brain damage can also be caused by a tumour, a congenital defect, or by the spread of a bacterial infection from another part of the body.	Urgent veterinary treatment is essential following an accident or fall, especially where head injuries are suspected. Most cats recover from a minor stroke, but they may need treatment for residual problems, such as loss of sight or recurring fits.
Meningitis	This uncommon nervous disease affects the membrane covering the brain and the spinal cord. It results in fever, dilated pupils, loss of appetite, and convulsions.	Urgent veterinary treatment is required. The vet may take a specimen of the spinal fluid for examination.
Encephalitis	Encephalitis is an inflammation of the brain itself and may be caused by some viruses such as rabies, or bacterial infection. Signs can be variable and include fever, dilated pupils, seizures, and paralysis.	Urgent veterinary treatment is required. The vet will need to establish the cause of the infection.
Fits and epilepsy	Fits and epilepsy are relatively rare in cats. They may be connected with brain damage, poisoning, a vitamin deficiency, or may even be inherited. Epileptic attacks may begin when a kitten is about six months old or they may suddenly start following an accident or blow to the head.	Consult a vet immediately. Do not move a convulsing cat. Fits and epilepsy can sometimes be controlled by anti-convulsant drugs.
Paralysis	The spinal cord and nerves supplying a part of the body may be damaged following an accident, resulting in paralysis of the affected area. This usually happens to a cat's tail or limb. The cat will be unable to bear any weight on the affected limb and may drag it along the ground.	If the nerve is severely damaged and the limb is fractured in an accident, amputation may be necessary. Most cats are able to cope surprisingly well with only three legs.
Feline Dysautonomia (Key-Gaskell Syndrome)	The cause of this rare condition, which affects a cat's nervous system, is unknown. Signs include rapid weight loss, appetite loss, vomiting, regurgitation of food, and pupil dilation.	Urgent veterinary attention is essential if there are to be any prospects of the cat recovering.
Poisoning	There are a number of household substances that are extremely poisonous to a cat should it ingest them. Poisoning may cause signs such as convulsions or muscle tremors.	Seek veterinary attention immediately if you suspect that your cat has been poisoned (see pages 166–167).
Loss of balance	Unsteadiness and lack of coordination when walking may be the result of faulty development, injury, vitamin deficiency, or a disorder of the inner ear (see page 107).	Seek veterinary attention immediately for a thorough examination of the cat.

TESTING REFLEXES

While half the nervous system is concerned with feeling, using the sensory nerves, the other half controls the cat's movement with the motor nerves. Examining a cat's reflexes is the first step in investigating any nervous disorder. A cat's reflexes (see page 159) give an indication of which part of the nervous system is not working normally. A vet may also test the ability of the cat's pupil to contract when a bright light is shone into the eye. A semi-conscious cat may be unable to react to stimulus if it is suffering from shock. X-ray examinations and samples of blood or fluid from the spinal cord may also be required if a cat is suffering from any suspected nervous disorder.

If there is no feeling in a limb, or an absence of reflexes, and the cat is unable to control its urine or faecal movements, the prospects for recovery are not very good. However, a cat can recover from some neurological injuries and an assessment must be carried out by a vet in every case.

Feline Dysautonomia (below)
Permanently dilated pupils are a sign of this rare disease.

BLOOD AND HEART DISORDERS

Disorders of the blood are more prevalent in cats than problems with the heart. Even though the heart is fairly small, it is well adapted to the feline lifestyle, spending a great deal of time just "ticking over", but rapidly boosting the blood circulation for the sudden bursts of action that are typical of cats. As the heart ages, these periods of activity become less frequent but it is only when there is advanced deterioration of the heart that the cat gets breathless and reluctant to move at all. Heart disease is not common, but can result from old age or be due to a nutrient deficiency, such as a lack of taurine in the diet, but this only follows gross errors such as feeding a cat exclusively on dog food.

Listening in
Part of any routine examination of a cat's circulatory system includes listening to the heart. A vet can usually assess heart function with a stethoscope, but other, more sophisticated techniques are also available.

THE CIRCULATORY SYSTEM

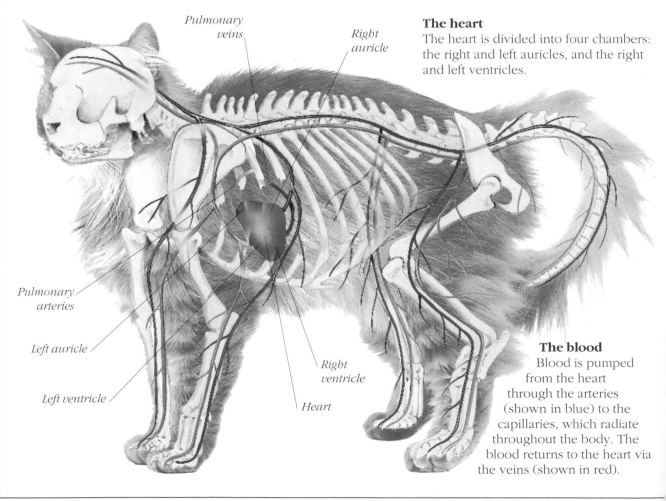

Pulmonary veins

Right auricle

The heart
The heart is divided into four chambers: the right and left auricles, and the right and left ventricles.

Pulmonary arteries

Left auricle

Left ventricle

Right ventricle

Heart

The blood
Blood is pumped from the heart through the arteries (shown in blue) to the capillaries, which radiate throughout the body. The blood returns to the heart via the veins (shown in red).

BLOOD AND HEART DISORDERS

Disorder	Description and signs	Action
Feline Leukaemia Virus (FeLV)	FeLV causes cancer of the white blood cells and lymph system. It can only be spread by direct contact with an affected cat and is most common in multi-cat households. Symptoms of the virus are not very specific but include weight loss, vomiting, diarrhoea, laboured breathing, and anaemia.	There is no effective treatment for FeLV. Blood tests are available to detect the virus. All cats that test positive must be isolated. a vaccine is now available.
Feline Immuno Deficiency Virus (FIV)	FIV is similar to the HIV virus that affects humans, but it is specific to cats. The virus suppresses the immune system, making the cat susceptible to infection. It is not transmitted sexually but is spread through the saliva of an infected cat. A cat with FIV may appear off colour at first, but it may then develop secondary infections such as anaemia (*see below*).	A blood test is available to diagnose the disease, but there is no treatment or vaccine to combat the FIV virus. Humans cannot catch AIDS from cats.
Anaemia	A cat suffering from anaemia has a shortage of red blood cells, which reduces the amount of oxygen carried in the blood. Signs of anaemia include pallor of the gums, lethargy, weakness, and loss of appetite.	Consult a vet immediately if you notice any signs of anaemia. Treatment depends on the cause of the illness.
Feline Infectious Anaemia (FIA)	FIA is caused by a small blood parasite that damages red blood cells and causes severe anaemia (*see above*). It is transmitted by blood-sucking parasites such as fleas and ticks.	FIA can be confirmed by a blood test Treatment involves antibiotics, iron supplements, and blood transfusions.
Heart disease	Kittens may occasionally be born with heart abnormalities – most of them die when they are under one year old. Other problems involve a deterioration of the heart muscle, causing it to become inflamed or damaged (cardiomyopathy). The heart valves may get weaker or become blocked in an elderly cat. Signs of heart disease include heavy breathing, a bluish tinge to the gums, and a tendency to tire easily.	Consult a vet immediately if a cat shows any signs of heart disease. Treatment depends on the heart problem but drugs can be prescribed for certain conditions.
Thrombosis	This is caused by clotted blood blocking a vessel and cutting off the blood supply. The first sign may be a sudden paralysis of the hind legs, which will feel cold to the touch.	Urgent veterinary treatment is essential. Surgery may sometimes be possible, but the recovery rate is low.
Heartworm	This uncommon feline disease usually occurs only in hot, humid parts of the world. Signs include breathing difficulties, weight loss, and a build-up of fluid in the abdomen.	If detected early, a vet can prescribe drugs to prevent the heartworm larvae from developing into adult worms.

HEARTWORM

In hot, humid countries, the heartworm (*Dirofilaria immitis*) can infest cats, although it prefers to parasitize dogs. Preventive drugs are given in high-risk areas, but treatment is difficult, since killing the adult worm can cause fatal blockage of a blood vessel. The microscopic larvae, meanwhile, are often difficult to detect in a cat's blood since they are not very numerous. However they can be prevented from developing into the harmful adult worms with a course of drug treatment.

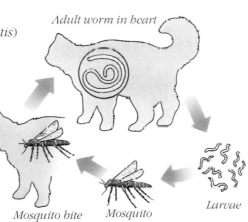

Adult worm in heart

Mosquito bite *Mosquito* *Larvae*

Life of a heartworm (*above*)
The worm's microscopic offspring are transmitted via a mosquito bite and develop in the heart.

BLOOD TESTING

Infectious anaemia is due to tiny organisms that can inhabit the red blood cells and destroy them. A vet can identify these parasites by taking a blood sample. Other serious feline blood disorders are cancer of the white blood cells due to Feline Leukaemia Virus, and the suppression of a cat's immune system as a result of Feline Immuno Deficiency Virus, a relative of the AIDS virus. There are blood tests available for the detection of these different, lethal viruses and isolation procedures to prevent infection spreading. Consult a vet if any of these conditions is likely.

DISEASES TRANSMISSIBLE TO HUMANS

The infectious diseases that can be passed between humans and other animals are called zoonoses. As far as cats are concerned, however, the risk to humans is small, mainly because cats are very clean animals. In addition, infectious micro-organisms tend to thrive only in particular species. For example, swine fever only affects pigs, and the common cold is confined to man. There are a few diseases that can be passed from animals to humans. The most important feline zoonoses include rabies, toxoplasmosis, and skin irritations, However, the risk of catching any disease from your cat is minimal.

Rabies
Rabies can be passed from wild animals to pets, and then to humans.

RABIES WORLDWIDE

Map of vectors
The map shows the main vectors of rabies in different parts of the world.

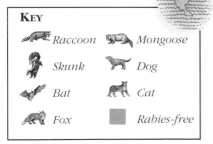

KEY	
Raccoon	Mongoose
Skunk	Dog
Bat	Cat
Fox	Rabies-free

VECTORS OF RABIES

The most serious disease that man can get from animals is rabies. All warm-blooded animals can be victims of rabies, but only a few animals are vectors, or carriers, of the disease. The main vectors are animals such as foxes, wolves, raccoons, skunks, bats, dogs, and mongooses. Only parts of Europe (including Great Britain), Iceland, Japan, Hawaii, the West Indies, Australia, New Zealand, and Antarctica are free of rabies. All these countries must take strict quarantine measures to safeguard their enviable status (see page 50).

DISEASES TRANSMISSIBLE TO HUMANS

Disease	Description and signs	Action
Rabies	Rabies is the most dangerous disease that can be passed from animals to humans. It is highly contagious and is transmitted through the saliva of an infected animal. There are three stages to the disease. The first stage is marked by a change in behaviour. A normally friendly cat may become nervous and try to hide itself away. The cat may become increasingly aggressive and excited in the second stage, and may try to bite and scratch anyone who approaches it. The final stage is paralysis and coma, which ends in death.	There is no known treatment for rabies once the cat (or human) is showing clinical signs of the disease. Routine preventive vaccination is required by law in some countries where rabies is present, such as the United States. A cat suspected of having rabies must be isolated and immediate veterinary treatment should be sought.
Bacterial enteritis	A cat may occasionally eat contaminated or badly cooked meat containing bacteria and suffer from enteritis (inflammation of the intestine). Salmonella bacteria are a rare cause of enteritis but can be transmitted to humans. Signs of infection are fever, vomiting and diarrhoea, and excessive drinking to replace lost fluids.	Consult a vet if vomiting or diarrhoea are severe or persist. The cat may require antibiotics to treat the bacterial infection. Good hygiene is essential, as an affected cat may be a potential human health risk.
Tuberculosis	Tuberculosis can infect cats and other domestic animals as well as man, but it is now uncommon in most countries. The disease is usually transmitted by a cat drinking infected milk, but it can also be passed on by owners to their pets. The lungs and abdomen are the main body systems affected. Signs include fever and severe loss of condition.	Treatment of an infected cat may be possible but the public health risks have to be considered.
Toxoplasmosis	This common disease is caused by a microscopic intestinal parasite that can infect many species of animal and can be transmitted to humans. A cat becomes infected by eating contaminated prey or raw meat. Most infected cats show no signs of illness, but signs of a severe infection may include fever, loss of appetite, weight loss, and breathing difficulties. Humans may be infected from handling contaminated cat faeces or, more likely, from handling infected raw meat.	The disease can be controlled by preventing a cat from scavenging and by cooking raw meat thoroughly. Pregnant women are at risk and should avoid handling soiled litter. Blood tests are available to screen those at risk.
Skin problems	Ringworm is a common fungal skin infection (*see page 101*) that is contagious to humans and other animals. It causes small, round, bald patches on a cat's head and ears and circular red patches on a human's arms and legs. Fleas, lice and fur mites may sometimes bite humans and cause skin reactions, such as itchiness and red blotches.	Prompt veterinary treatment and disinfection of bedding and grooming equipment is advisable if your cat has ringworm. Fleas and other parasites can be controlled by treatment of animals and their environment.

TOXOPLASMOSIS

Cats are sometimes carriers of the microscopic Toxoplasma parasite that can also infect humans. A cat is infected by eating contaminated raw meat, and cysts are then shed in the animal's faeces. The risks to humans are greatest from handling infected, raw meat. Most infections are harmless, but pregnant women are particularly at risk, since the disease may cause abnormalities in the unborn child. Although cats are very careful about burying their droppings, sensible hygiene precautions should be followed when handling soiled cat litter.

BITES AND SCRATCHES

Few cats are aggressive towards humans without provocation. Many of the bites and scratches humans experience are related to clumsy handling or action that is frightening to the cat (*see pages 40–41*). A cat's mouth contains bacteria and a bite can become infected if it is not cleaned and treated with antiseptic. If a cat bite becomes swollen or painful, you should seek medical attention. Cat scratches can also introduce infection, and even fever (known as cat-scratch fever), and should always be washed carefully.

Teeth and claws (*above*)
When provoked, a cat can use its teeth and claws to defend itself.

Chapter 7

NURSING

UNWELL OR injured cats and those recovering after a surgical operation require careful observation, loving support and attention, and a degree of privacy. Try to create a quiet, clean, comfortable area as the feline sick room. Keep a medicine chest well stocked with essential items, such as a thermometer, syringe, and dosing gun, ready in case of illness. Sick cats may need to be tempted to eat a few nourishing morsels to keep their strength up. You should administer medicines in a gentle but purposeful way, so that you cause the sick cat the least possible distress. Consult the vet about any special nursing or feeding requirements for your cat's condition.

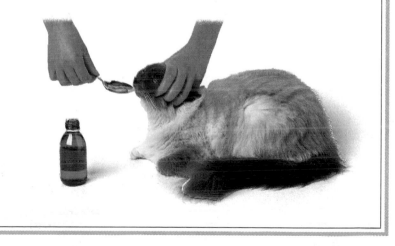

RESTRAINING A CAT

Most cats are not difficult to handle and restrain, but they do have to be taken in their own time with a kindly and gentle approach. Your aim should always be less rather than more restraint. It is unwise for untrained people to attempt to restrain a cat that is not used to being handled; feral cats and most farm cats are particularly resistant to being held. A lively pet may need to be restrained when being examined by a vet.

The methods of firm restraint shown on these pages should only be carried out to control a difficult cat. It is important not to use any unnecessary force, since this will frighten the cat and could even cause it injury. You may find it easiest to wrap an uncooperative cat in a towel when administering medicines at home. A cat needs to be held very still when it is being given a tablet or when applying eye and ear drops. Always talk to a cat while it is being examined or restrained to reassure it.

HOLDING A CAT FOR EXAMINATION

Examining the head
A veterinary nurse restrains the cat by holding its front legs gently but firmly. Her forearms hold down the cat's body, allowing the vet to examine its head.

Examining the body
A calm cat is easily restrained by holding the shoulders while the skin and coat are examined by the vet.

RESTRAINING A DIFFICULT CAT

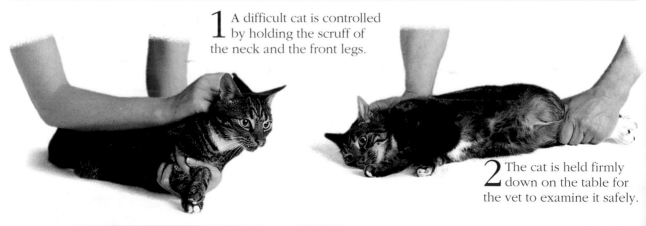

1 A difficult cat is controlled by holding the scruff of the neck and the front legs.

2 The cat is held firmly down on the table for the vet to examine it safely.

WRAPPING A CAT IN A TOWEL

1 When maximum restraint is needed a large, thick towel is useful. The cat is held firmly on the towel by the scruff. It is best not to let the cat use the towel beforehand.

Hold the cat firmly on the towel

The paws must be wrapped in the towel

2 The cat is wrapped quickly in the towel, keeping hold of the scruff all the time.

3 A towel wrapped firmly around the cat prevents the cat from scratching when being treated or examined.

SCRUFFING A CAT

Scruffing may help control a difficult cat

Clothes pegs
One or two broad-ended clothes pegs placed on the scruff of the neck can immobilize a cat in the same way as lifting it up by the scruff.

HANDLE WITH CARE

Do not attempt to restrain an angry or frightened cat by holding it by the scruff or by using the "clothes-peg" method unless you are experienced in handling cats. You should never prolong any restraint if it is causing the animal distress. This applies to all methods of handling and restraint.

ADMINISTERING MEDICINE

You may be given some tablets or medication to administer at home after visiting the vet. Getting your cat to take the medicine it needs but does not want requires a gentle but purposeful approach. It is best if the cat is placed on a table or other raised surface, and some cats will need to be restrained by an assistant. If the cat tries to scratch or bite, it should be wrapped in a towel (*see page 129*). You should not try to hide medicine in food since a cat can usually detect any additions to its food bowl by smell and may refuse to eat.

GIVING A TABLET

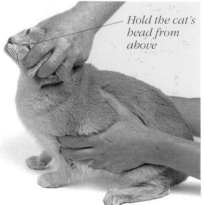

Hold the cat's head from above

1 While an assistant holds the cat, gently enclose its head with your fingers. Do not ruffle its whiskers.

2 Grasp the head between forefinger and thumb and tip it back. Press lightly on the jaw to open the cat's mouth.

3 Place the tablet as far back as possible on the tongue at the back of the cat's mouth.

4 Close the cat's mouth and gently stroke the throat to encourage it to swallow the tablet.

GIVING A TABLET ON YOUR OWN

1 If your cat is gentle and docile, you can give it a tablet without any assistance. Grasp the cat's head with one hand and open its mouth with the other.

Tablet

2 Put the tablet on the back of the cat's tongue. Hold the mouth closed until the cat has swallowed as shown above.

GIVING A TABLET USING A DOSING GUN

Fire the tablet into the cat's mouth

1 An alternative method of giving a tablet is to use a pill or dosing gun, which you can obtain from your vet.

2 Open the cat's mouth as shown opposite and "fire" the tablet with a little water to the back of the throat. Hold the mouth closed until it has swallowed.

GIVING MEDICINE WITH A SYRINGE

Using a plastic syringe, slowly squirt the liquid into the cat's mouth. Administer the medicine slowly so that it does not go down the wrong way.

GIVING AN INJECTION

An injection is the most effective way of administering medicine to a cat and this is almost always done by a vet. However, where daily injections are required, for instance in the treatment of diabetes, you may have to carry out this procedure yourself. Your vet will supply you with sterile syringes and discuss the procedure with you.

Draw the medicine into the syringe

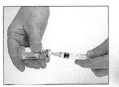

1 Hold the cat firmly and make a little "tent" of loose skin at the scruff of the neck.

2 Insert the needle under the skin at the cat's neck and slowly inject the medication.

TREATING EYES AND EARS

There are several feline eye and ear conditions that require treatment with drops or ointment prescribed by a vet. After consulting your vet you will probably be given a course of medicines to administer at home. (Never try to treat your cat with medicines intended for humans or without getting proper advice.) The vet or veterinary nurse will be happy to demonstrate the best way to apply eye and ear medications.

You should administer eye and ear drops quickly and carefully, using the minimum amount of restraint (*see pages 128–129*). Follow the directions given by the vet and, even if the problem appears to clear up, continue the course of treatment for as long as advised to ensure that the condition does not recur.

APPLYING EYE OINTMENT

1 Hold the cat's head still with one hand. Using the other hand, gently squeeze a line of ointment on to the eyeball. Do not let the tube touch the eye.

2 Close the eyelids and hold closed for a few seconds to allow the ointment to spread over the eyes.

APPLYING EYE DROPS

1 Gently clean the area around the eyes, wiping away any discharge from the corners of the eyes with a small piece of dampened cotton wool.

2 Holding the cat's head firmly with one hand, apply the required number of eye drops in both eyes.

3 Allow the eyes to bathe in the drops for a few seconds. Gently hold the eyes closed as above.

ADMINISTERING EAR DROPS

Massage the drops into the ears

1 Using a piece of dampened cotton wool, wipe away any dirt from the inside of the ear.

2 Holding the cat's head firmly, fold the outer ear back and administer the required number of drops in both ears.

3 Be careful not to poke the dropper into the cat's ears. Gently massage the ears.

INHERITED EYE AND EAR PROBLEMS

Deaf white cats
Deafness can be associated with the gene that gives a white cat its coat colour. It causes a degeneration of the inner ear

Longhaired cat
Some pedigree longhaired cats are very prone to blocked tear ducts, which result in runny eyes.

Siamese cat
Some Siamese cats suffer from reduced binocular vision or double vision which they compensate for by squinting. Careful breeding has reduced the number of cats affected.

Abyssinian cat (*right*)
Certain breeds, such as Abyssinian and Siamese cats, are prone to inherited eye problems.

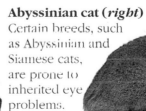

SURGERY AND AFTERCARE

Most cats will need to undergo surgery under a general anaesthetic at some point in their lives. Although modern techniques of surgery have reduced the dangers to a minimum, there is still a small risk involved with any type of operation. A cat makes a good surgical patient; it adapts well to cage rest and it recovers quickly after major operations.

After an operation, a cat needs to be kept warm and quiet, and its behaviour should be closely observed. If the cat is restless or has a fractured limb, it may have to be confined to a pen. A cat recovering from an illness may need to be kept indoors.

Convalescence
A cat must be kept quiet and carefully watched for a couple of weeks after an operation. Try to keep it confined to one room and prevent it from biting its stitches or removing its dressing.

SURGICAL OPERATIONS

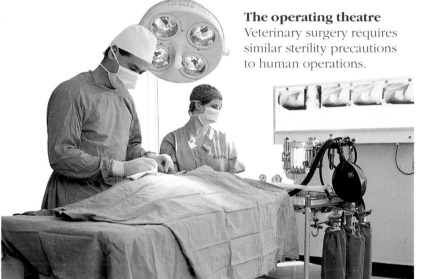

The operating theatre
Veterinary surgery requires similar sterility precautions to human operations.

PRE-OPERATIVE CARE

If your cat is to undergo a routine operation, such as neutering or teeth scaling, arrange for it to be done when you have some time to care for your pet. The cat will not be allowed to eat or drink for 12 hours prior to the operation. This may seem hard, but it is important because it reduces the risk of the cat vomiting while under the anaesthetic. When you deliver your cat to the hospital or surgery, you can ask when you can telephone to find out about its progress. A cat will usually be allowed to go home the same day.

ANIMAL HOSPITALS

At the animal hospital or veterinary surgery, the cat will be kept in a recovery cage until it has recovered from the anaesthetic. When it comes round it will be unsteady on its feet for several hours. You will be allowed to take the cat home only when the vet is satisfied that it is on the mend. The cat may need to be kept at the surgery for a couple of days for observation following a serious operation.

Cage rest
A cat is usually put in a recovery cage after a surgical operation to allow for close observation and undisturbed rest. Some hospitals have television monitors to help watch cover the animals after surgery.

POST-OPERATIVE CARE

Bandages
If a cat has a dressing covering a wound, it may do its utmost to remove it. Cover it with an elastic bandage to keep it in place for as long as possible. Keep a cat confined as directed.

General nursing
A cat recovering from an operation must be kept warm and quiet. Make the cat comfortable by wrapping it in a large towel or blanket, or by putting it in a cardboard box.

Elizabethan collar
A cat should be prevented from pulling out its stitches. An Elizabethan collar, fitted by a vet, is a simple solution that will prevent a cat from worrying a wound. Consult a vet if you notice any swelling or discharge from the wound site.

Veterinary care
If you notice any change in your cat's condition after an operation, report it immediately to a vet.

ALTERNATIVE MEDICINE

There is a growing interest and awareness in alternatives to established conventional medicine for treating cats and dogs. While homoeopathic and herbal approaches can be used to treat certain ailments, you still need to consult a vet to get a proper diagnosis. Some vets even specialize in alternative medicine and can prescribe a suitable treatment for your cat. Alternative medicine cannot cure serious conditions that require surgery, but it can be used to treat many minor disorders and prevent them from recurring. For example, homoeopathic creams can be used to help various common feline skin complaints.

Garlic
Garlic is reputed to act as a flea repellent and may increase a cat's resistance to infections.

NURSING A SICK CAT

A sick cat that is recovering from an operation, or that needs to be nursed at home through an illness, requires special care. For the best results, it should be cared for in familiar surroundings by people it knows and trusts. Try to make your sick cat comfortable by keeping it clean, warm, and dry. Your vet will give you instructions if your cat requires a special diet.

KEEPING WARM

The sick room
To make a sick bed for your invalid pet, cut a hole in one side of a large cardboard box. Line it with newspaper, a towel, and a lukewarm hot-water bottle. The box should be placed in a quiet corner.

FEEDING A SICK CAT

Loss of appetite
A sick cat often needs to be coaxed to eat. Feed small, frequent meals, warmed to blood heat.

Spoonfeeding
If a cat refuses to eat or drink, try feeding it liquids with a spoon. Allow the cat to swallow after every few drops.

Spoonfeeding medicine
A calm cat can be spoonfed liquid medicines. This can be messy, but try to get as much of the medicine as possible into the cat's mouth.

Forcefeeding
A weak cat can be fed small amounts of liquidized food with a dropper or a syringe (*see page 131*).

GROOMING A SICK CAT

1 Clear any discharge from around the cat's eyes with a piece of cotton wool dampened in clean, warm water. You can apply a little petroleum jelly to any sore places, but do not put it too near the cat's eyes.

2 Gently wipe away any nasal discharge and crusting around the cat's nostrils. The cat will be able to breathe more easily and will feel better with some of its sense of smell restored.

SAFE DISINFECTANTS

Disinfectants containing phenol are poisonous. Use a dilute solution of sodium hypochlorite or hydrogen peroxide to clean the sick room.

Gently wipe the cat's mouth

3 Clean up any saliva or vomit from around the cat's mouth. Clean up the cat's behind if there is any diarrhoea, and change the bedding if it becomes soiled.

NURSING EQUIPMENT

Dropper   *Dosing gun*

Thermometer   *Syringe*

Lagged hot-water bottle   *Disinfectant*   *Medicinal paraffin*   *Diarrhoea medicine*   *Petroleum jelly*   *Skin cream*   *Worming tablets*

You should keep your cat's medicine chest stocked with everything you will need in case of illness. Never give a cat medicine intended for humans or without having consulted a vet.

CARING FOR AN ELDERLY CAT

Old age is not a specific disease, and comes to us all. As a cat gets older, the vital organs of its body deteriorate at different rates. Changes in the heart, brain, kidneys, and liver are the most life-threatening. Fortunately, these major organs have reasonable reserves of functional activity; more than half of the kidney function may, for example, be lost without the cat showing any signs of illness. Given plenty of loving care and close veterinary management, many cats with quite advanced kidney failure may lead fairly normal, active lives.

Regular health check-ups by a vet can improve the quality of life of an elderly cat. An older cat will generally become less active and spend more time sleeping. Try not to disturb its daily routine and ensure that it has a warm bed which is kept in a cosy spot out of draughts.

SIGNS OF OLD AGE

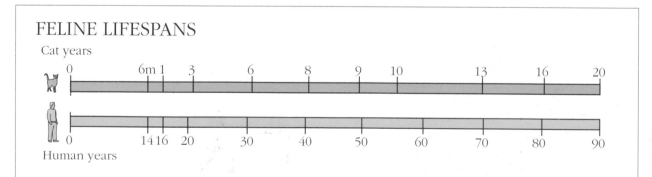

Hearing may become less acute

Eyesight may deteriorate

The coat may become less thick and lose condition

Heath checks
You should keep a careful check on the health of an elderly cat. Watch out for any signs of abnormal behaviour and examine its eyes, ears, mouth, and coat regularly. Pay particular attention to its mouth and, if your cat will allow it, brush its teeth once a week.

The joints and muscles may become stiff and less supple

The claws may need regular trimming if the cat is inactive

FELINE LIFESPANS

Cat years

0   6m 1   3   6   8   9   10   13   16   20

0   14 16   20   30   40   50   60   70   80   90

Human years

Many people believe that cats age about seven years for every one human year. In fact, their development accelerates in the early years and slows down in middle age, as shown in the lifespan chart above. After the age of ten, signs of old age begin to appear and the time scale is more like ours. Cats over 20 years of age can be looked upon as feline centenarians.

SPECIAL CARE

Feeding
Some cats need less food and fewer calories as they age; others may need more due to poor absorption and digestion (*see page 61*).

Constipation
Elderly cats may become constipated. Spoon two or three teaspoonsful of medicinal liquid paraffin into the cat's mouth to relieve constipation.

Weighing
If your cat loses weight while continuing to eat substantial amounts, consult your vet. On the other hand, an older cat that becomes much less active but continues to eat the same amounts of food may become obese.

Veterinary check-ups
Regular check-ups become more necessary as your cat starts to show the signs of age. They should be carried out every three to six months or whenever your vet advises.

EUTHANASIA
There may come a time when your cat's life needs to be brought to a peaceful end. Any cat that has an untreatable condition, which is causing it pain or distress, can have its life ended gently and with dignity. Vets usually inject an overdose of an anaesthetic into a vein, putting the cat into a deep sleep to a point where the animal will not regain consciousness. Your vet will be able to advise you and help you make the difficult decision if your pet is very unwell. You may wish to plant a small rose bush or tree, or make a donation to an animal charity to perpetuate the best memories of your pet.

Pet cemeteries
You can bury your cat in a special pet cemetery.

Chapter 8

BREEDING

THE WORLD would certainly be a better place for cats if only wanted kittens were born. Consider carefully the responsibilities of breeding from your cat and decide whether or not neutering is the best course of action. Cats are very fertile and, provided that your queen is in good health, it is fairly straightforward to plan the mating. Make preparations for the birth by setting aside an appropriate place for the kittening box. Remember that kittens are demanding; they disrupt your home, take up your time, require vaccinations, and need to be found homes.

HEREDITY AND BREEDING

Every cat inherits certain physical characteristics from both its parents. These characteristics are determined by genes. They represent a set of instructions that determine the cat's coat colour, the length of its coat, and the colour of its eyes. For every kitten in a litter, the genes are arranged in a different order, so each individual is generally unique, no matter how similar it is in appearance.

If you wish to breed a show cat, look for a tom cat with suitable characteristics for your female to be mated with.

Mother and kitten
This little kitten has a different coat colour from both its parents.

A CAT FAMILY TREE

Determining coat colour
Kittens with very different coat colours result from the mating of Chocolate and Blue Burmese cats. One of the kittens is the same colour as the mother and one is identical to the father, but four have lighter coats. This is because the male is carrying a gene that dilutes the coat colour from a silver-grey (Blue) to a lavender-grey (Lilac).

Chocolate Burmese mother

Blue Burmese father

Lilac female kitten

Blue female kitten

Chocolate male kitten

Lilac male kitten

Lilac female kitten

Lilac male kitten

INHERITED CHARACTERISTICS

A "Stumpy" Manx has a residual tail

Manx cat (*left*)

The Manx cat is a very old breed, but if someone applied today for its official recognition, this would probably not be granted. The Manx carries a gene that causes the deformity of taillessness, which is deadly if it is passed on by both parents. The mating of two Manx cats usually results in the kittens dying before or shortly after birth.

Rex cat (*right*)

Despite their similar appearances, there are two distinct breeds of curly coated Rex cat, namely the Devon and the Cornish Rex. Both breeds are believed to have developed from separate mutations.

Tortoiseshell cat (*above*)

The orange gene that results in a tortoiseshell coat is linked to the gene that determines the cat's sex. This means that nearly all tortoiseshell cats are female. The very rare male tortoiseshell is usually sterile.

Rogue genes (*left*)

There are a few genes that are passed on from parents to offspring that cause deformities. While some inherited traits, such as a kitten being born with extra toes (polydactyly) are relatively harmless, others, such as heart defects, are fatal.

Siamese cat

The Siamese is really a black cat with its coat colour diluted by an albino-type gene. This is what gives a Siamese cat its unique, pale-coloured coat with darker markings on the head, paws, and tail. Selective breeding has intensified the coat colour, so that the body is darkest in the Seal-point Siamese.

PLANNING A LITTER

Breeding from your cat is an important decision, which must be given careful consideration. A female cat is sexually mature from about six months old and a male cat from about ten months old. A queen comes into heat in two-week cycles, and each "oestrus" lasts for two to four days. Even if you take precautions, an unneutered queen is almost certain to be mated. It is very difficult to confine a female cat on heat since she will become restless and "call" or howl, attracting every local tom.

CHOOSING A SUITABLE MATE

The stud cat
If you plan to breed from your pedigree queen, you will need to find a suitable stud cat. Make enquiries at local cat shows or through the relevant breed club, which will be able to supply you with a list of reputable breeders.

COURTSHIP AND MATING

The queen may be hostile to the tom at first

1 The queen is taken to the breeder's stud cat when she comes into heat and starts to "call".

MATING A CAT
• Choose a reputable breeder.
• Cats must be vaccinated and free of Feline Leukaemia Virus.
• Never mate a cat that is not perfectly fit and healthy.
• Keep your cat indoors after she returns from the stud.

2 When the female begins to show an interest in the tom, the two cats are put together in the same pen. Clip both cats' claws beforehand to prevent injuries in case there is a fight.

The queen sniffs the tom

3 The queen signals that she is ready for mating by rolling provocatively to attract the tom's attention.

The neck-bite immobilizes the queen

4 As part of the courtship ritual, the female rejects the first advance. The tom retreats but renews his overtures a few moments later.

5 The queen raises her rear and makes a "paddling" movement with her back legs. As the tom mounts, he grasps her by the scruff.

6 The tom penetrates the queen and ejaculates immediately. The female cat may call out at the moment of penetration. Ovulation is stimulated by the act of mating.

Post-coital behaviour
After mating, both cats separate and groom themselves. The whole mating sequence will need to be repeated several times over a period of two to three days to ensure that the queen is pregnant.

PREGNANCY AND PRE-NATAL CARE

The queen will not come into heat as usual two or three weeks later if a mating is successful. A pregnant cat shows the first signs of her condition soon after this. Her nipples become redder and the surrounding fur may recede slightly. At around three to four weeks, a vet can confirm the pregnancy by gently palpating the cat's abdomen. A healthy cat does not require any special care other than being fed a well-balanced diet. The queen's appetite will increase and she will gradually put on weight.

SIGNS OF PREGNANCY

The queen will put on about 1–2 kg (2–4 lb)

The nipples are prominent

The abdomen is distended

A pregnant queen
A cat is noticeably fatter after the sixth week of pregnancy. Her abdomen becomes rounded and the nipples redden and become very prominent.

CARING FOR A PREGNANT CAT

Feeding
A pregnant cat must be fed a nourishing, well-balanced diet and your vet may also recommend additional feeding during the last weeks. The number of meals should be gradually increased from about the fifth week of pregnancy (*see page 61*). Consult your vet about dosing your pregnant cat with worming tablets.

Kittening box (*above*)
Provide the queen with a warm and comfortable place to give birth. Make a kittening box out of a cardboard box, cut down at one side and lined with newspaper.

Active pregnancy
A healthy cat will remain lively throughout the pregnancy. She can be allowed to go outside and will continue to play, jump, and climb, although she may slow down these activities.

A pregnant cat is still interested in playing games

DEVELOPMENT OF THE FOETUS

Length of pregnancy
The average length of pregnancy is 65 days or about nine weeks from the date of the mating. An ultrasound scan can be used after six weeks into the pregnancy.

Embryo

Placenta

Yolk sac

Umbilical cord

2 At 22 days the embryo's head, eyes, and limbs are developing.

3 At 28 days the foetus is about 2.5 cm (1 in) long and all its internal organs have developed.

4 Between 40–45 days the bones of the skeleton form.

1 At 18 days the embryo is still attached to the yolk sac, which provides it with nutrients.

5 The foetus develops rapidly during the last three weeks before the birth. Kittens born earlier than 58 days do not usually survive. Kittens born later than 70 days are likely to be bigger than normal.

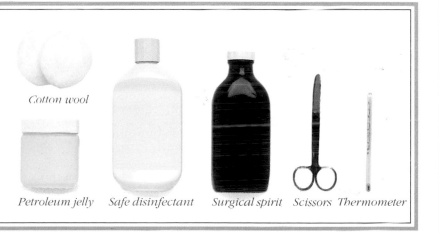

KITTENING EQUIPMENT
Prepare for the kittens' birth by making a kittening box and having some essential items to hand. This equipment may be needed if you (or the vet) have to assist with the delivery (*see pages 174–175*). A thermometer may record a drop in the cat's temperature (about 1°C/2°F) a few hours before kittening.

Cotton wool

Petroleum jelly   *Safe disinfectant*   *Surgical spirit*   *Scissors Thermometer*

KITTENING

Keep a careful watch on the queen during the last week of the pregnancy. Make sure that she is accustomed to the kittening box and do not allow her to wander off or to hide herself away. The queen's behaviour will warn you when the birth is imminent. She may refuse food or vomit before the labour begins. Many kittens are born at night.

GIVING BIRTH

1 The queen starts to breathe heavily, pant, or purr, but not in pain. A clear vaginal discharge may be seen. This first stage of labour can last as long as six hours but is usually shorter.

2 The second stage of labour begins when the queen starts "bearing down". Make a note of the time that she starts to strain and if a kitten is not born within 30 minutes, contact the vet.

The membrane around the kitten can just be seen

3 In an ideal birth, a kitten enclosed in a bubble-like membrane will appear between 15–30 minutes later. Most kittens are born head first, but some may be born hind legs first.

4 As soon as a kitten is born, the queen licks it to remove the membrane surrounding it and to stimulate its breathing. The third stage of labour is marked by the expulsion of the afterbirth, which the queen may eat.

HELPING AT THE BIRTH

An inexperienced mother cat may require assistance with the kittening. If a queen ignores a new-born kitten or a kitten is only partially delivered, you need to take emergency action immediately or the kitten may die (*see pages 174–175*). Make sure that your vet is on stand-by when the kittens are due.

5 Usually, the mother cat instinctively knows what to do. She bites through the umbilical cord with her teeth.

WHEN TO CALL THE VET

Most cats do not need any help with kittening. Keep interference to a minimum. Contact a vet if the cat is distressed (*see page 174*).

6 Allow the mother cat to lick the kittens straightaway. The queen may take a short rest after one or two kittens have been born and resume her straining a few moments later.

A new-born kitten looks for a teat

7 The new-born kittens may need a little help in finding a teat to feed on. Make sure that the kittens are placed near to their mother's abdomen and encourage them to suckle as soon as possible.

8 An average litter numbers between two and six kittens and the labour may last for several hours. If the queen shows signs of weariness, she can be revived with a little milk or some of her favourite food.

Happy families

Once the kittening is complete, leave the mother and kittens to rest. Make sure that the queen is provided with water, food, and a litter tray. She may be reluctant to leave her kittens.

POST-NATAL CARE

New-born kittens are totally dependent on the mother cat. The cat family should be kept in the kittening box, in a warm place. Keep a watch on the kittens, particularly if the queen is inexperienced. As long as the mother is healthy, she will do all that is necessary. The queen will require at least three times more food than usual (*see page 61*).

MATERNAL CARE

Each kitten has its own preferred teat

Bonding
Shortly after a kitten is born, the mother cat will gently guide it to a teat and it will start to suckle. The milk produced by the mother cat in the first few days after kittening is called "colostrum" and is packed with nutrients and antibodies that will protect the kittens from infections.

The mother cat washes her kittens frequently

Washing
Once the kittens have finished suckling, the mother cat will wash them all over. The queen licks the kittens' bottoms to stimulate excretion of waste products. She will do this until the kittens start to eat solid food.

Suckling
By kneading its mother's body with its paws, a kitten stimulates the flow of milk. If the kittens are restless and cry a lot, this may be a sign that the queen is not producing enough milk. Consult the vet if you suspect that the kittens are not getting enough milk.

Keeping watch

The mother cat carefully guards her litter and dislikes leaving the kittens too often. If any of the kittens strays from the nest, she retrieves it by carrying it by the scruff of the neck. Do not let children pick up or handle the kittens without supervision. Try not to disturb the mother and offspring any more than is necessary.

A straying kitten is closely watched by its mother

FOSTERING KITTENS

The mother cat will not notice one or two extra mouths to feed

Foster mothers

If the mother cat has died, rejected her litter, or cannot produce milk, you will need to find a foster mother. A newly kittened queen with a small litter of her own will accept one or two orphan kittens.

Shared nursing

If there is another newly kittened queen in the household, some of the kittens from a large litter can be fostered by the other cat. Introduce the kittens to the foster mother cat as soon as possible after birth.

ARTIFICIAL FEEDING

Bottle feeding

It is possible to rear orphan kittens by hand. Start by feeding the kittens every two hours with a cat milk replacer. The kittens must also be kept clean and warm. Ask your vet for guidance.

FEEDING EQUIPMENT

Feeding bottle   Dropper Syringe

All feeding equipment must be sterilized and the milk made up according to the directions.

EARLY KITTEN CARE

For the first few weeks of their lives, kittens are at their most helpless and need a lot of attention. The mother cat will provide for all their needs up to the age of about three weeks, when they begin to explore their surroundings and become more independent. The kittens should gradually be weaned off their mother's milk and introduced to solid food. By the age of ten to twelve weeks, the kittens should be fully weaned and ready to leave their mother.

RAISING KITTENS

One day old
A new-born kitten is completely dependent on its mother. Its eyelids are closed and its ears are folded back, so it cannot see or hear.

The kittens instinctively huddle together to keep warm

Three weeks old
A couple of weeks later, the kittens are fully mobile and eager to explore. They are now ready to be given a little solid food (*see opposite*).

One week old
The kittens' eyes open at about seven days old. The litter is still very vulnerable and helpless without the mother cat, and the young sleep huddled together for security and warmth.

Four weeks old
Once the kittens are eating solids, they can be trained to use a litter tray. Place the tray in a quiet spot and put the kittens on it after each feed. Never rub a kitten's nose in any accidental mess that it makes.

Five weeks old
Feed the kittens a range of different foods to encourage good eating habits in later life. Finely minced cooked meat and poached white fish can be given to add a little variety to the diet as an alternative to canned kitten food.

Six weeks old
The kittens learn how to hunt by pouncing on toy prey. Boisterous games with littermates allow them to try out offensive and defensive roles.

Seven weeks old
Regular weighing and monitoring of the kittens' weights (*see page 58*) allows you to keep an eye on their development – however, you may have a problem getting them to sit still on the scales.

Nine weeks old
At eight to nine weeks of age, the kittens should be vaccinated against Feline respiratory disease and Feline Infectious Enteritis. A kitten should not go outside until it has been vaccinated.

WEANING KITTENS

Age	Type of food	Number of
3 weeks old	Powdered cat milk substitute, a little finely chopped, cooked meat or canned kitten food, and mother's milk.	Place in a saucer and give 4–6 times daily.
4 weeks old	Powderded cat milk substitute, finely chopped, cooked meat or canned kitten food, and mother's milk.	Place in a saucer and give 4–6 times daily.
5 weeks old	Finely chopped, cooked meat or canned kitten food as well as mother's milk.	Provide solid food 4–5 times daily.
6–8 weeks old	Increase the amount of solid food given and decrease the kittens' access to mother cat's milk.	Provide solid food 3–4 times daily.
8 weeks and older	The kittens are fully weaned. Give cow's milk (if tolerated) or low-lactose milk until they are six months old.	Provide solid food 3–4 times daily.

PREVENTING PREGNANCY

Unless you are the owner of a pedigree cat that you intend to show or breed from, you should consider having it neutered to prevent unwanted kittens. "Doctoring" is a routine operation and should ideally be carried out when a kitten is between four and six months old. Neutering prevents the production of the hormones that govern a cat's sex drive and the development of undesirable behaviour. An unneutered tom cat marks its territory by spraying it with pungent urine. An unspayed queen comes into heat every few weeks, when she "calls" to attract males in the vicinity.

Double pregnancy
Two pregnant cats mean double the care when the kittens arrive.

MALE CATS

A castrated cat
A neutered male cat makes a very affectionate and loving pet, which is less likely to stray from home or to get into fights than a tom cat.

The head, neck, and shoulders are less muscular than in an entire cat

A tom cat (*below*)
A tom cat is dominated by its sex drive. The secondary sexual characteristics of a tom are unpleasant for humans and make it a difficult pet to keep indoors. It marks its territory by spraying it with pungent urine.

Fight wounds around the eyes and ears are very common

NEUTERING CHECKLIST

• A cat can be castrated or spayed at any age provided that it is healthy.
• Early castration prevents a male cat from developing undesirable behaviour.
• Alternative methods of birth control are avilable to postpone a queen from coming into heat.

FEMALE CATS

A spayed cat
A spayed cat looks the same as an unspayed female. Contrary to popular belief, there are no benefits in letting your cat have one litter of kittens before being spayed.

A queen on heat attracts toms by her scent

Sexual behaviour (*above*)
A queen on heat is restless and noisy. If she is confined indoors, she will become frustrated and do her utmost to escape.

A spayed cat looks the same as a queen

Spay wound on the flank heals quickly

The queen (*right*)
The process of giving birth and raising young will take its toll on a female cat and may cause premature ageing. It is cruel to allow a cat to go through the rigours of kittening, only to have the unwanted kittens destroyed.

THE NEUTERING OPERATIONS

Castration
A male cat should ideally be neutered at about six months old. Castration is a routine operation and involves the removal of the cat's testes under a general anaesthetic. There are normally no stitches. A healthy cat will be back to normal a day after the operation.

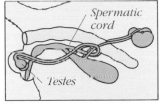

Spermatic cord

Testes

Tom cat

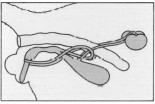

Neutered male

Spaying
A female cat should ideally be neutered at around four or five months old. A queen cannot be neutered while on heat. The operation involves the removal of the cat's uterus and ovaries under a general anaesthetic. There will be a small wound on the cat's flank.

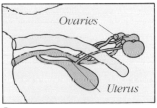

Ovaries

Uterus

Queen

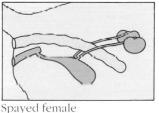

Spayed female

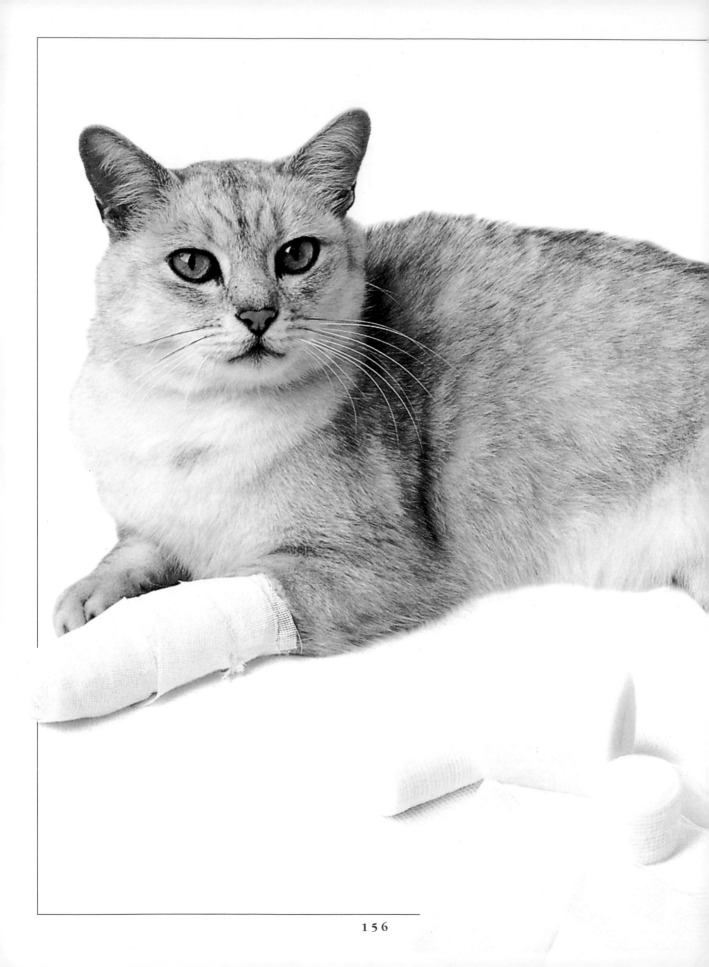

Chapter 9

FIRST AID

LEARN HOW to handle the most common emergencies. Prompt action in such cases as poisoning, choking, drowning, burns, bites, and stings, can save life and prevent unnecessary suffering. First aid does not mean setting up a do-it-yourself veterinary surgery. Your primary objectives must be to prevent further injury to the cat, to alleviate pain and distress, and to help begin the recovery process. Getting help from a vet is the highest priority. You should restrict yourself to taking only immediate necessary action to stabilize the cat's condition until veterinary assistance is available.

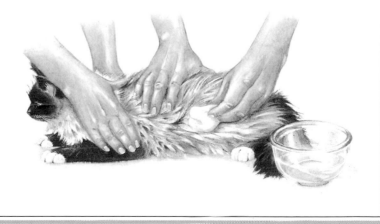

PRINCIPLES OF FIRST AID

First aid is important as an interim measure before professional veterinary help is available and it may save your cat's life in an emergency. An injured cat may require urgent first aid to stop bleeding, treat shock, and restart or clear its breathing. The objectives of first aid should be to prevent the cat's condition from worsening; to remove any source of harm; to alleviate pain and suffering; and to help with the recovery process. The absolute rule is to do no harm. Take essential action only and seek advice on the next course of action from a vet as soon as possible.

FIRST-AID EQUIPMENT

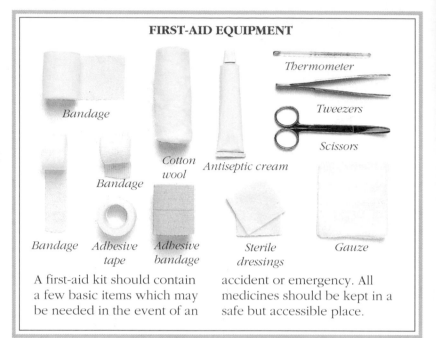

Bandage

Thermometer

Tweezers

Scissors

Cotton wool

Antiseptic cream

Bandage

Bandage   Adhesive tape   Adhesive bandage

Sterile dressings

Gauze

A first-aid kit should contain a few basic items which may be needed in the event of an accident or emergency. All medicines should be kept in a safe but accessible place.

ASSESSING AN INJURED CAT

1 Open the cat's mouth and pull the tongue forwards. Clear the mouth of mucus using a piece of cotton wool. The head should be tilted downwards so that no fluids are inhaled.

2 Count the number of breaths in or out (but not both) over a couple of minutes. The rate should be 20–30 breaths per minute.

3 Feel the cat's pulse on the inside of the hind leg. Count the number of beats per minute. The rate should be 160–240 beats per minute. The heartbeat can be felt behind the cat's elbow.

Feeling the pulse

Feeling the heartbeat

CHECKING REFLEXES

Eyelid reflex
You can check the eyelid reflex by gently touching the corner of the cat's eyelid. Do not touch the eyeball itself. A cat should automatically blink if it is at all conscious.

Foot reflex
Gently pinch the web of skin between the toes. A cat should automatically react by flexing or moving its leg if it is at all conscious.

Ear reflex
Touch or gently flick the tip of the ear flap with one finger. If a cat is at all conscious, it should automatically react by twitching its ears.

FIRST AID WARNING

A semi-conscious cat may feel stimulus and be unable to react if it is in shock. Never persist with an examination longer than needed.

COLLAPSE AND SHOCK

Recognizing shock
A cat may go into a state of shock following a serious accident. It will feel cold to the touch and its breathing and pulse will be rapid.

Conserve heat (*left*)
Make the cat as comfortable as possible. Keep it warm (unless it is suffering from heatstroke) by wrapping it loosely in a blanket or towel. Do not constrict the cat's breathing.

EMERGENCY ACTION

Do not let an unconscious cat lie on one side for more than 5–10 minutes. Do not give an unconscious cat anything by mouth.

Recovery position
If a cat is unconscious or having difficulty breathing, place it on its side with the head tilted downwards. Open the mouth and ensure that the airway is clear.

ACCIDENTS

The most important thing to do in the event of an accident is to contact a vet as soon as possible. Even if a cat appears to have no external injuries, it should be given a check-up, since there may be internal damage. A vet or his trained staff can advise you on immediate first aid measures. If time is critical, ask someone to telephone the surgery and warn the vet that you are on the way.

Accidental falls
A cat is unlikely to injure itself if it falls from a tree, but injuries do occur with falls from greater heights. Keep all accessible windows closed if you live on an upper floor of a building.

MOVING AN UNCONSCIOUS CAT

1 More the injured cat out of harm's way if it is necessary. A blanket or coat will serve as an improvised stretcher. Lay the blanket out flat and then gently ease the cat on to it.

2 With the help of an assistant, gently lift the blanket up, taking care not to let the cat slip off. If the cat is conscious, you may need someone to restrain it.

3 Ensure that the airway is clear by removing any fluid from the mouth and pulling the tongue forward (*see page 158*). Stop any severe bleeding by covering the wound with a pressure bandage or gauze pad (*see page 170*).

4 It is advisable to transport an injured cat in a secure container. An unconscious cat can be lowered on the blanket into a large box so as not to disturb it.

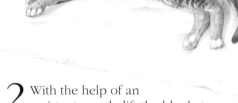

MOVING AN UNCOOPERATIVE CAT

1 An injured cat will be frightened and perhaps in pain. Talk to the cat to reassure it, approaching it very slowly and cautiously. A frightened cat may be aggressive and defensive, even to people it knows.

2 Cover the cat with a blanket to restrain it and to prevent it from running off. It may be advisable to wear gloves to protect your hands.

Make sure paws are enclosed

3 With one hand holding the scruff of the neck, wrap the blanket quickly but securely around the cat's body, leaving the head exposed (*see page 129*).

4 Maintaining a firm grip on the cat's scruff, pick the cat up and put it into a carrier for transportation to the vet. Do not release your hold until you are about to fasten the carrier.

FRACTURED LIMBS

Lifting an injured cat
If you suspect that a cat has a fractured limb, handle it very carefully. Lay it on a blanket and pick it up, keeping the injured limb uppermost. Avoid twisting or bending its body. Put the cat in a carrier and get it quickly to a vet.

FIRST AID WARNING

Transport and handle a cat with a fractured limb so as to cause it the minimum disturbance. Do not attempt to apply a splint yourself since this will distress an injured cat and probably do more harm than good.

RESUSCITATION

Prompt action taken in an emergency situation, such as a road traffic accident (*see pages 160–161*), may save your cat's life. Fortunately, such emergencies are rare, but they usually occur without warning and allow little or no time to get professional help. If a cat is unconscious and its breathing and heartbeat have stopped, get someone to telephone the vet for you in order to obtain immediate advice while you try to resuscitate the animal.

Resuscitation must be carried out following the guidelines given opposite (or by a vet), to ensure that a cat has the best chance of recovery. A cat may suffer respiratory and heart failure following drowning, electric shock, or poisoning. For the cat to survive, its breathing or heart must be restarted within a few minutes.

ARTIFICIAL RESPIRATION

The mouth should be open to ease breathing

1 Remove the cat's collar. Lay the cat on one side in the recovery position (*see page 159*). Open the mouth and clear the airway of any fluid (*see page 158*).

2 If the cat has stopped breathing but the heart is still beating, proceed with artificial respiration. Using a towel, pull the tongue forward to clear the throat. This may stimulate breathing, causing the cat to regain consciousness.

3 If the cat remains unconscious, place your hands on the chest and apply gentle pressure. This expels air from the lungs, allowing them to be refilled with fresh air. Repeat every five seconds until the cat breathes.

CARDIAC MASSAGE

If a cat is unconscious and there is no sign of a heartbeat or breathing, direct stimulation of the heart may be attempted. Place your fingers on the chest at the point of the elbow and press down gently but firmly. Repeat five or six times at one-second intervals. Alternate with artificial respiration for up to ten minutes, after which the procedure is unlikely to be successful.

MOUTH-TO-MOUTH RESUSCITATION

1 If the chest cavity has been damaged, the lungs may not refill automatically and you will have to blow air into them. Hold the unconscious cat in an upright position with its mouth closed.

2 Breathe into the nostrils for two to three seconds to inflate the lungs. The movement of the chest will be clearly visible. Pause for a two-second rest, then repeat.

Support the cat's body

3 Continue with resuscitation until the cat starts to breathe on its own. An alternative method involves breathing simultaneously into the cat's nose and open mouth.

FIRST AID WARNING

The resuscitation methods described here should only be attempted if a cat is unconscious and does not respond to normal stimuli. Do not use an excessive amount of force since this can injure the cat.

DROWNING

1 Most cats dislike going too near water but accidents do happen – for example, a kitten may fall into a pond or a swimming pool.

2 Take the cat out of the water and dry it quickly with a towel. If the cat is motionless, drain any water from the lungs. Hold the cat upside down by firmly gripping its hind legs above the hock joints.

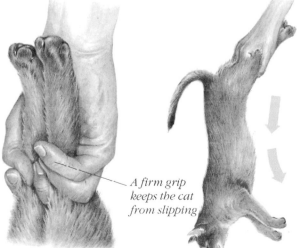

A firm grip keeps the cat from slipping

3 Swing the cat vigorously (but not violently) downwards to remove water from the lungs. If there are still no signs of the cat resuming breathing, resuscitation should be started (*see opposite*). Get the cat into warm surroundings as soon as possible.

CHOKING AND FOREIGN BODIES

Professional help from a vet is essential if a cat is having any difficulty with its breathing. However, in the unlikely event of a foreign body becoming lodged in your cat's throat, you may not have time to call a vet. You will need to take emergency action. A cat with an object such as a fish bone lodged in its throat will be distressed and make convulsive choking noises and may paw at its mouth. This should not be confused with a cat that is coughing up a hairball.

CHOKING

1 If the cat is making coughing and choking noises and gasping for air, try to get a look at the back of the throat. Get someone to contact a vet for advice, meanwhile restrain the cat and open its mouth (*see page 130*) to identify the object. As with all first-aid treatments, keep the cat as calm and still as possible.

FIRST AID WARNING

Do not put your fingers in a cat's mouth if it is choking, since you are likely to get bitten. It will help if the cat is restrained by being wrapped in a towel (*see page 129*).

2 Locate the object using a small torch. Try to remove the object with tweezers or the handle of a teaspoon. If this does not work, try to dislodge the object by turning the cat upside down.

FOREIGN BODY IN THE MOUTH

1 A carelessly discarded fish hook can occasionally become lodged in a cat's mouth. If the hook is superficial, the barb can be carefully cut off with pliers or wire cutters.

2 The remains of the hook can then be removed safely. Do not pull on a fishing line or thread that has been swallowed. Consult a vet immediately to locate and remove the hook or needle.

FOREIGN BODY IN THE EYES

1 Grass seeds and tiny pieces of grit are the most common objects to become lodged in a cat's eyes. Hold the eyelids open and examine the eye carefully. If something has penetrated the eyeball, do not touch it.

2 If the foreign body is loose or under the eyelid, you may be able to float it out with eye drops or a couple of drops of olive oil. If you are in any doubt contact a vet.

OTHER FOREIGN BODIES

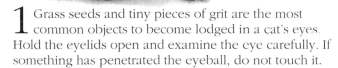

Foreign body in the ears
Similar techniques to those above can be used to remove objects, such as grass seeds, from just inside the ear. Float out seeds using ear drops or a couple of drops of olive oil.

FIRST AID WARNING

Never poke tweezers or anything else into a cat's ears or eyes. A great deal of damage is done this way by well meaning owners who do more harm than good. Remember: if in doubt, it is always best to call in a vet.

Foreign body in the paws
Grass seeds and burrs can become stuck in the fur between the toes, or a cat can get a splinter in its paw. If a cat cannot remove the object with its teeth, it may need to be dislodged by hand or using tweezers. Do no try to remove any object that is embedded in the paw pad. It is advisable to consult a vet if the injury is more than a superficial scratch.

POISONING

Poisoning is not a common occurrence since cats are extremely careful feeders and also vomit very readily if they have eaten anything harmful. However, a cat may ingest a poison accidentally by eating either plants that have been treated with insecticides, or poisoned prey. If a cat's coat becomes contaminated with chemicals, it will lick them off in an attempt to clean itself. Two common household poisons are slug killer and painkillers such as aspirin.

POISONS

Treating poisoning
Contact a vet immediately and tell him what the cat has eaten. Signs of poisoning are usually dramatic. Do not induce vomiting unless advised to by a vet.

COAT CONTAMINATION

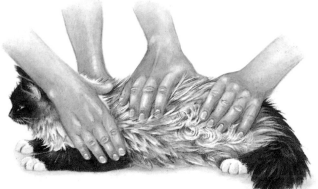

1 Soften paint or tar with petroleum jelly to help with removal. It is essential to remove any contaminant from the coat immediately to prevent the cat from licking it off while grooming.

2 Cut away any heavily contaminated fur, taking care not to cut the cat's skin. Antifreeze, bleach, and disinfectant can all be fatal if ingested.

FIRST AID WARNING

Never use solvents or paint stripper to remove paint from a cat's coat, since these are very toxic. A cat with a badly contaminated coat needs veterinary treatment. If possible, take a sample of the contaminant with you when you visit the surgery.

3 Wash as much contaminant off the coat as possible, using a dilute solution of baby shampoo and warm water. Wrap the cat in a towel, if necessary, to prevent it from licking its coat.

COMMON POISONS IN THE HOME

Poisonous plants
Many plants are toxic to cats. Most felines enjoy chewing on greenery but usually prefer grass to the leaves of plants. A cat may occasionally develop a taste for a particular plant and will need to be discouraged from eating it.

Poinsettia

Christmas cherry

Spotted dumb cane

Sweet pea

Clematis

Azalea

Oleander

Delphinium

Rhododendron

Lupin

Christmas rose

HOUSEHOLD POISONS

Poison	Signs of poisoning	Action
Rodent poisons (e.g. arsenic, strychnine, thallium, warfarin)	Restlessness, abdominal pain, vomiting, bleeding, and diarrhoea. Potentially fatal.	Conult a vet immediately. Antidotes to some types of poison are available.
Antifreeze	Lack of coordination, vomiting, convulsions, followed by coma. Potentially fatal.	Consult a vet immediately. An injection may block the effect.
Alcohol, methylated spirits	Depression, vomiting, collapse, dehydration, and coma. Potentially fatal.	Consult a vet immediately. Note what type of poison has been eaten.
Painkillers (e.g. aspirin, disprin, paracetamol)	Lack of coordination, loss of balance, and vomiting. The gums will be blue if a cat has swallowed paracetamol. Potentially fatal.	Consult a vet immediately. Painkillers intended for humans are toxic to cats.
Disinfectants, household cleaners (e.g. phenols)	Severe vomiting, diarrhoea, nervous signs, staggering, and coma. Potentially fatal.	Consult a vet immediately. Note what type of poison has been eaten.
Insecticides and pesticides (e.g. chlorinated hydrocarbons)	Muscle twitching, drooling, convulsions (sometimes triggered by handling), and coma. Potentially fatal.	Consult a vet immediately. There is no specific antidote.
Slug and snail poisons (e.g. metaldehyde, baysol)	Continous salivation, muscle twitching, vomiting, diarrhoea, lack of coordination, convulsions, and coma. Potentially fatal.	Consult a vet immediately. Treatment is often effective if given promptly.

BITES AND STINGS

When a cat is allowed to go outdoors, fights with other felines over territory are likely. Cat bites can quickly become infected and form abscesses, which require veterinary treatment. Insect bites and stings are rare, but can cause considerable pain and distress. In tropical countries, venomous snakes, spiders, scorpions, and toads are other hazards. Cat are usually more inquisitive raher than aggressive towards these creatures, but they can get too close. Kittens play-hunting are especially liable to being bitten.

INSECT BITES AND VENOM

Bee and wasp stings
Sudden swelling and pain result from stings around the face or feet. Urgent veterinary treatment is essential if a cat is unsteady or disoriented, or has trouble with its breathing.

Treating stings (*right*)
A bee sting, which looks like a splinter in a red, swollen area, can be removed with tweezers. Bathe with a weak solution of sodium bicarbonate. An ice pack will help reduce swelling.

Snake and spider bites
Try to identify the type of creature that has bitten the cat since this will help with the treatment. A snake bite will be visible as two deep puncture wounds, and the cat will keep licking the affected area.

Treating bites (*right*)
Slow the spread of the venon by applying a cold compress and then a pressure bandage just above the bite (*see page 170*). Contact a vet immediately.

Toad venom
Some species of toad secrete a venom on their skin. If a cat picks up a toad, this venom causes its mouth to become painful and inflamed.

Treating toad venom (*left*)
If the cat will allow it, flush out the mouth immediately with clean water, being careful to prevent the cat from inhaling any fluid. Wipe away excess saliva and keep the cat quiet. Seek veterinary help.

CAT BITE ABSCESS

1 Where a cat bite is not detected at the time it happens, it is likely to become septic. After a few days, it will be swollen and very tender. If the cat will allow it, clean the area around the abscess and clip away surrounding fur.

2 Bathe the swollen area with hand-hot water or a weak salt solution (one teaspoonful in a glass of water). Frequent bathing should bring the abscess to a "head". Do not try to lance the abscess.

Expel any remaining pus once the abscess has burst

3 After bathing for 24 hours, the abscess should burst, producing foul smelling pus. Once the pressure has eased, the cat will feel much better.

4 Keep the wound clean and continue bathing so that the abscess does not re-form. The cat may need antibiotics to control infection

FIGHT WOUNDS

Occasionally a cat may return home in a very dishevelled state, signifying that it has been in a fight. Some of its fur may be missing, ears and eyelids may be torn, and teeth or claws broken. Any minor cuts or lacerations should be cleaned up (*see page 170*). A bite from another cat is not normally visible at the time. In many cases, this turns septic in a few days and the wound becomes swollen and painful to the touch. If you know that your cat has been in a fight and if it seems to be distressed, it is best to take it to a vet for a thorough examination.

Ears may be torn and bleeding

Neck may be bitten

Base of the tail is a common site for abscesses

EMERGENCY ACTION

Call a vet immediately if an abscess is very large or does not rupture 24 hours after bathing. The abscess may need to be lanced and drained by a vet. Antibiotics may sometimes be required to prevent the abscess from re-forming and to eliminate bacterial infection.

Assessing an injury
Examine the cat to determine its condition. Stop any bleeding and consult a vet if an injury is serious.

BANDAGING WOUNDS

Since most cats lead quite adventurous lives, they risk the odd injury every now and again. The most common causes of wounds are bites and scratches from other cats (*see page 169*). If your cat is injured, the primary first-aid aim is to control shock and minimize blood loss. The best way to stop bleeding is to cover the wound with a gauze pad and apply pressure. A handkerchief or strips of cloth can be used in an emergency.

CUTS AND LACERATIONS

1 Examine the cat, keeping it as calm as possible. Gently wipe away any blood or dirt, using a damp piece of cotton wool. Contact a vet if the injury is more than superficial.

2 With the help of an assistant to steady the cat, trim away any matted fur. Petroleum jelly applied around the edges of the injury will prevent hair from falling into the open wound.

3 Minor cuts and lacerations can be treated with a mild antiseptic suitable for cats, such as dilute hydrogen peroxide solution.

STOPPING BLEEDING

Apply a cold-water compress

1 Contact a vet at once if an injury is bleeding heavily. Meanwhile staunch the flow of blood with a gauze pad soaked in cold water.

2 The bleeding should stop after a minute or two. If it does not, secure the gauze with a bandage and put another pad over the top.

3 Wrap another bandage around the cat to keep the gauze pads in place. Maintain pressure on the bleeding points. Consult a vet.

APPLYING DRESSINGS

1 Simple dressings can be applied to minor wounds or to control bleeding, but bandaging of more serious injuries should be done by a vet. First cover the wound with a gauze pad.

2 Secure the gauze pad over the wound by covering with bandages. The bandage should be firm but not too tight, since this may restrict the circulation. Do not apply a tourniquet without veterinary advise.

SERIOUS INJURIES

Torso wounds
When there are very extensive injuries or bruising, a complete body bandage can be made out of an old, clean pillow case, in order to reduce further injury on the way to the vet. All dressings should be changed daily or when there is evidence of blood or discharge seeping through.

BANDAGING A MINOR WOUND

FIRST AID WARNING

Never bandage a limb too tightly since this may constrict the circulation. Do not move a limb if there is pain or swelling, since bones may be broken.

1 When bandaging a paw, first clean up the site of the wound (*see opposite*). Put small tufts of cotton wool between the cat's toes to prevent rubbing and discomfort.

Insert cotton wool between the toes

2 Cover the wound with an absorbent pad 1 cm (½ in) thick. Do not use cotton wool, since the fibres may stick to the wound and disturb any clot that is forming.

3 Secure the pad in position with adhesive tape, looped under the foot, then around the leg. Be careful not to restrict the blood supply. Check the wound regularly to make sure that it is healing.

BURNS AND OTHER INJURIES

Even though cats are always getting into inaccessible places, they usually manage to avoid getting burnt or scalded. Their thick coats may also give them some added protection. When accidents do occur, they are usually caused by boiling water, hot fat, or open fires. Shock is associated with burns and cold-related injuries, so it is vital to consult a vet at once.

SCALDS

1 If a cat has been scalded, the affected area of its body must be swabbed with cold water as soon as possible. Do not apply any butter or skin cream to the wound.

Swab wound with cold water

2 Make an ice pack with ice cubes in a freezer bag or wrapped in a piece of clean cloth. Apply this to the burn while contacting the vet.

3 Apply petroleum jelly to the wound (if the cat will allow it). Do not cut away any surrounding fur. Do not cover the wound.

CHEMICAL BURNS

1 Wash any chemical off the coat at once. Weak solutions of sodium bicarbonate or vinegar may help neutralize the effects of acid and alkali respectively.

Use only water where chemical is unknown

2 Put an ice pack on the injured area while contacting the vet. An affected limb can be placed under a cold-water tap for several minutes. It may be advisable to wear rubber gloves when touching any chemicals.

ELECTRICAL BURNS AND SHOCK

1 Kittens are most likely to chew or bite through electrical wiring. Even if a cat only suffers mild burns to the tongue and to the corners of its mouth, it needs to be examined by a vet since there may be other injuries or complications.

SUNBURN

Apply sunblock cream to ears

Sunburn on the ear tips
Cats in hot, tropical countries are prone to sunburn on their ears. As a precaution, cats with pale-coloured coats should be kept indoors during the hottest part of the day and their ears protected with a sunblock cream.

2 Switch off the current before touching the injured cat. If this is not possible, use a broom handle to move the live wire away from the cat. Contact a vet.

EMERGENCY ACTION

Severe electrical shock can be fatal or result in heart failure. The cat may require emergency resuscitation (*see pages 162–163*). Contact your vet immediately for further advice.

FROSTBITE AND HYPOTHERMIA

Frostbite
The parts of a cat's body that can be affected by frostbite in severe weather are the paws, tail, and ears. Paws can be gently warmed by immersing in warm water.

Hypothermia
This involves a cooling down of the whole body and can result in death. The cat should be placed in a warm, sheltered place and covered with blankets. Warm the cat up gradually.

OTHER EMERGENCIES

Even though most cats have no trouble with kittening, problems do sometimes occur. You should contact a vet if your cat seems to be distressed or in pain, or has been straining for more than half an hour without producing a kitten. A mother cat and new-born kittens may occasionally need immediate first aid while a vet is on the way or if veterinary help is not available. This may mean the difference between life and death. Other emergencies needing urgent first-aid treatment include heatstroke and asphyxia.

LABOUR PROBLEMS

When to call a vet

Keep a close but discreet watch on your cat as she goes into labour. If she seems distressed and has not delivered a kitten within 30 minutes after she has started straining, you should contact a vet.

KITTENING PROBLEMS		
Disorder	**Description and signs**	**Action**
Miscarriage	Premature labour is rare in cats, but can be caused by an accident, infection, stress, or an abnormal foetus. Symptoms may include straining, vomiting, diarrhoea, and bleeding from the vulva.	If you know the kittens are not due, contact a vet immediately. Keep the cat warm and quiet. There is not much that can be done to prevent miscarriage once it begins.
Uterine rupture	This may occur as the result of an accident in late pregnancy, or just before or during the delivery. The queen may show signs of shock or abdominal discomfort, or she may fail to go into labour. If the queen is in shock, she may collapse, breathe rapidly, and have a racing pulse and diluted pupils.	Contact a vet immediately. Shock requires urgent veterinary treatment. Keep the cat warm and calm, reassuring it by gently speaking to it until it can be treated by a vet.
Vulval discharge and haemorrhage	Some vulval discharge is normal for a few days after the birth, but if it is brown or foul-smelling, it may indicate an infection or retained foetal membranes. Bleeding from the vulva signifies internal haemorrhage and can be life-threatening.	Consult a vet immediately. Keep the queen warm and quiet to prevent her from going into shock. Put a pad of gauze against the vulva to soak up any discharge or blood.
Fading Kitten Syndrome	Sometimes kittens may be born underweight, deformed, or fail to suckle. In some cases, apparently normal kittens will fade away and die after a few days or weeks.	There is often not much that can be done to save affected kittens, although you may be able to feed them by hand. Severely deformed kittens may need to be humanely destroyed by a vet.
Rejected kittens	Occasionally, a queen may not be able to produce sufficient milk or be unable to nurse her litter. She may reject the kittens shortly after the birth, or the runt of the litter may be ousted by its siblings. Like many animals, a cat produces several offspring to allow for some not surviving to adulthood in the wild. Rejected kittens may be fostered by another queen or reared by hand (*see page 151*).	Consult a vet for advice. Orphan kittens must be kept warm, well-fed, and clean. To begin with, they must be fed every two hours with special replacement cat milk. After feeding, the anal area of a kitten needs to be gently wiped with a piece of damp cotton wool to encourage elimination of waste products. The mother cat may accept the kittens back when they are partially weaned.

HELPING WITH KITTENING

1 If a kitten is stuck partly out of the vulva and the queen seems to be in difficulty, you need to act immediately. Wash your hands, then lubricate the vulva with petroleum jelly. Firmly grasp the kitten and gently ease it out as the queen bears down.

2 If the queen ignores the kitten, you must pull off the membrane covering it, and clear its mouth and nostrils of mucus. Rub it dry with a towel. When it is breathing, soak some cotton and scissors in antiseptic. Tie the cotton around the umbilical cord about 3 cm (1 in) from the navel.

3 Cut the umbilical cord on the side attached to the placenta. Alternatively the cord can be separated by hand. Do not pull on the cord, since this may damage the kitten. Encourage the kitten to suckle.

> ### FIRST AID WARNING
> If a kitten's head or one of its limbs are held up inside the birth passage, do not attempt to force it out. Seek veterinary help immediately.

HEATSTROKE AND ASPHYXIA

Heatstroke
A cat suffering from heatstoke may collapse. Lower its temperature by wrapping it in towels soaked in cool (but not ice-cold) water.

Asphyxia
A cat may collapse if it inhales carbon monoxide fumes. It must be allowed to breathe fresh air as soon as possible and encouraged to move about to stimulate circulation.

Chapter 10

SHOWING

BREEDERS WHO exhibit pedigree cats at shows are striving to achieve perfection within the standards of their chosen breed. Competition for what is judged to be the best of breed, with the most striking eye colour, head shape, and so on, is always intense. The formalities for entering a show and the ways in which different types of show are organized vary around the world. Shows often have classes for household pets and this is probably a good place for a beginner to start off. The competitive drive of showing can become totally absorbing, so be warned.

CAT SHOWS

Breeders constantly strive to produce the finest cats for exhibition in competitive cat shows, so visiting a show can be a rewarding and educational experience. Every breed you have ever heard of is likely to be present at a large cat show, and probably a few rare ones not generally seen. In each country, shows are run by the controlling authority for all cat clubs and societies. In Great Britain, the Governing Council of the Cat Fancy (GCCF) is responsible for the show rules and has approved standards for all the pedigree breeds. In the United States, the Cat Fanciers' Association (CFA) establishes the breed standards, registers pedigrees, and approves the dates of major shows.

THE HISTORY OF CAT SHOWS

First pedigree breeder
An early North American breeder, Mrs. Clinton Locke, pictured with her two Siamese cats.

The first modern cat show (*below*)
Crystal Palace in London was the venue for the first large cat show, which took place in 1871. Longhairs and British Shorthairs were among the cats exhibited. The first North American cat show was held in New England for the Maine Coon breed at about the same time.

HOW A SHOW IS ORGANIZED

Kitten class

Cats under nine months of age have separate open classes for all breeds. Kittens compete with others of the same breed, sex, and colour. At a large show, kitten classes for popular breeds may be divided by sex or by age.

Open class

The most important of all the classes. At a large cat show there will be open classes for all the breeds represented. To become a champion, a cat must win three open classes at different shows.

Neuter class

Pedigree cats that are castrated males or spayed females have separate open classes of their own. They compete against other neuters of the same breed and are judged according to the same breed standards as entire cats.

Household pet class

Neutered cats of unknown or unregistered parentage can be entered in the class for household pets. There is no written standard for non pedigree cats. They are judged for their uniqueness, any unusual markings, and temperament.

BRITISH AND AMERICAN SHOWS

Shows in Great Britain

All cat shows operate under the Governing Council of the Cat Fancy. After a veterinary inspection, cats are given a number. Pens are numbered but carry no other distinguishing marks. Judging takes place on a table that is wheeled from pen to pen (*see page 183*).

Shows in the United States

The Cat Fanciers' Association is the largest of the eight cat authorities in the United States. Classes are divided into "allbreed" or "specialty", with a separate household pet competition. Judging takes place on tables set up in full view of the public attending the show.

JUDGING SHOW CATS

Over the past century, interest in pedigree cats has played a central role in creating the rich spectrum of breeds we see today. Selective breeding programmes have been used to enhance certain physical characteristics and to create cats that look attractive to the human eye. Fortunately, in contrast to dog breeding, there have been few instances of this having harmful effects. A pedigree cat is judged against a standard that specifies how a perfect example of its type should look. Points are awarded for the appearance of the cat's head, eyes, body, and coat.

Registering a kitten
Register your pedigree kitten with the appropriate cat fancy organization.

EXAMPLES OF HOW CATS ARE JUDGED

British Blue Shorthair (*left*)
The British Shorthair is a compact and powerful cat, with a strong, muscular body on short legs. It has a broad head, with round eyes, and ears set well apart.

Head (20 points)
Round face, with full cheeks and a strong chin.

Body (25 points)
"Cobby" type, low on legs, with a broad, deep chest.

Tail (10 points)
Thick and of medium length.

Eyes (10 points)
Copper, orange, or deep gold in colour.

Coat (35 points)
Short and dense (not over-long or fluffy). Colour should be light to medium blue with no tabby markings or silver tipping.

Tail (10 points)
Short and bushy, but in proportion to body length.

Head (25 points)
Round and broad, with a short nose and a strong chin.

Eyes (10 points)
Deep orange or brilliant copper.

Cream Shaded Cameo Longhair (*right*)
This classic Pedigree Longhair cat has a "cobby" build, with a sturdy, rounded body and short, thick legs. It has a broad head, with round eyes and small ears.

Coat (40 points)
Long and thick, and fine in texture. Colour should be white with cream tipping (with no tabby markings).

Body (15 points)
Stocky or "cobby" in build, with short, thick legs.

Head (20 points)
Wedge-shaped face, long and narrow, with pricked ears.

Eyes (20 points)
Clear, bright vivid blue. A squint is a fault.

Tail (5 points)
Long and tapering, with no kink at the end.

Red-point Siamese (*left*)
The Siamese has a unique, pale-coloured coat and darker markings on its face, paws, and tail. It has a long, slim, oriental build, with slanted eyes, and elegant legs and feet.

Body (20 points)
Long, svelte, oriental build, with slim legs.

Coat (35 Points)
Very short and fine. Colour should be white, shading to apricot on the body and reddish-gold on the points (barring is permissible).

Usual Abyssinian (right)
The Abyssinian's ticked coat, in which each hair has several different-coloured bands, is very distinctive. The build of this cat is muscular and lithe, and the head is less elongated than that of the Siamese.

Head (15 points)
Round and gently wedge-shaped, with large, preferably tufted, ears.

Eyes (10 points)
Amber, hazel, or green A light eye colour is undesirable

Head (20 points)
Medium, wedge-shaped head, with a distinct nose break.

Eyes (25 points)
Golden-yellow eyes preferred. Green eyes are a serious fault in Brown Burmese, but Blue Burmese may show a slight fading of colour.

Coat (20 points)
Short and glossy, with a satin finish. Colour should be a mixture of blue and cream, without any obvious barring.

Coat (45 points)
Short, fine, and close-lying, with double or preferably treble ticking. Colour should be a ruddy brown ticked with black. A pale overall colour is a fault and so are black or grey base hairs.

Body (30 points)
Medium in length, and lithe and muscular in appearance. A "cobby" build is not permissible.

Body (35 points)
Medium in size, feeling muscular and heavier than it appears.

Blue Tortoiseshell Burmese (*left*)
The Burmese cat is prized for its smooth and glossy coat. Its build is more round-bodied and muscular than that of the Siamese. The British Burmese is more oriental in appearance than the sturdier North American variety.

TAKING PART IN A CAT SHOW

The preparations for showing your cat should begin several weeks, or even months, beforehand. If your cat has not been shown before, you will have to get it accustomed to being confined in a pen and to being handled. Maintaining a show cat involves good feeding and daily grooming.

GROOMING FOR SHOWING

A cat's eyes and ears must be spotlessly clean

1 A longhaired cat needs to be bathed before a show to ensure that its coat is in perfect condition *(see pages 76–77)*. On the show day, remove any staining around the eyes with damp cotton wool.

2 Final grooming takes place in the pen. Carefully brush the shorter hairs on the cat's face with a small toothbrush. Do not put the toothbrush too close to the eyes.

3 As a finishing touch, use a slicker brush to make the cat's fur stand out fully from its body. The fur around the cat's neck should frame the face.

SHOWING EQUIPMENT

The only items allowed in a cat's pen are a litter tray, blanket, and water bowl. You will also require the following: cat food; a white ribbon or elastic collar on which the cat's entry number can be pinned; vaccination certificates; show documentation; and brushes and combs.

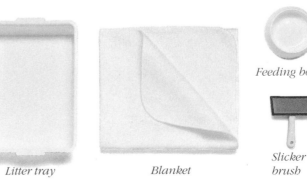

Feeding bowl   *Water bowl*

Litter tray   *Blanket*   *Slicker brush*   *Toothbrush*

THE DAY OF THE SHOW

Vetting in (*left*)
Any cat entered for competition in a cat show should be in good health. In some countries every cat is examined by a vet. An animal that is unwell will not be allowed to take part in the show.

A cat is scrutinized by a judge

Awarding points (*below*)
A pedigree cat is judged against its breed standard. A maximum of 100 points is awarded for its head, eyes, condition, and coat (*see pages 180–181*).

Judging (*right*)
Cats are judged at a movable table near their pens. In North American shows, cats are examined in public.

Prizewinning cat
A well-trained show cat sits proudly in its pen and enjoys all the attention that it receives. Rosettes are pinned on the pens of the winners.

Best in show (*below*)
The climax of a cat show comes when all the entries have been judged. This is when the best cat in the show is announced.

GLOSSARY

Abscess Collection of pus forming painful swelling. Usually the result of a cat bite.
Ailurophile Cat lover.
Ailurophobe Cat hater.
Albino Lack of pigment melanin, causing white fur and pink eyes.
Angora Breed of cat with long hair and slim, long body. Lacks woolly undercoat of true longhaired cats.
Anoestrus Female who is not in season.
Awn hair Bristly hair of undercoat with thickened tips.

Back-cross Offspring of mating between adult cat and its own kitten.
Bicolour Coats consisting of white hair mixed with one other colour.
Boarding cattery Establishment that boards cats while owners are away.
Breed A type of cat, named for its colour, size, and shape.
Breed standard A description of ideal characteristics against which each breed of cat is measured. This is determined by the national cat society of each country.

Calico American name for Tortoiseshell-and-White cat.
Canker *See* Otitis.
Carpal pad Extra fleshy pad above others on front paws, thought to help stop skidding when a cat lands after jumping.

Castrate To remove testicles to prevent reproduction and sexual behaviour.
Cat flap Hinged flap set in a door that enables a cat to come and go as it wants.
Cat flu *See* Feline respiratory disease.
Catnip The herb *Nepeta cataria*, which gives off a scent that most cats find irresistible. Used in some cat toys.
Chinchilla Longhaired cat whose white fur is tipped with black.
Chlamydial disease Affects cat's eyes and the respiratory system.
Chromosomes Tiny strands of DNA that store genetic information.
Cobby A stocky, rounded body shape, with short legs and long fur.
Coccidiosis Caused by protozoan parasite that affects the digestive system.
Colourpoint A cat whose face, ears, legs, feet, and tail are of a different colour to the rest of its body.
Conjunctivitis Inflammation of the thin outer layer of the eye, causing watering and soreness. Associated with Feline respiratory disease.

Dermatitis An inflammation of the skin.
Dew claw Extra toe on hind leg above paw. Its function is not known.
DNA Chemical substance that makes up chromosomes, from which all life begins.
Dominant gene The gene that over-rides a recessive gene in a pairing of chromosomes, so that its characteristics are always evident in the offspring.
Down hairs Soft hairs under guard hairs that insulate body.

Ear mites Tiny parasites living in ear canal, causing irriation.
Elizabethan collar Cardboard or plastic funnel fitted over head to prevent cat interfering with wounds.
Entire An unneutered cat.

Feline Calici Virus (FCV) One of the two common viruses causing Feline respiratory disease. Signs include coughing, sneezing, watery eyes, and runny nose. *See also* Feline respiratory disease and Feline Viral Rhinotracheitis.
Feline Dysautonomia Nervous disorder causing persistent pupil dilation, regurgitation, and rapid weight loss. Once known as Key-Gaskell Syndrome.
Feline Infectious Anaemia Disease caused by parasite in blood. Signs are fever, weight loss, and lethargy.
Feline Immuno Deficiency Virus (FIV) A relative of the HIV virus, which weakens the immune-system, causing death. Highly contagious to other cats, but not to humans or other animals.

Feline Infectious Enteritis (FIE) Virus causing loss of white blood cells, and fatal in most cases. Signs include depression, severe diarrhoea, vomiting, and abdominal pain. Also called Feline Panleukopenia.
Feline Infectious Peritonitis (FIP) Usually fatal virus disease. Signs include fluid accumulation in the abdomen, jaundice, and anaemia.
Feline Leukaemia Virus (FeLV) Virus affecting lymphatic system, suppressing immunity to disease. Usually fatal. Signs include weight loss, vomiting, diarrhoea, and difficulty in breathing.
Feline Panleukopenia *See* Feline Infectious Enteritis.
Feline respiratory disease Sometimes known as "cat flu". See Feline Viral Rhinotracheitis and Feline Calici Virus.
Feline Urological Syndrome (FUS) Inflammation of bladder and urethra. Sandy deposits in bladder and urethra can lead to blood in urine and difficulty in urination. Obstruction is a real emergency.
Feline Viral Rhinotracheitis (FVR) The more serious of the two common viruses that cause Feline respiratory disease. Signs include high fever, and a discharge from the eyes and nose. May sometimes be fatal, especially in kittens and elderly cats. *See also* Feline respiratory disease and Feline Calici Virus.
Feral Domestic animals that have reverted to a wild state.
Flea collar Special collar in which chemical is impregnated to kill fleas.
Fleas The most common parasite found on a cat's skin. Live by feeding on blood. Cats my be sensitive to bites or flea dirt.
Flehming Grimacing and lifting the upper lip to bring a scent into contact with the Jacobson's organ for detailed examination. Usually related to sexual behaviour of tom cats.
Flukes Parasites found in intestine and liver, causing diarrhoea and anaemia.
Foreign Another term for a cat of oriental appearance, such as a Siamese cat.

Gastritis Inflammation of the stomach walls causing vomiting and inappetence.
Gene Tiny head of DNA on chromosomes that carries information on physical characteristics such as coat colour, eye colour, length of coat, and many others.
Gene pool The total number of genes available within a breed.
Glaucoma Enlargement of eyeball caused by increased pressure from within.
Groom To brush or comb a cat's coat.
Guard hairs Thick, coarse hair that protects softer down hairs underneath, in some cats providing a waterproof layer.

Haematoma Blood blister in ear flap usually due to scratching and bursting of a blood vessel.

Harvest mites Parasites that appear in the autumn and can cause skin irritation. Also known as chiggers.

Haw *See* Third eyelid.

Heat *See* Oestrus.

Heartworms Parasites found in tropical areas of the world. Transmitted by mosquitoes and lives in heart.

Hock A cat's ankle.

Hookworms Blood-sucking worms that live in small intestine. Can cause weight loss, diarrhoea, and anaemia.

Jacobson's organ A sensory organ above the roof of the mouth that analyzes smells and tastes, and sends a signal to the brain.

Keratitis Inflammation of cornea, resulting in eye becoming cloudy.

Key-Gaskell Syndrome *See* Feline Dysautonomia.

Kitten pen Wire cage in which a new cat or kitten can live briefly while being introduced to a household.

Lactational Tetany Due to inadequate calcium levels in blood during nursing. Causes vomiting and staggering. Also known as Milk Fever.

Lice Parasites that suck blood, causing anaemia in a severe infestation.

Litter The absorbent granules used in a cat's toilet tray. Also a family of kittens.

Litter tray Shallow tray filled with litter.

Longhaired Cat whose coat has long top hairs, with a thick, woolly undercoat.

Mange mite Minute parasites that burrow into a cat's skin, causing chronic hair loss, irritation, and inflammation.

Manx Tailless breed of cat, caused by mutant gene which can be associated with lethal characteristics.

Mastitis Infection of milk glands.

Metacarpal pads Thick pads of tissue on paws to stop a cat slipping.

Middle ear disease Infection of inner ear. Signs include tilting of head to one side, staggering, and partial deafness.

Milk Fever *See* Lactational Tetany.

Neuter To castrate males or spay females to prevent reproduction and unwanted sexual behaviour.

Nictitating membrane *See* Third eyelid.

Odd-eyed Cat with one blue eye and the other orange. Blue eyes in white cats may be associated with deafness.

Oestrus Periods during which a female cat is sexually responsive to a male, commonly known as heat or season.

Oriental Foreign breeds with almond-shaped eyes, wedge-shaped heads, and long limbs. Examples are the Abyssinian, Siamese, and Burmese.

Otitis A term for inflammation of outer ear, caused by mites, bacteria, or foreign bodies. Also known as canker.

Pedigree A record of ancestry, showing a cat's family tree over several generations.

Pedigree Longhair Pedigree cat with a long outer coat. Also known as Persian.

Peritonitis An inflammation of the peritoneum in the abdomen. *See also* Feline Infectious Peritonitis.

Persian *See* Pedigree Longhair.

Points The face, ears, legs, feet, and tail, which may be a different colour to the rest of the body, as in a Siamese cat.

Polydactyly Having extra number of toes.

Prolapse Condition in which internal organs such as uterus or rectum are pushed outside body by straining.

Quarantine All cats and dogs entering certain countries, such as Great Britain, Australia, and New Zealand, must be kept in quarantine for a specified period to prevent the spread of rabies.

Queen Unspayed female cat.

Rabies Serious virus disease affecting nervous system. Transmission is by bite from an infected animal.

Recessive gene One whose characteristics are over-ridden by a dominant gene in each pairing of chromosomes, so that it is not evident in the resulting offspring.

Register List of pedigree cats. In order to be allowed to enter cat shows, each pure-bred cat must be registered upon birth with the national cat authority.

Ringworm Form of fungal infection that causes scaly skin and irritation.

Roundworms Parasites found in cat's digestive tract, feeding on digesting food. Can cause diarrhoea, especially in kittens.

Scent marking A cat marks its territory with urine, or with scent from glands on the head, sending a clear message to any intruding cats. It may also scratch furniture and trees, sharpening its claws and leaving a scent from glands on its paw pads.

Scratching post A covered post upon which a cat can exercise its claws without damaging furniture. It will also mark the post with scent to denote its territory.

Scratching *See* Scent marking.

Season *See* Oestrus.

Selective breeding Breeding of pedigree cats by planned matings to enhance certain physical characteristics, such as eye colour.

Self Coat of only one colour.

Siamese Oriental, shorthaired cat, with pale-coloured coat and points of a different colour.

Spay Operation to remove ovaries and uterus to prevent oestrus and pregnancy.

Stud Uncastrated tom cat used specifically for breeding purposes.

Tabby Cat with striped, blotched, or spotted markings. Pattern used in the wild for breaking up the body shape so that the cat can hide itself in the undergrowth.

Tapeworms Intestinal parasites that feed on cat's partly digested food. Fleas are needed to complete the life cycle.

Taurine An amino-acid that must be present in a cat's diet. A deficiency can lead to blindness.

Territory Area patrolled by a cat, which it considers to be its own. A cat will fiercely defend its territory against intruders.

Third eyelid Eyelid that is sometimes visible at corners of a cat's eyes.

Ticks Parasites that bury their heads into a cat's skin to feed on blood. Some types of tick can transmit diseases.

Tipped Coat whose top hairs are tipped with a different colour to the undercoat.

Tom cat An uncastrated male cat.

Topcoat Outer layer of hair that forms overall colour of cat.

Tortoiseshell Coat resulting from linkage of dominant and recessive orange genes, both carried by female chromosome. Tortoiseshell cats are usually female.

Toxoplasmosis Disease caused by parasite, often in raw meat, which affects digestive system. Causes diarrhoea. Can sometimes be transmitted to humans.

Tumour Swelling on or beneath skin due to abnormal growth. Can be cancerous.

Undercoat Thick layer of insulating fur under topcoat.

Vetting in Examination by a vet upon entry into a British cat show. No longer required in American cat shows.

Weaning Gradual change in a kitten's diet from mother's milk to solid food.

Zoonoses Diseases that can be passed between vertebrate species including man.

CAT CARE RECORD

Cat's name: ....

Breed: ....

Pedigree name: ....

Names and breeds of parents: ....

....

Date of birth: ....

Sex: ....

Colour of coat: ....

Colour of eyes: ....

Favourite foods: ....

VETERINARY RECORD

Name and address of veterinarian: ....

....

....

Telephone number: ....

Emergency telephone number: ....

Medical history (any recent illnesses with dates of

visits to the vet):..

....

....

....

VACCINATIONS

Date of first vaccination: ....

Date annual booster due: ....

Other vaccinations: ....

....

BREEDING RECORD

Name and address of stud breeder: ....

....

....

Telephone number: ....

Birth date of litter: ....

Names and sexes of kittens: ....

....

....

BOARDING

Name and address of cattery: ....

....

....

Telephone number: ....

Name and address of cat sitter: ....

....

....

Telephone number: ....

ADDITIONAL INFORMATION

USEFUL ADDRESSES

Veterinary organizations
British Small Animal Veterinary Association
Kingsley House,
Church Lane,
Shurdington,
Cheltenham,
Gloucestershire GL51 5TQ

British Veterinary Association
7 Mansfield Street,
London W1M 0AT

Royal College of Veterinary Surgeons
32 Belgrave Square,
London SW1X 8QP

Charities
Blue Cross
1 Hugh Street,
London SW1V 1QQ

Cat's Protection League
17 Kings Road,
Horsham,
West Sussex RH13 5PP

Feline Advisory Bureau
235 Upper Richmond Road,
London SW15 6TL

People's Dispensary for Sick Animals
Whitechapel Way,
Priorslee,
Telford,
Shropshire TF2 9PQ

Royal Society for the Prevention of Cruelty to Animals
The Causeway,
Horsham,
West Sussex
RH12 1HG

Society for Companion Animal Studies
7 Botanic Crescent Lane,
Glasgow G20 8AA

Wood Green Animal Shelters
Kings Bush Farm,
London Road,
Godmanchester,
Cambridgeshire PE18 8LJ

Registration organizations
Cat Association of Great Britain
Cat Association Central Office,
Hunting Grove,
Lowfield Heath,
Crawley,
West Sussex RH11 0PY

Governing Council of the Cat Fancy
4–6 Penel Orlieu,
Bridgwater,
Somerset TA6 3PG

FURTHER READING

Allan, Eric, Bonning, Lynda, & Blogg, Rowan, *Everycat*, Methuen, 1985
Bessant, Claire, *How To Talk To Your Cat*, Smith-Griffon Ltd, 1992
Bush, Barry, *First Aid for Pets*, 2nd edition, A & C Black, 1984
Clutton-Brock, Juliet, *Eyewitness Cat*, Dorling Kindersley, 1991
Clutton-Brock, Juliet, *The British Museum Book of Cats*, British Museum Publications, 1988
Dale, Rodney, *Louis Wain, The Man Who Drew Cats*, Michael O'Mara, 1991
Dale-Green, Patricia, *The Cult of the Cat*, Heinemann, 1963
Edney, Andrew (ed.), *The Waltham Book of Dog and Cat Nutrition*, Pergamon, 1988
Edney, Andrew, & Hughes, I. B., *Pet Care*, Blackwell Scientific, 1986
Evans, J. M., & White, Kay, *Catlopaedia*, Henston, 1988
Fogle, Bruce, *Know Your Cat*, Dorling Kindersley, 1992
Fogle, Bruce, *The Cat's Mind*, Pelham Books, 1991

Fortunati, Piero, *First Aid for Animals*, Sidgwick & Jackson, 1989
Foucart, Walter, & Pierre, Elizabeth and Rosenberg, *The Painted Cat*, Rizzoli, 1987
Gettings, Fred, *The Secret Lore of the Cat*, Grafton, 1989
Humphries, John, *Cat Breeding, A Complete Guide*, Cat World, 1991
Lewis, Martyn, *Cats in the News*, Macdonald, 1991
Loxton, Howard, *The Noble Cat*, Merehurst, 1990
Macbeth George, & Booth, Martin, *The Book of Cats*, Penguin, 1980
McHattie, Grace, *Supercat*, Mandarin, 1989
Morris, Desmond, *Catwatching*, Jonathon Cape, 1986
Neville, Peter, *Do Cats Need Shrinks?*, Sidgwick & Jackson, 1990
Parsons, Alexandra, *Amazing Cats*, Dorling Kindersley, 1990
Pocock, Robine (ed.), *The Burmese Cat*, The Burmese Cat Club, 1991
Reiner, Traudl and Walter, *Yoga for Cats*, Victor Gollancz, 1991
Robinson, Roy, *Genetics for Cat Breeders*, Pergamon Press, 1977
Royston, Angela, & Burton, Jane, *See How They Grow: Kitten*, Dorling Kindersley, 1991
Sayer, Angela, & Findlay, Michael, *The Encyclopaedia of the Cat*, W.H. Smith Books, 1979
Segal, Mordecai (ed.), *The Cornell Book of Cats*, Villard Books, 1989
Silkstone Richards, Dorothy, *A Cat of Your Own*, Salamander, 1988
Silkstone Richards, Dorothy, *A Practical Guide to Selecting a Cat*, Salamander, 1988
Suares, Jean-Claude, *Indispensable Cat*, Webb & Bower, 1983
Tabor, Roger, *The Rise of the Cat*, BBC Books, 1991
Tabor, Roger, *The Wild Life of the Domestic Cat*, Arrow, 1983
Taylor, David, *The Ultimate Cat Book*, Dorling Kindersley, 1989
Taylor, David, *You & Your Cat*, Dorling Kindersley, 1986
Viner, Bradley, *The Cat Care Manual*, Stanley Paul, 1987
Wilson, Michael, *V & A Cats*, Victoria & Albert Museum, 1989
Wright, Michael, & Walters, Sally, *The Book of the Cat*, Pan, 1980

INDEX

ACKNOWLEDGMENTS

Author's acknowledgements

Any work of this kind requires an enormous effort from a large number of people. All of these deserve my sincere gratitude. The team at Dorling Kindersley is unsurpassed. In the forefront of this admirable group are Project Editor Alison Melvin, Art Editor Lee Griffiths, and Managing Editor Krystyna Mayer. It is these tireless people who create the book. The author is only one of the team. The photographs produced by Dorling Kindersley set the highest standards. Steve Gorton and Tim Ridley approaching the notoriously difficult task of capturing cats in every pose with humanity, immense skill, and inextinguishable good humour.

My former colleagues at the Waltham Centre for Pet Nutrition, especially Dr. Helen Nott, Dr. Jo Wills, Dr. Ivan Burger, Dr. Kay Earle, Helen Munday, and Dr. Ian Robinson have been most helpful, as have Pedigree Petfoods, the Pedigree Education Centre, and Denise Reed. Many veterinarians and the BSAVA have given help and encouragement, particularly Dr. Bruce Fogle. The Royal Veterinary College, my own *alma mater*, was very helpful. I am grateful to the Principal, Professor Lance Lanyon, and the staff of the Queen Mother Hospital and its Director, Professor Roger Batt. Polly Curds and Liz Ravenor of the RVC Animal Care Trust provided much cheerfully given assistance. Professor Oswald Jarrett and Dr. Helen Laird of Glasgow University Veterinary School kindly sent information on feline viruses.

Among the countless individuals who I must thank are Betty Thomas and Sophie Hamilton-Moore of the Feline Advisory Bureau, Peter Neville, everyone at the Wood Green Animal Shelter, and Benita Horder, librarian at the Royal College of Veterinary Surgeons.

Publisher's acknowledgments

For providing animals for photography: Ben and Vicky Adams (*Ferret*); Rosemary Alger (*Champion Typha Plush Velvat, also known as "The Toy Boy"*); Stacey Berenson (*Tammy*); Jenny Berry (*Hamster and Puffin*); Maria Dorey (*Bella*); Moyra Flynn (*Sydney, Biancia, Bill, and Ben*); Janice Hall (*Seamus*); Pat Heller (*Phoebe*); Intellectual Animals (*Jules, Wilma, Cherry, and Glynis*); Sue Kempster (*Harry and Melissa*); Krystyna Mayer (*Mruczek*); Alison Melvin (*Nelson and Winston*); Christina Oates (*Cloud*); Eunice Paterson (*Soames and Fleur*); Sally Powell (*Violet*); Sue Roberts (*Blue Boy and Hoppy*); Pauline Rogers (*Misty, Lulu, and Ollie*); Di Sanderson (*Billy*); Celia Slack (*Bluey and kittens*); Katy Slack (*Chockie and kittens*); Karen Tanner (*Cherami, Fortune Cookie, and kittens*); Hazel Taylor (*Maisie*); Amanda Topp (*Tiddles*); Alison Trehorne (*Lollipop and Humbug*); RVC Animal Care Trust (*Chloe*); Beany Smith (*Smudge*).

For modelling: "Cookie" Baran and Stacey Berenson.
For handling cats: Kate Forey, Jenny Berry, Etta Rumsey, and Di Sanderson.
For supplying equipment and materials: Animal Fair, Kensington, London W8.

For design assistance: Colette Cheng.
For editorial assistance: Lynn Parr.
For page make-up and computer assistance: Patrizio Semproni.
For picture research: Diana Morris.

Dorling Kindersley wish to thank Terence C. Bate BVSc, LLB, MRCVS of the RSPCA for his valuable advice on the text.

Illustrations

Angelica Elsebach: 157, 158–159, 160–161, 162–163, 164–165, 166, 168–169, 170–171, 172–173, 174–175
Christ Forsey: 13, 45, 47, 51, 98, 99, 100, 102, 104, 106, 108, 109, 110, 112, 114, 116, 118, 120, 122, 124

Photography

KEY: t *top*, b *bottom*, c *centre*, l *left*, r *right*
All photography by Steve Gorton and Tim Ridley except for:
Animals Unlimited: 46bl, 70t, 71bl, 179bl
Ardea: 13c
Bodleian Library, Oxford: 12t
Jane Burton: 5tl, 8tl, 10, 16t, 17r, 18t, 18b, 19cr, 21cr, 25b, 27b, 34c, 36r, 42b, 44c, 44b, 46t, 56t, 58t, 71br, 78–79, 80–81, 82–83, 84–85, 86–87, 98b, 100t, 105bl, 110b, 114t, 119b, 120t, 121b, 124t, 125b, 133cl, 143bl, 154b, 179tl
Bruce Coleman Ltd: 13tr, 44t Hans Reinhard
Eric Crichton: 167cl, 167cr, 167brc
Tom Dobbie: 167t
E.T. Archive: 12br
John Glover: 167crc, 167blc
Jerry Harpur: 167clc, 167bl, 167br
Marc Henrie: 101b
Michael Holford: 12c, 12bl
Larry Johnson: 179br
Dave King: 7tr, 9b, 11cl, 11b, 19cl, 2lt, 22–23, 26t, 26c, 27t, 70b, 71t, 71c, 88, 89t, 89c, 92–93, 94, 133bl, 143t, 143c, 143br, 154c, 179c, 180c, 180b, 181
Oxford Scientific Films: 13tl Frank Schneidemeyer, 50b London Scientific Films
David Ward: 134b
Matthew Ward: 130t, 131, 133cr, 133br

The Illustrated Atkins New Diet Cookbook

The Illustrated Atkins New Diet Cookbook

OVER 200 MOUTHWATERING RECIPES TO HELP
YOU FOLLOW THE INTERNATIONAL NUMBER ONE
WEIGHT-CONTROL PROGRAMME

By Dr Robert C Atkins, with Fran Gare, M.S.

We would like especially to acknowledge Nancy Mahoney, M.S., R.D., for her nutritional research
on the recipes.

1 3 5 7 9 10 8 6 4 2

Text copyright © The Estate of Robert C Atkins, 2004
Photography copyright © Ebury Press, 2004
Design copyright © Ebury Press, 2004

First published in the United Kingdom in 2003 by Vermilion as *Dr Atkins New Diet Cookbook*
This illustrated and revised edition first published in the United Kingdom in 2004 by
Vermilion
Random House UK Ltd
Random House
20 Vauxhall Bridge Road London SW1V 2SA

Random House Australia (Pty) Limited
20 Alfred Street, Milsons Point, Sydney,
New South Wales 2061, Australia

Random House New Zealand Limited
18 Poland Road, Glenfield,
Auckland 10, New Zealand

Random House (Pty) Limited
Endulini, 5A Jubilee Road, Parktown 2193, South Africa

Random House UK Limited Reg. No. 954009
www.randomhouse.co.uk

A CIP catalogue record is available for this book from the British Library.

Editor: Grace Cheetham
Designed by Ghost Design
Project Managed by Claire Wedderburn-Maxwell
Photography by Martin Brigdale
Food Styled by Linda Tubby and Angela Boggiano
Stylist: Helen Trent
Edited by Gillian Haslam
Proofread by Annie Lee

ISBN: 0 091 89470 0

Printed and bound in Germany by Appl Druck Wemding

Contents

Introduction

You have all seen cookbooks that promise to help you lose weight, but I suspect that you haven't seen one like this. This isn't a copycat cookbook. It doesn't attempt to refurbish and enliven the repetitious regimes that pretend it is possible to cook delicious meals by cutting out most fat and offering instead mini portions that could barely satisfy a small child, much less an active adult. Forget about those so-called cookbooks and instead be prepared for the shock of your life as you page through the delectable recipes and mouthwatering photographs. 'Where's the diet?' you may ask. What happened to self-denial, austerity and limited food choices? Can following The Atkins Nutritional Approach™ really be the path to a healthy goal weight?

Just glance at the wonderful recipes in this book. They don't look like recipes from many of the diets you may have tried before because they are not restricted in fat. You will quickly see the inclusion of tasty foods such as olive oil, butter, mayonnaise, sour cream, cheese and avocado. How can you eat these fatty foods and still lose weight? Be assured, these are the very foods, including poultry, fish, shellfish, beef and pork, that will help you lose weight. (Along with these proteins and fats, you will also enjoy an array of salad greens and other vegetables. And after you have lost your initial weight, you can start eating berries, nuts, seeds and more.) If you are relying on fat restriction to get you thin, this is not the cookbook for you. If you have cut fat from your diet before but still gained weight or have been unable to lose it, you may have an inkling that restricting fat is not all it is cracked up to be.

On the other hand, if you understand that by eating these foods, while controlling your carbohydrate intake, you actually start up your body's own fat-burning engine, this book is the guide you need to put delicious meals on the table for breakfast, lunch and dinner. And even if you don't understand it yet, this cookbook and the principles and guidelines upon which it is based are exactly what you need.

You need a new start, new principles and a new way of eating that promises immediate results and can become a permanent healthy lifestyle. A controlled carbohydrate programme is the answer. Such programmes have recently been shown in one research study after another to be as effective as – if not more effective than – limiting calories and fat. However, since the 1970s – and until very recently – a simplistic theory of weight loss that focused obsessively on dietary fats (and by implication taught the stale doctrine that gaining or losing weight is just a matter of calorie consumption) had dominated.

To understand how simplistic it is to look at weight control that way, you only have to consider different people you know, their various body types, and their differing appetite levels. Undoubtedly, you have friends who eat constantly and who eat whatever they want and never seem to gain any weight, while others live on salads and skinless chicken breasts but can't seem to slim down. Right away you'll see that there's no necessary connection between how much you eat and how heavy you are or between eating a lot of fat and being fat. You've probably noticed people who eat bacon and eggs for breakfast but are not overweight. Nor necessarily are people who eat steaks or butter. Yet the restriction of fat has become the basis of a whole weight-loss industry and a huge category of food products.

Despite the obsession with fat and with avoiding dietary fat, the Western world is in serious trouble weight-wise. The United States has the dubious distinction of leading the way as a nation of overweight and obese individuals. At this time, more than 64 per cent of the adult population is overweight and 30 per cent are clinically obese. The United Kingdom is not far behind, with 17 per cent of men and 21 per cent of women obese, and millions more seriously overweight and on the road to obesity. Public health policy has clearly failed to stem this tide and should be reviewed. Indeed, the Food Standards Agency advice of five portions of fruit and vegetables a day, combined with regular exercise, offers little for those who are already overweight or obese. The risk to individual health through associated conditions of diabetes and cardiac disease is very serious, and the burdens on the National Health Service are huge. The National Audit Office has estimated the annual cost of obesity and related conditions to the NHS to be half a billion pounds, with wider economic costs of two billion pounds every year.

This is serious food for thought. Speaking of food, remember that this book promises to be a source of the richest and most diverse dining pleasure. Most diet books focus on carrot and celery sticks, skimmed milk, plain toast and skinless chicken. In their attempt to deploy a few delicious salads (though none more delicious than those in this book), they are fundamentally working from poverty. Fine cuisine has always been firmly rooted in luxurious fat. That's why we feel confident that you are going to relate to a weight-control programme and a cookbook that allows you to enjoy Guacamole, Pizza Burgers, Chicken Croquettes, Steak au Poivre and Duck In Red Wine, as well as puddings and cakes such as Butter Pecan Ice Cream, Lemon Pie and Chocolate Brownies.

You are probably already salivating, but before you rush to the kitchen and start cooking up a storm, you need to understand the basic principles of controlled carb nutrition. (Before his death, Dr Atkins spent almost 40 years advising overweight patients at The Atkins Center for Complementary Medicine in New York City. He repeatedly saw that despite the media storm of the preceding years, most overweight men and women are not particularly sensitive to dietary fat.)

In fact, what makes most people fat and keeps them fat is an impaired metabolism. They are eating a diet that is very high in carbohydrates – most of them heavily processed and refined – and their bodies cannot efficiently metabolize all of them. When the carbohydrates they eat are turned into glucose and not burned for energy, then the glucose is stored as body fat. For such people, trying to lose weight by reducing fat is torture because it simply does not address the core of their problem: excessive carbohydrate intake.

WHAT TO EXPECT

In addition to delicious food, what will you experience on the Atkins Nutritional Approach?

When you do Atkins, you can:

- Eat until you are satisfied but not stuffed.
- Control your appetite.
- Enjoy rich and luxurious foods.
- Snack when you are hungry.
- Benefit from a metabolic advantage that allows you to eat more calories.
- Experience steady weight loss, even if you have failed on other diets.
- Adopt a permanent way of eating that lets you maintain your weight loss.
- Enjoy improvements in health problems associated with being overweight.

When you do Atkins, you won't:

- Experience constant hunger.
- Count calories.
- Eat tiny portions.
- Cut out butter, mayonnaise, cream and other fats.

All these promises are explained in detail in *Dr Atkins New Diet Revolution*, which is the natural companion to this book.

DIET IS AT THE HEART OF MOST HEALTH PROBLEMS

Many of our major health problems and most of our weight problems are indeed nutritional, but they spring from eating the refined, processed and devitalized food of the modern world, not from eating too many lamb chops or roasted chickens. In actuality, the foods waiting to ambush your health are sugar, corn syrup and other sweeteners, hydrogenated oils and white flour.

Do you realize that if you are overweight, there is a 60 per cent chance that you have a problem with blood sugar and insulin levels? There is a very good probability that you're already on the path to diabetes if you are not already diabetic. You are putting yourself at risk for heart disease. You may suffer from fatigue and irritability that is totally curable if you follow a controlled carbohydrate nutritional programme.

You should be following the Atkins Nutritional Approach not just because it will slim you down but because it is the path to lifetime health and well-being and reduces risk factors for certain diseases.

Doing Atkins properly can reverse hypertension (high blood pressure), head off or control the progression of diabetes, correct many eating disorders, and generally reduce the exposure to food intolerances. You deserve to be a healthy person as much as you deserve to eat delicious meals.

Because not all doctors and nutritionists are familiar with Atkins, it is a good idea for you to have a complete physical and certain blood tests before you begin doing Atkins. First, a complete examination may uncover health problems unrelated to the way of eating you are about to embark upon; second, you want markers against which you can measure your progress after a couple of months of doing Atkins. Your doctor should check your blood pressure, your fasting blood sugar and insulin levels two hours after a carbohydrate meal, your high-density lipoprotein (HDL) and low-density lipoprotein (LDL) cholesterol and your triglycerides. There's nothing like watching these numbers improve as you get slim and having any doubting friends see the two working in tandem as well.

If, like many people, you are overweight because you are sensitive to carbohydrates, then your weight problem is likely to be caused by how your body processes insulin, a hormone produced by your pancreas. Obese people almost always also have a condition called hyperinsulinism or insulin resistance. In plain English, this means that your body releases an excessive amount of the hormone. When you eat carbohydrates, your body produces blood sugar (glucose), and when you eat the refined carbohydrates mentioned above, your glucose level goes up rapidly. Your pancreas releases insulin to lower that level by transporting the glucose to your cells, where it is used for energy or stored as fat. That's why insulin is sometimes referred to as the fat-producing hormone.

Once you understand the basics of this process, you have a weapon to wage your battle against flab. By controlling the intake of foods that stimulate excessive insulin release, you can be in control of your weight. Carbohydrates provide that kind of stimulation, but fats and protein generally do not. (You should know that if you eat huge portions of protein, some of it converts to glucose.) This strategy for success doesn't stop when the weight comes off; it helps you maintain a healthy weight once you have slimmed down.

Regaining weight is the demon that bedevils most people who have been (briefly) successful on a diet. They may have put time, great effort and high hopes into adhering to a programme, lost that nasty excess weight, only to find that six months or a year later the weight has returned to the same level as it was before. It's almost worse than never having lost it in the first place.

You'll be happy to know that there is no need for that exercise in frustration when you do Atkins. The Pre-Maintenance phase of Atkins is a natural transition from the weight-loss phases of the programme. Once you have achieved your goal weight and move on to the Lifetime Maintenance phase you can enjoy your newly slim shape for good. At this point, you can eat poultry, fish, red meat, cheese, vegetables, nuts and seeds, as well as fruits, legumes and grains in moderation.

THE ROLE OF LIPOLYSIS/KETOSIS

For most people who do Atkins after trying a variety of low-fat, low-calorie diets, the most remarkable experience is that they are not obsessed with hunger. While you can always have a snack if you are hungry between meals, most people find a significant change in their appetite level. That is because eating the controlled carbohydrate way actually controls appetite. How can that be? Your cavemen ancestors' bodies were actually designed for periods of feast and famine. If you have ever fasted or talked to someone who has done so, you will be familiar with the fact that after a couple of days hunger disappears. Controlling carbs produces a similar phenomenon.

What does your body use for energy when you fast or control your carbohydrate intake? It burns off its own stored fat. Unlike a fast, where the body also burns off muscle tissue to meet its protein requirements, which is undesirable and can be dangerous, controlling carbohydrates allows your body to burn off only fat.

This happens because there is a pecking order when it comes to preferred fuel. The body will always burn glucose first. Remember that glucose comes from carbohydrates in food. But when you significantly control your carbohydrate intake, as you do on the Induction phase of Atkins, only the obligatory amount of glucose is produced in your blood stream after you eat. For two days your body can metabolize its stores of glucose (called glycogen), then it has to turn to another source for energy for your back-up fuel system. The next fuel in the pecking order is body fat, which is when you begin to lose weight.

When your body starts to burn the fat, you enter a state called lipolysis, which means 'the dissolving of fat'. Among the by-products of fat burning are compounds called ketone bodies, which become your newfound source of energy. Rest assured, your body is just as happy using ketones as it is using glucose. The use of fat, the body's back-up energy source, is a perfectly natural process. As you go into lipolysis and the resultant state of ketosis, your appetite is under control. Because this usually results in a decrease in the intake of calories, your rate of weight loss accelerates.

YOUR METABOLIC ADVANTAGE

The accelerated weight loss is the result of a side benefit of controlled carbohydrate eating that is called the metabolic advantage. Very simply – and this has been demonstrated in numerous research studies – individuals eating the same number of calories on a controlled carbohydrate programme lose more weight than those following a low-fat programme. (Some studies demonstrate that even when an individual consumes more calories than those following a low-fat programme, they still lose more weight.)

This means that you do not have to focus on counting calories and restricting foods such as steak or cream. All you have to do is keep your intake of carbohydrate foods low enough so that you enjoy the metabolic advantage. As long as you are continuing to lose weight and inches at a steady pace, you know that you are burning fat for energy. The side benefit of appetite control helps you to continue losing even more. Lipolysis/ketosis diminishes hunger and with it the need for willpower. After two or three days in this state most people feel better and more energetic than they have felt in years.

Kick-starting weight loss by getting your body into lipolysis/ketosis means severely controlling your carbohydrate intake. That's why you must initially cut your intake to two to three small salads or a salad and a portion of cooked vegetables each day. This translates into three cups of salad or two cups of salad and a one-cup serving of most vegetables. During the Induction phase you will not be eating bread, pasta, cereal and other foods made with flour and/or sugar. As you move into Ongoing Weight Loss (OWL), you will gradually add other carbohydrate foods and increase the amount of carbohydrates you eat. Even in Lifetime Maintenance, however, you will be eating far less than the 200 to 300 grammes of carbohydrate that most people eat on a daily basis.

OTHER ESSENTIALS

Another crucial aspect of the Atkins Nutritional Approach is nutritional supplementation. The foods you will be eating are tasty and nutrient rich, but when you go down to a low level of vegetable consumption during Induction, you may be getting inadequate portions of certain nutrients. We stress *may* because if you choose nutrient-dense foods, it is easy to consume adequate amounts of most vitamins and minerals.

The real reason you'll need supplements is because of the way you are likely to have been eating for years. If you have been on a low-fat diet, you will have to play catch-up to make up for possible deficiencies of essential fatty acids, vitamin B_{12}, and the fat-soluble vitamins A, D and E. Several minerals are also in short supply on most low-fat diets. And if you've been eating junk food full of sugar and bleached flour, then you've been consuming anti-nutrients, and your nutritional needs are even greater. When you eat such foods you're doing more than just depriving yourself of sufficient supplies of important vitamins and minerals. Metabolizing those empty refined foods uses up what little stores of nutrients remain.

The third reason you need what we like to call 'vitanutrients' is to maximize your body's ability to function optimally as a fat-burning unit.

In order to get the nutrients you need each day, we suggest you take the following:

1. A broad multiple vitamin and mineral supplement that contains considerably more than the recommended daily intake (RDI) of B complex factors and vitamin C and at least 30 other different nutrients. Chromium picolinate (between 200 and 600 mcg), which helps burn fat, should be included. Unless your doctor has found you to be deficient in iron, take a multivitamin that does not contain iron, as high iron intake can be a risk factor for cardiovascular disease.
2. The second essential supplement is called just that – essential fatty acids (EFA). EFA-deficiency may be the most prevalent dietary shortage in our culture, thanks to the misguided obsession with avoiding dietary fat and the over-consumption of trans fats (found in hydrogenated and partially hydrogenated oils) instead of healthy natural fats. An EFA supplement should include gamma-linolenic acid (GLA) – primarily found in primrose or borage oil – and omega-3 fatty acids from fish oil, flaxseed oil or linseed oil. (You can, of course, also eat salmon and other cold-water fish.)
3. If you have sugar cravings, you should also include 500 to 1,000 mg of L-glutamine before each meal. L-glutamine has been shown to curb alcohol addiction as well. If you previously ate lots of carbohydrates, this will help to ease the transition to controlled carbohydrate eating.
4. You also should be supplementing with psyllium husks or another form of fibre to prevent constipation.

Specific details of the supplements you should take appear on page 220.

EXERCISE AND NUTRITION GO HAND-IN-HAND

In addition to good food and vitamin–mineral supplements, there is one more vital component integral to doing Atkins properly: exercise. If you're considerably overweight, many types of exercise may be difficult for you right now. But while you may not be ready to run a marathon, you can still make a concerted effort to become more active. A walk around the park or climbing the stairs a few times a day may be all you can handle at first. Water aerobics are a good option, and there are also chair exercises appropriate for very heavy people. You will eventually find that the exercise feels good.

However, if you're over 35, significantly overweight or have not been physically active, it is important to consult your doctor before initiating an exercise programme.

Not only will exercise make you feel good and look better, but it also builds muscle. Muscle cells burn more energy than fat cells do even while you're sleeping, so the more you exercise and the more muscle you build, the more you're shifting the metabolic balance of your body towards slimness. Exercise provides a long-term advantage in your effort to maintain an ideal weight.

Half-an-hour a day of exercise is the bare minimum. It is advisable to aim for an hour – but feel free to divide it up throughout the day. Thirty minutes on the stair climber at the gym in the morning, a speedy, 15-minute walk during your lunch break and another 15 minutes of strength training while you watch your favourite sitcom, all count towards your daily goal. Ideally, you should do both aerobic exercise, such as brisk walking, jogging, swimming and biking – which will work your heart and lungs – and anaerobic exercise, which is any kind of weight bearing exercise.

PREPARE YOUR NEAREST AND DEAREST

When you are planning a new dietary programme, you need all the support you can get. Start by telling the people you live with just what you intend to do. Tell them that you take your weight-control programme seriously and you'd appreciate their doing the same. If they are unfamiliar with the controlled carbohydrate approach or concerned by the lack of restriction on fat consumption, you can do two things. Send them to www.atkins.com for more information, including numerous recent studies that validate the efficacy of the controlled carbohydrate approach. Or, if you can bear to part with it, lend them your copy of *Dr Atkins' New Diet Revolution*. Otherwise, tell them just to sit back and watch the changes they are about to see in you. When they see how terrific you look and how good you feel, their criticisms should melt away as fast as the fat on your hips.

Be diplomatic, and gentle but firm with anyone questioning you. Eating is fraught with all sorts of emotional issues, and changes in the way you eat affect everyone around you. Nonetheless, this is your body, your life and your way of eating, not that of your relatives.

PREPARE YOUR KITCHEN

If you live alone, it will be easy to 'remodel' your kitchen before starting Atkins. Either invite over some friends for a final high carb bash or give those foods away to friends and neighbours. If you live with others and they are not going to join you doing Atkins, you'll need to put the foods that you will not be eating aside for others, preferably where they are not calling to you regularly. If you are the main cook, you may have to prepare some foods that you are not going to eat yourself. In general, meal planning should be easy enough. For example, if you are having chicken and salad for dinner, just cook some brown rice or another starchy side dish for the rest of the family. You'll also want to fill your fridge and store cupboard with many of the foods listed in the next chapter, so check out the meal plans that represent the various phases of the Atkins Nutritional Approach.

A Four-Phase Weight-Control Programme

This chapter is designed for those of you who have not read *Dr Atkins New Diet Revolution*. It provides a simplified description of the four phases of the Atkins Nutritional Approach™. These four phases are an effective way of breaking up what will become a permanent way of eating. Induction gets you losing weight with a bang; Ongoing Weight Loss carries you through the weeks or months as you continue to slim down to near your goal weight; in Pre-Maintenance you work off that last bit of extra weight and make a graceful transition into the most important phase: Lifetime Maintenance. This final phase is your lifetime ticket to health and slimness.

PHASE ONE: Induction

Induction, which kick-starts weight loss, controls carbohydrates more than any of the following phases. *Because of its rigour, this and the other weight-loss phases of Atkins are not appropriate for pregnant or nursing women or for people with severe kidney disease.* You will be eating only 20 grammes of Net Carbs per day in the form of salad greens and other vegetables. Net Carbs are the only carbs that matter when you do Atkins because they are the only carbs that have a significant effect on blood sugar. They are called Net Carbs because they represent total carb grammes minus the grammes of carbs that don't impact on blood sugar. In the USA, Net Carbs reflect total carbs minus fibre and certain carbohydrates such as polyols (sugar alcohols), including glycerine and maltitol, which act as sweeteners. Because food labels in the UK distinguish the fibre content from the carb content, if there are no sugar alcohols in a product, the number of grammes of total carbohydrates and of Net Carbs is the same. But if you are looking at labels on foods from countries that list fibre as a carbohydrate, make sure you subtract the grammes of fibre from the carbohydrate grammes to get the Net Carb count.

In the case of unprocessed foods such as vegetables and berries, you may need to use a carbohydrate gramme counter, such as *Dr Atkins New Carbohydrate Counter*. If the gramme counter includes fibre in its totals, make sure you subtract the fibre from the total carb count.

The purpose of this restrictive regimen is to ensure that your body goes into lipolysis/ketosis, which will control your appetite, and that after the first two or three days your body begins to burn its own fat for energy. Once you are in lipolysis, your body has made the transition from burning carbohydrate (glucose) for fuel to employing its alternative metabolic pathway that evolved millions of years ago to enable humans to survive periods of famine. You now break down fat, and the byproducts of fat metabolism – ketones – are consumed for energy.

1. Consume no more than 20 grammes of Net Carbs daily. This allows for approximately 3 servings of salad vegetables (loosely packed) or 2 servings of salad and 1 serving of cooked vegetables from the acceptable foods list (see pages 17–18). Depending on which vegetables you choose from this list, you may actually be able to eat more than 3 servings in total. This is a good time to begin counting grammes of Net Carbs, which you will have to do when you are in the next phase.
2. Eat pure protein, pure fat and mixtures of protein and fat. This means you can eat shellfish, fish, poultry, meat, cheese and eggs, as well as butter, olive oil, mayonnaise, cream and other oils. Foods combining fat and carbohydrate or carbohydrate and protein are not allowed.
3. Each day you can also eat the Special Category Foods found on page 18.
4. When hungry, eat enough to make you feel satisfied but not stuffed. If you are not hungry at mealtimes, eat a small snack with your vitamin supplements to avoid low blood sugar levels.
5. Do not go more than six waking hours without eating as you may become ravenous and over-eat.
6. Eat nothing that is not on the acceptable foods list, not even 'just one bite' of it.
7. Drink eight 250ml/8floz glasses of water a day to hydrate your body and remove toxins.
8. Don't eat any food unless you know its Net Carb count by referring to a carbohydrate gramme counter or the food label.
9. Stay on Induction for a minimum of 14 days. You can safely remain on Induction for up to six months or more if you have a lot of weight to lose and are highly motivated.

1. The Induction phase contains no fruit, bread, grains, starchy vegetables, or dairy products other than butter, cream and most cheeses.
2. Most so-called 'diet' products are not suitable for doing Atkins because they are fat restricted, not carbohydrate controlled. Avoid them unless they specifically state 'no carbohydrates' or they are foods designed for controlled carbohydrate eating plans and state their precise carb count. Controlled carb food products (including those produced by Atkins Nutritionals, Inc.) can make it even easier to enjoy what is already a sumptuous way of eating.
3. The word 'sugar-less' on a product is not enough. The label must state the carbohydrate content.
4. Many condiments, such as ketchup, are also full of sugar. As always, read labels carefully.
5. Many non-food products, such as chewing gum, cough syrups and cough sweets, also contain lots of sugar or other calorific sweeteners and must be avoided.

ON INDUCTION YOU CAN EAT LIBERAL AMOUNTS OF THE FOLLOWING:

Meat

All meats, such as beef, veal, lamb, pork, ham, bacon and venison, except delicatessen meats with nitrates, nitrites or added sugar, or products that are not exclusively meat, such as meatloaf.

Fish

All fish, such as tuna, salmon, flounder, sole, trout, sardines, herring, haddock and halibut, except fish cured with nitrates, nitrites or sugar and products that are not exclusively fish such as imitation crab.

Fowl

All fowl, such as chicken, turkey, duck, goose, guinea fowl, quail and pheasant.

Shellfish

All shellfish, such as oysters, mussels, clams, squid, prawns, lobster and crab. Limit oysters and mussels to 110g/4oz per day.

Eggs

Any style of eggs, including scrambled, fried, poached, soft-boiled, hard-boiled, devilled and omelettes.

Cheese

All matured cheeses, cow's and goat's cheese, cream cheese, Swiss cheese, cheddar, mozzarella and tofu (soy) 'cheese' (but check the carbohydrate content). Note that all cheeses have some carbohydrate content, and quantities are governed by that factor (see a carbohydrate gramme counter or the food label).

Individuals who have a yeast intolerance must avoid cheese.

You cannot eat fresh cheeses such as ricotta, cottage cheese, diet cheese, cheese spreads, whey cheese or imitation cheese products.

Spices

All spices to taste, but make sure that spice blends do not contain any sugar.

Vegetable Oils	All vegetable oils are allowed ('cold pressed' oils retain the most nutrients), including olive, grapeseed, canola (rapeseed), walnut, sesame, sunflower, safflower and flaxseed (do not heat flaxseed).
Fats	Butter, mayonnaise (unless you have a yeast intolerance) and cream (double, single, whipping or crème fraiche), but no more than 3 tablespoons daily. You do not need to trim the fat from meat or poultry.
Beverages	Water, mineral water, spring water, club soda, essence-flavoured seltzer (must say 'no calories'), decaffeinated coffee and tea (but see controlled beverages, page 19), herb tea (if it is not sweetened with barley, dates, figs or sugar), diet soda water (preferably sweetened with sucralose, brand name Splenda®), iced tea with low carb sweetener, carbohydrate-free powder with low carb sweetener used for making fruit-flavoured drinks, clear consommé/bouillon (not all brands; check label for carb count).

YOU CAN HAVE UP TO THREE SERVINGS OF SALAD INGREDIENTS:

Salad Vegetables	One serving: Alfalfa sprouts (40g/1^1/2oz), bean sprouts (40g/1^1/2oz), celery (125g/5oz), chicory (75g/3oz), cucumber (125g/5oz), endive (50g/2oz), escarole (50g/2oz), fennel (90g/3^1/2oz), jicama (125g/5oz), lamb's lettuce (50g/2oz), lettuce (50g/2oz), mâche (50g/2oz), morels (75g/3oz), mushrooms (75g/3oz), olives (125g/5oz), pak choy (75g/3oz), peppers (125g/5oz), radicchio (40g/2^1/2oz), radishes (100g/4oz), rocket (50g/2oz), romaine (cos) (50g/2oz), spring onions (100g/4oz), sorrel (125g/5oz) and tomato (150g/6oz).
Salad Herbs	Basil, chives, coriander, dill, oregano, parsley, rosemary and thyme. For salad dressing, use the desired oil plus vinegar (not balsamic) or lemon juice and herbs and spices.

Anchovies, grated cheese, chopped hard-boiled eggs, crumbled crispy bacon, sautéed mushrooms and sour cream.

YOU CAN HAVE ONE SERVING OF THE FOLLOWING INSTEAD OF A SERVING OF SALAD:

Cooked Vegetables

Artichoke hearts (125g/5oz), asparagus (125g/5oz), aubergine (75g/3oz), bamboo shoots (150g/6oz), beet greens (40g/1½oz), broccoli (75g/3oz), Brussels sprouts (90g/3½oz), cabbage (100g/4oz), cauliflower (100g/4oz), celeriac (150g/6oz), chard (40g/1½oz), christophene (100g/4oz), courgette (100g/4oz), dandelion greens (60g/2½oz), hearts of palm (100g/4oz), kale (75g/3oz), kohlrabi (125g/5oz), leeks (90g/3½oz), mangetout (60g/2½oz), okra (100g/4oz), onion (150g/6oz), pumpkin (125g/5oz), rhubarb (125g/5oz), spaghetti squash (100g/4oz), spinach (30g/1oz), spring greens (40g/1½oz), stringless beans (100g/4oz), summer squash (125g/5oz), turnips (125g/5oz) and water chestnuts (125g/5oz).

SPECIAL CATEGORY FOODS

Each day you can also eat 10 to 20 olives, half a small avocado, 30ml/1floz of sour cream or 90ml/3floz of unsweetened double cream, as well as two to three tablespoons of fresh lemon or lime juice. If you are losing weight slowly, adjust your intake of these foods.

FOODS TO BE CAREFUL OF

Diet Foods

Avoid foods marketed as diet foods, which typically replace fat with sugar, making them higher in carbohydrates. That is the same reason that cream is allowed on Atkins while skimmed milk is not and why sour cream is acceptable but yogurt is not. Similarly, you can pan-fry chicken but you cannot use a low-fat breadcrumb mix.

Fats and Oils

Natural fats, especially certain oils, are essential to good nutrition. Olive oil (monounsaturated) is particularly valuable. Do not cook polyunsaturated oils, such as corn, soybean and sunflower oil, at high temperatures or allow to brown and smoke. You want to eat a balance of omega-3, omega-6 and omega-9 fatty acids. You should have a source of GLA (gamma linolenic acid) and omega-3s, which are found in salmon oil, linseed oil and flax oil. Although you can eat butter, margarine should be avoided because it is usually made of trans fats (hydrogenated or partially hydrogenated oils), which are a serious health hazard. Some non-hydrogenated margarines are available in health food stores and selected supermarkets.

Controlled Beverages

Avoid all caffeine if you suspect you are caffeine-dependent; others can consume limited quantities (perhaps one cup a day). Grain beverages, i.e. imitation coffee substitutes, are not allowed. Alcoholic beverages are not part of Induction, but those low in carbohydrate are, in moderation, an option for the later phases of the programme.

Artificial Sweeteners

Consumed in moderation, artificial sweeteners make it possible for those trying to lose weight to enjoy the taste of sweets. Individuals must determine which artificial sweeteners agree with them

Sucralose (marketed as Splenda®) is the preferred sweetener; it is the only sweetener made from sugar. It does not raise blood sugar, and the US Food and Drug Administration approved it in 1998 after reviewing more than 100 studies. Saccharin (marketed as Sweet 'N Low®), cyclamate, and acesulfame-K are all acceptable as well.

Saccharin has been extensively studied, and harmful effects could only be produced in rats when extremely high doses were given. The FDA has removed saccharin from its carcinogen list, citing a thorough review of the medical literature. Saccharin can be safely consumed in moderation, meaning no more than three teaspoons a day.

Remember each teaspoon of sugar substitute will contain a little less than 1 gramme of carbohydrate, which must be counted.

PHASE 2: Ongoing Weight Loss (OWL)

After the first 14 days on Induction you can decide whether to stay on this phase or to move on to Ongoing Weight Loss (OWL). Ask yourself the following questions:

1. Are you bored with Induction?
2. How much weight do you have to lose?
3. Are you losing weight slowly?
4. Are you willing to slow down the pace of weight loss in exchange for more food choices?

If you are bored, and this boredom could lead to not complying with the rules of Induction, by all means move on to OWL after two weeks. However, if you are comfortable staying in this phase, and you still have a lot of weight to lose, you can do Induction safely for six months or more. If you do not have much more weight to lose, it is important to advance to OWL so you can cycle through all the phases of the programme.

After two weeks of doing Atkins, if you are like most people, you will be losing weight and will also feel healthier than you have in years. Most people feel energized by a controlled carbohydrate regimen. On the weight-loss front, losses of 2.25 to 4.5kg/5 to 10lb are common, although results vary from individual to individual, depending on metabolism, age, gender, hormonal status, fitness level and genetics.

In the Induction phase, you were at a fairly strict level of carbohydrate control. Now, you're going to liberalize your intake ... a bit. This has to be done slowly and carefully because you don't want to go past a certain level that, numerically speaking, will differ for each of you. This is called your Critical Carbohydrate Level for Losing (CCLL). During this phase, which may continue for as many weeks or months as it takes to get close to your goal weight, you will continue to shed weight, but at a slower pace. This is deliberate, enabling you to learn eating habits that will allow you to keep the weight off for good.

This minor liberalization of carbohydrate consumption is, of course, not permission to go back to your old way of eating. Instead, you will be increasing your daily carb intake by 5g of Net Carbs per week. This will give you more variety in your eating, it will allow you to restore a few favourite foods, and it will put more wonderfully healthy vegetables back in your food choices. Many people doing Atkins actually end up eating more vegetables and salads than they've ever eaten before.

More salad and other vegetables on the acceptable foods list

Fresh cheeses (as well as more aged cheeses)

Seeds and nuts (but not chestnuts)

Berries

You can also add 125ml/4floz of dry wine, 185ml/6floz of a light beer or 30ml/1floz of whisky or gin daily

The crucial fact about OWL is that it's a steady, ongoing process. Aim to increase your carbohydrate intake by one level every week as long as you continue to lose weight at a slow but steady pace. A level is defined as 5 grammes of Net Carbs daily. You'll continue to lose weight – at a much-reduced rate, of course, but still losing. If you stop losing, you simply back down a level and you should have found your CCLL. You'll also be learning to make healthy carbohydrate choices. This is not just a numbers game, but a way of eating that ensures good health if followed properly. Your 5-gramme increments should not include refined or processed carbohydrates. The purpose of Atkins is not to lose weight in a hurry but to get it off and keep it off. By slowing down your rate of loss, you gradually get into a permanent way of healthy eating.

INCREASING YOUR DAILY CARB INTAKE

These small additions are typical 5-gramme Net Carb increments that you can make as you proceed through your weeks or months on OWL.

40g/1$\frac{1}{2}$oz almonds	40g/1$\frac{1}{2}$oz fresh soybeans	125ml/4floz tomato juice
50g/2oz sunflower seeds	25g/1oz steamed spinach	60g/2$\frac{1}{2}$oz fresh blueberries
60g/2$\frac{1}{2}$oz Brussels sprouts	60g/2$\frac{1}{2}$oz cottage cheese	180g/6oz fresh strawberries

PHASE 3: Pre-Maintenance

Once you have passed your weeks or months on OWL and have only 2.5 to 5kg/5 to 10lb to lose, it's time to move on to the Pre-Maintenance phase, which is the gateway leading to the end of the weight-loss phases of Atkins and the beginning of permanent weight control. Many people find it difficult to postpone when the goal is within reach but it is very, very important to proceed at a snail's pace.

It is actually easier to lose weight than to keep it off. You may have lost weight in the past only to regain it after you went back to your old way of eating. You have certainly seen this happen to friends. Lose that final bit of excess weight with excruciating slowness so that by the time you say, 'I'm there,' you'll virtually be eating the way you will be eating for the rest of your life.

In Pre-Maintenance, if you have not already starting doing so in OWL, it is time to reintroduce some additional carbohydrate foods:

FOODS YOU CAN ADD DURING PRE-MAINTENANCE

Legumes (black beans, lentils etc.)
Fruits other than berries
Starchy vegetables
Whole grains

Your goal is to increase your grammes of Net Carbs to the point where you're losing less than $^1/_2$kg/1lb a week. Increase your weekly carbohydrate intake in levels consisting of 10g of Net Carbs per day, gradually introducing foods from the above groups. Or you may prefer to allow yourself one or two servings of your favourite nutrient-rich higher carbohydrate foods each week. Perhaps have half a cantaloupe melon at lunch one day, or a small portion of wild rice at dinner another evening. However, such foods must be added gradually and one at a time. You want to see how you react to these additions. As long as you continue to lose weight slowly, that is great. If, on the other hand, such foods stimulate weight gain or cause cravings or if you are unable to stop with a small portion, you should cut them out for a while.

THE ATKINS CARBOHYDRATE EQUILIBRIUM™

Pre-Maintenance is designed to allow you to identify what we call your Atkins Carbohydrate Equilibrium™, or ACE. This is a position of metabolic equilibrium, a balance point between carbohydrate restriction (which causes weight loss) and carbohydrate indulgence (which causes weight gain).

Here's how to find your ACE: if you maintain your weight after eating 60 grammes of Net Carbs a day for several days, try going to 70 grammes. Keep inching up each week by 10-gramme increments as long as you do not gain weight. If you do put on a little weight, back off 5 or 10 grammes and you should have found your ACE. On the other hand, if you initially gain weight after a few days at 60 grammes a day, cut back to 50 grammes and see if you can maintain your weight at that level. Continue to play with that number of carbohydrate grammes until you are neither losing nor gaining. At that point, you have found your ACE!

Each person has his or her individual ACE. A young, active man will have a considerably higher ACE than a sedentary, older woman. Depending on your gender, metabolism, activity level, hormonal status, age and genetics, your ACE may range anywhere from 45 to 100 grammes or more of Net Carbs. Once you have found your ACE and maintained your goal weight for at least one month – and preferably three months – at this level, you are officially in the Lifetime Maintenance phase of Atkins. It's important to understand that Pre-Maintenance segues seamlessly into Lifetime Maintenance.

Prawn Stir-fry

PHASE 4: Lifetime Maintenance

In this permanent phase, you will continue to enjoy a wide range of delicious foods staying at or just below your ACE. Of course you still need to keep an eye on your carbohydrate intake. Just skip the junk food and use your carb grammes on nutrient-rich foods such as whole, unrefined grains and a variety of fruits and vegetables.

After your battle with weight loss, this probably sounds easy. But be aware of your own tastes and tendencies in Lifetime Maintenance, and don't go back to eating the way you were.

At your ACE, you will still be controlling your carbohydrate intake enough to keep your blood sugar level normal and avoid the roller-coaster ride of high and low blood sugar. This control will ensure some curbing of your appetite, but the benefits of constant fat-burning experienced in Induction and OWL are not as pronounced. As long as you are not storing fat, you are teetering between fat-burning and glucose-burning. Instead, you will have to rely more on your willpower, although adequate fat, protein and fibre will help stabilize your appetite.

Here is a list of suggestions for individuals who have successfully attained their goal weight. These are simultaneously the rules of Lifetime Maintenance:

1. Understand that fish, fowl, meat, vegetables, eggs, cheese, nuts, seeds and occasional fruits and nutrient-dense starches are the foods on which your body is naturally adapted to thrive. Learn to think of those foods whenever you think of food.
2. Avoid processed foods and all foods that contain sugar, corn syrup, honey, dextrose, fructose, cane sugar, molasses, etc. These so-called foods act as slow poison, however sweet they taste. Also avoid cornstarch and white flour. Of course, being human, you will have the occasional indulgence, just make sure that these exceptions to your good eating habits are few and far between.
3. Consider the programme of vitamin and mineral supplementation (see page 220).
4. Individualize your meals and sample new recipes. Try high-protein foods you've never had the opportunity to try before.
5. Use caffeine and alcohol in moderation.
6. Know your addictions and be aware of them. They can only be handled through abstinence.
7. If you gain more than 2.5kg/5lb of weight, return to an earlier phase or simply decrease your daily carbohydrate intake in 5-g increments. If absolutely necessary, return to Induction. Don't allow yourself to be more than 2.5kg/5lb overweight. Weigh and measure yourself once a week and track your progress in your personal progress diary.
8. Enjoy moderately vigorous daily exercise, which is essential to weight control and good health.

Are you ready to be happy?

We can't guarantee that you'll be wealthy and wise, but we have every intention of making you happy in your body. That doesn't just mean being slim, it also means being healthy and thrilled by the food you eat. It's simply essential that your foods thrill you. If they don't, how can we fulfil our promise that for you doing Atkins will be a satisfactory and satisfying lifetime way of eating?

We want your new meals to provide you with every bit as much emotional satisfaction as your normal pre-Atkins way of eating did. Hopefully more. If we succeed at this, then there will be no reason for you to return to your old way of eating – the way that didn't work for you.

If you follow the suggestions outlined in this book, you will probably end up a better cook than you were before. Add to that the fact that on the Atkins Lifetime Maintenance phase, you will still be eating enough fat to produce satiety and avoid disruptive blood sugar highs and lows and you should be an odds-on favourite to succeed.

Here's one parting tip: one of the advantages of fat and protein in your diet is that they moderate changes in blood sugar levels, thereby suppressing the craving for sweets. The successful effort to lower the amount of fat in the diet during the last three decades has been purchased at a crippling price. During this same period, consumption of sugar has increased dramatically. This is not only a catastrophe for people watching their weight, it is a health catastrophe.

As someone who has taken the first step to avoidance of this catastrophe, you have our sincerest congratulations. But, more importantly, you can celebrate your own success by sticking with a programme you know is effective and easy to maintain for the rest of your (healthy) life.

Peanut Butter Cookies

Induction

These meal plans contain no more than 20 grammes of Net Carbs per day. Dress salad greens with oil and vinegar unless otherwise specified.

DAY 1

Breakfast

Two-cheese Omelette (see page 44)
3 rashers of bacon
2 slices of tomato

Lunch

Chicken Salad Ham Rolls (see page 73)
Small tossed green salad

Dinner

Greek Salad (see page 74)
Luscious Lamb (see page 98)
Roasted green beans

Snack

Gouda cheese and olives

DAY 2

Breakfast

Crab and Mushroom Omelette (see page 41)
2 turkey sausages

Lunch

Spicy Burgers (see page 109)
Cucumber and radish salad with Vinaigrette
    Cream Dressing (see page 89)

Dinner

Cream of Chicken Soup (see page 61)
Halibut Roll-Ups (see page 134)
Small green salad and steamed broccoli

Snack

Guacamole (see page 55) with endive spears

DAY 3

Breakfast

Whitefish salad
2 scrambled eggs

Lunch

Chicken Croquettes (see page 119) on lettuce
2 slices of tomato

Dinner

Egg Dumpling Soup (see page 67)
Fennel Red Mullet (see page 134)
Coleslaw (see page 72)
Confetti Mould (see page 185)

Snack

Sour Cream Clam Dip (see page 200) with
    celery sticks

DAY 4

Breakfast

2-egg vegetable omelette
2 turkey sausages

Lunch

Courgette Soup (see page 62)
Poached Salmon Salad (see page 73)
Celery and red pepper strips with Italian
    Dressing (see page 87)

Lemon-basted Roast Chicken (see page 114)
Sautéed asparagus
Small tossed green salad

Snack
Cheese cubes

DAY 5
Breakfast
Smoked salmon with cream cheese
2 hard-boiled eggs

Lunch
Smoked turkey breast
Alternative Potato Salad (see page 204)

Dinner
Japanese Egg Custard (see page 203)
Prawn Stir-fry (see page 130)
Small tossed green salad

Snack
Fran's Special Pâté (see page 56)

DAY 6
Breakfast
Bacon and Onion Omelette (see page 38)
Sautéed mushrooms

Lunch
Sliced roast pork
Horseradish Cream (see page 158)
Small tossed green salad

Dinner
Egg Dumpling Soup (see page 67)
Gourmet Poussins (see page 112)
Green Beans and Artichokes (see page 149)

Snack
Sardine Snack (see page 58)

DAY 7
Breakfast
2 Scrambled Eggs (see page 47)
2 slices of ham

Lunch
New England Fish Chowder (see page 68)
Chicken salad (see page 204) with small
    tossed green salad

Dinner
Mother's Roast Beef (see page 101)
Buttered green beans
Green onion and cucumber salad

Snack
Roast beef rolled around pickle spears

Ongoing Weight Loss (OWL)

These meal plans contain no more than 45 grammes of Net Carbs per day. Your personal Critical Carbohydrate Level for Losing (CCLL) may be higher or lower.

DAY 1

Breakfast

Two-cheese Omelette (see page 44)

3 rashers of bacon

1 small roasted tomato

Lunch

Stuffed Aubergine (see page 151)

Small tossed green salad with Italian Dressing
(see page 87)

Dinner

Cod with Hollandaise Sauce (see page 156)

Roasted broccoli florets

Baked Cheesecake (see page 182)

Snack

Smoked almonds with cheese

DAY 2

Breakfast

Cottage cheese with 80g/3oz raspberries

1 hard-boiled egg

Lunch

Gazpacho (see page 62) and celery sticks

Avocado stuffed with chicken salad (see
page 204)

Dinner

Enchiladas (see page 141)

Baked cauliflower and red pepper strips

Small tossed green salad

Coffee Cream Layer Cake (see page 191)

Snack

Slice of ham wrapped around a dill pickle

DAY 3

Breakfast

2 eggs with smoked salmon and
goat's cheese

80g/3oz raspberries

Lunch

Dr Atkins' Fromage Burgers (see page 106)

Tomato and cucumber salad

Dinner

New England Clam Chowder (see page 68)

Grilled lobster with butter

Green Beans Almandine (see page 154)

Snack

Olives and cheese cubes

DAY 4

Breakfast

Cottage cheese with 60g/2^{1}/2oz blueberries

2 slices high-fibre flat bread

Lunch

Greek Salad (see page 74)

1 170-g/6-oz can of tuna

Dinner

Roast Beef with Horseradish Cream
    (see page 158)
Endive with vinaigrette and Parmesan
    shavings
Asparagus with brown butter

Snack

2 Peanut Butter Cookies (see page 192)

DAY 5
Breakfast

Ham and Artichoke Omelette (see page 40)
1 slice low carb bread

Lunch

Creamy Pumpkin Soup (see page 65)
Courgette stuffed with Cream Sauce
    (see page 156)
Sliced smoked turkey

Dinner

Chinese Mangetout (see page 147)
Grilled prawns
Small tossed green salad
Lemon Lime Mousse (see page 216)

Snack

Fran's Special Pâté (see page 56)

DAY 6
Breakfast

Ricotta cheese with cinnamon
110g/4oz mixed berries
1 soft-boiled egg

Lunch

Swordish Topped with Goat's Cheese
    (see page 133)
Small tossed green salad
Spice Cake (see page 188)

Dinner

Tricolor Salad with Three Cheeses
    (see page 76)
Steak with grilled mushrooms
Broccoli

Snack

Cheese and olives

DAY 7
Breakfast

Smoked whitefish with spring onion
    cream cheese
1 slice low carb bread
1 small sliced tomato

Lunch

Grilled turkey burger
Tossed green salad
Swede Fries (see page 145)

Dinner

Chicken Croquettes (see page 119) served on
    spaghetti squash
Sautéed spinach with garlic
Pecan Orange Macaroons (see page 192)

Snack

80g/3oz raspberries with cottage cheese

Pre-Maintenance

These meal plans contain no more than 60 grammes of Net Carbs per day. You may or may not be able to consume this level of carbs in Pre-Maintenance. Some people can consume even more grammes of carbs.

DAY 1

Breakfast

2 turkey sausages

Scrambled Eggs (see page 47)

1 slice wholegrain bread

Lunch

Crunchy Seafood Salad (see page 204)

60g/2$\frac{1}{2}$oz strawberries with cream

Dinner

Moussaka (see page 94)

Roasted vegetable salad

Poached Peaches (see page 186)

Snack

2 Chocolate Brownies (see page 218)

DAY 2

Breakfast

40g/1$\frac{1}{2}$oz whole milk yogurt with

110g/4oz blackberries

1 hard-boiled egg

Lunch

Fresh Tuna and Avocado Salad (see page 79)

1 slice rye bread

Dinner

Manicotti (see page 142)

Small tossed green salad with Italian dressing

(see page 87)

Coconut Panna Cotta (see page 174)

Snack

Chicken Wings (see page 56)

DAY 3

Breakfast

1 slice wholegrain French toast

Ricotta cheese

$\frac{1}{2}$ grilled peach

Lunch

Hot Beef Salad (see page 70)

180g/6oz mixed berries

Dinner

Roast chicken

Baked Spinach (see page 147)

Small tossed salad with Creamy Celery-seed

Dressing (see page 89)

Snack

Butter Pecan Ice Cream (see page 170)

DAY 4

Breakfast

Herb Omelette (see page 42)
1/2 orange

Lunch

Salad Niçoise (see page 82)
1 slice wholegrain bread

Dinner

Enchiladas (see page 141)
Small tossed green salad with Mustard
    Vinaigrette (see page 84)
Sautéed green beans

Snack

Crêpes with Strawberry Coulis (see page 180)

DAY 5

Breakfast

Smoked salmon with cream cheese and
    capers on 1 slice wholegrain bread

Lunch

Stuffed Aubergine (see page 151)
Small tossed green salad with Italian Dressing
    (see page 87)
1 small apple

Dinner

Tuna Bake (see page 137)
Roasted cauliflower and carrots
Chocolate Ice Cream (see page 165)

Snack

Macadamia nuts

DAY 6

Breakfast

2-egg spinach and feta cheese omelette
1 slice pumpernickel bread

Lunch

1 grilled burger
Tricolor Salad with Three Cheeses (see page 76)

Dinner

Cauliflower Soup with Dill and Caraway
    (see page 67)
Pork chops
Sautéed spinach with garlic
Cantaloupe Granita (see page 173)

Snack

Sardine Snack (see page 58)

DAY 7

Breakfast

Cottage cheese with 12.5g/1/2oz pineapple
1 slice wholegrain bread

Lunch

Cold Avocado Soup (see page 203)
Chicken Salad (see page 204)
110g/4oz mixed berries

Dinner

Roast Turkey with Almond Stuffing
    (see page 209)
Irene's Turnips (see page 145)
Roasted green beans

Snack

Devilled-salmon Eggs (see page 58)

Lifetime Maintenance

These meal plans are designed not to exceed 75 grammes of Net Carbs per day. Depending on your Atkins Carbohydrate Equilibrium (ACE), you may be able to consume fewer or more grammes of Net Carbs.

DAY 1

Breakfast

40g/1¹/₂oz whole milk yogurt
15g/¹/₂oz wholegrain cereal
180g/6oz mixed berries

Lunch

Swedish Meatballs (see page 55)
Spaghetti squash
Small tossed green salad

Dinner

Steak au Poivre (see page 92)
Sautéed courgette
Gnocchi (see page 212)
Baked apple with cream

Snack

Vegetable sticks with hummus

DAY 2

Breakfast

2 Scrambled Eggs (see page 47)
1 slice wholegrain toast
1 grilled tomato

Lunch

Not Just Another Tossed Salad (see page 81)
Pineapple Cheesecake (see page 182)

Dinner

Consommé
Tarragon Lobster Tails (see page 211)
Small tossed green salad

Snack

1 pear with almonds

DAY 3

Breakfast

2 slices wholegrain French toast
¹/₄ cantaloupe melon

Lunch

Gazpacho (see page 62)
Poached Salmon Salad (see page 73)

Dinner

Spicy Spareribs (see page 97)
Mixed roasted vegetables
80g/3oz brown rice

Snack

Mocha Hazelnut Ice Cream (see page 169)

DAY 4

Breakfast
Two-cheese Omelette (see page 44)
1 slice wholegrain bread
1 tangerine

Lunch
Chicken Salad Ham Rolls (see page 73)
Coleslaw (see page 72)
110g/4oz cherries

Dinner
Veal Scaloppine (see page 98)
Manicotti (see page 142)
Small tossed green salad
Frozen Blood Orange Mousse (see page 173)

Snack
Celery stuffed with sugar-free peanut butter

DAY 5

Breakfast
Puffed wholegrain cereal
125ml/4floz whole milk
1/2 grapefruit

Lunch
Tuna salad over greens
80g/3oz cannellini beans
Peanut Butter Cookies (see page 192)

Dinner
Moussaka (see page 94)
Greek Salad (see page 74)

Snack
80g/6oz grapes with cheese

DAY 6

Breakfast
Oatmeal with 125ml/4floz whole milk
110g/4oz mixed berries

Lunch
Brit Burger (see page 106)
Roasted green beans
Small tossed green salad with French Dressing
    (see page 85)

Dinner
Lemon-basted Roast Chicken (see page 114)
1/2 sweet potato
Sautéed chopped greens

Snack
Apricots with ricotta cheese

DAY 7

Breakfast
Salmon Soufflé (see page 48)
1/2 orange

Lunch
Open roast beef sandwich on wholegrain bread
    with Horseradish Cream (see page 158)
Small tossed green salad

Dinner
Fennel Red Mullet (see page 134)
2 small boiled potatoes
Endive and tomato salad
180g/6oz mixed berries

Snack
Spice Cake (see page 188)

Breakfast and Brunch

EGGS

Eggs are the perfect protein and we recommend them, especially free range, organic eggs. The chickens that lay these eggs have not been injected with antibiotics or hormones and have not been fed chemicals. Always check the date on the box to ensure that the eggs are fresh.

During Induction (and any of the following stages) you can eat any style of eggs, so boiled, fried, scrambled and poached are allowed, as well as Cheese-baked Eggs and Eggs Florentine. Furthermore, you can have Salmon Soufflé during OWL. You can also have most of the omelettes during Induction, but will need to wait until OWL for the Ham and Artichoke and Herb Omelettes; and until Pre-Maintenance for the Peaches and Cream Omelette.

Soft-boiled Eggs

serves 1

2 large eggs, at room
  temperature

With an 'egg pricker' or skewer make a small hole in the large end of the egg. This stops the egg from cracking during cooking.

Place the eggs in a saucepan full of cold water and bring to the boil. Boil for 3 minutes for loose eggs, 4 minutes for runny yolks and firm whites, and 5 minutes for firm yolks and whites. Run under cold water to stop the eggs from cooking further, then crack open the tops and serve in egg cups.

> Per serving: Net Carbs: 1.2g • Fibre: 0g • Protein: 12.6g
> Fat: 10.6g • Calories: 156

Hard-boiled Eggs

serves 1

2 large eggs, at room
  temperature

With an 'egg pricker' or skewer make a small hole in the large end of the egg.

Place the eggs in a saucepan of cold water and bring to the boil. Cover the pan and turn off the heat. Allow the eggs to remain in the water for 20 minutes, then drain and cool.

> Per serving: Net Carbs: 1.2g • Fibre: 0g • Protein: 12.6g
> Fat: 10.6g • Calories: 156

Sunny-side Up and Over Easy Eggs

Melt the butter in a non-stick frying pan. Break the eggs, one at a time, into a flat saucer and slide them into the pan. Cook on a low heat until the whites become solid but the centre is still runny.

If Sunny-side Up is your preference, remove from the pan after about 2¹/₂ minutes; for Over Easy use a spatula or fish slice and carefully flip the eggs over, then cook for 30 seconds more. Sprinkle with salt and pepper to taste.

serves 1

15g/¹/₂ oz unsalted butter
2 eggs
salt and pepper to taste

> Per serving: Net Carbs: 1.2g • Fibre: 0g • Protein: 12.4g
> Fat: 13.8g • Calories: 184

Poached Eggs

Fill a saucepan half full with cold water, add the vinegar and heat the water to a simmer. Break the eggs, one at a time, into a flat saucer and slide into the simmering water. Allow to simmer for 3 minutes until the whites are no longer transparent, then remove from the water with a slotted spoon. Place on a plate and season with salt and pepper.

serves 1

1 teaspoon vinegar
2 eggs, at room temperature
salt and pepper to taste

> Per serving: Net Carbs: 1.2g • Fibre: 0g • Protein: 12.6g
> Fat: 10.6g • Calories: 156

Basic Omelette

serves 2

2 tablespoons butter
4 eggs
1 tablespoon double cream
1/2 teaspoon salt
freshly ground black pepper to
    taste

Melt the butter in a non-stick frying pan or omelette pan. Tilt the pan so it is well covered with the butter.

Beat the eggs with the cream, salt and pepper. Pour into the pan and tilt to spread the eggs to the edges of the pan.

Cook over a low heat until the eggs begin to set, then loosen the eggs from the sides of the pan with a spatula. Tilt the pan again to allow the uncooked eggs to run to the sides and cook until set. When cooked, carefully fold the outer edges of the omelette into the centre to resemble a flat cone. Slide the omelette out of the pan and serve.

If you are filling the omelette, spoon the mixture on to the centre of the omelette before folding the edges into the centre.

Per serving: Net Carbs: 1.4g • Fibre: 0g • Protein: 11g
Fat: 26g • Calories: 290

Bacon and Onion Omelette

serves 4

9 rashers streaky bacon
40g/1 1/2 oz onion, chopped
2 Basic Omelette recipes
    (see above)

Cut the bacon into small pieces and fry in a small non-stick frying pan or omelette pan until crisp. Add the onion and sauté until translucent. Pour off the fat. Set aside.

Follow the *Basic Omelette* instructions, using half the egg mixture. When cooked, place half the bacon and onion in the centre of the omelette before folding over. Fold over and cook for 1 minute more, then move to a serving plate and cover to keep warm. Make the second omelette in the same way, then cut the omelettes in half and serve immediately.

Per serving: Net Carbs: 1.6g • Fibre: 0g • Protein: 17g
Fat: 34g • Calories: 400

Lunch Omelette

serves 4

2 tablespoons olive oil
6 shiitake mushrooms,
    thinly sliced
4 spring onions, thinly sliced
12 sugar snap peas, trimmed
    and blanched
2 slices sun-dried tomatoes,
    diced
6 eggs
2 tablespoons double cream
1 tablespoon finely chopped dill
    (or 1 teaspoon dried)
30g/1oz herbed goat's cheese
30g/1oz unsalted butter
salt and freshly ground black
    pepper to taste

Heat the oil in a non-stick frying pan or omelette pan over a medium heat. Sauté the mushrooms and spring onions for 2 minutes. Add the sugar snap peas and sun-dried tomatoes and cook for another 3 minutes (the peas will remain crunchy).

Whisk the eggs with the cream and dill; pour carefully over the vegetables and cook until nearly set. Dot the centre of the omelette with the goat's cheese and butter, then fold over the sides. Season with salt and pepper.

> Per serving: Net Carbs: 6.3g • Fibre: 1.5g • Protein: 11g
> Fat: 23.5g • Calories: 282

Ham and Artichoke Omelette

serves 4

1 x 180-g/6-oz jar marinated
    artichoke hearts, drained
2 tablespoons grated
    Parmesan cheese
8 eggs
3 tablespoons mascarpone
    cheese
salt and freshly ground black
    pepper to taste
120g/4½ oz ham, thinly sliced

Place the artichoke hearts on kitchen paper and pat the excess oil off. Roll the hearts in Parmesan cheese and set aside.

Beat the eggs, mascarpone cheese and salt and pepper together in a bowl until smooth. Follow the *Basic Omelette* instructions (see page 38) to make the omelette.

When the egg mixture is set, cover the surface with ham slices. Place the artichoke hearts in the centre and fold the sides over. Slice into four pieces before removing from the pan, then serve hot.

> Per serving: Net Carbs: 5.6g • Fibre: 1.6g • Protein: 19.7g
> Fat: 18.9g • Calories: 275

Crab and Mushroom Omelette

Melt the butter in a non-stick frying pan or omelette pan. Add the mushrooms and onion and sauté until light brown. Stir in the crabmeat and simmer for 3 minutes. Add the sherry and simmer for 1 minute more. Remove half of the crab mixture from the pan.

Beat the eggs and cream together, then pour carefully over the crab mixture in the pan. Cook until set, fold in half, then place the reserved crab mixture over the top of the omelette.

serves 4

30g/1oz butter
6 shiitake mushrooms, thinly sliced
2 tablespoons chopped spring onion
110g/4oz white crabmeat
1 tablespoon sherry
6 eggs
45ml/1½floz double cream

> Per serving: Net Carbs: 4.7g • Fibre: 0.6g • Protein: 15g
> Fat: 18g • Calories: 243

Peaches and Cream Omelette

Combine all the ingredients except for the butter and chopped peaches in a bowl and beat until smooth.

Cook the omelette following the *Basic Omelette* instructions (see page 38).

When the centre is firm, spoon the peaches on to the centre and fold over the sides. Slide out of the pan and serve.

serves 4

225g/8oz full fat soft cream cheese, softened
8 eggs
pinch salt
60ml/2floz double cream
2 teaspoons granular sugar substitute
30g/1oz butter
5 tablespoons chopped Poached Peaches (see page 186)

> Per serving: Net Carbs: 9.5g • Fibre: 0.5g • Protein: 15.9g
> Fat: 41.5g • Calories: 475

Aubergine and Cheddar Omelette

serves 4

80g/3oz peeled and
    cubed aubergine
4 tablespoons olive oil
1 clove garlic, peeled and
    chopped (or $1/4$ teaspoon
    garlic powder)
125ml/4floz prepared tomato
    sauce or passata
8 eggs, beaten
$1/2$ teaspoon salt
60g/$2^{1/2}$oz Cheddar cheese,
    grated

Soak the aubergine cubes in a bowl of cold water for 30 minutes. Drain and dry well.

Place 3 tablespoons of the olive oil in a frying pan or omelette pan. Add the aubergine and garlic or garlic powder and sauté until the aubergine begins to brown. Add the tomato sauce or passata and heat through, then set aside.

Heat the remaining tablespoon of olive oil in a large non-stick frying pan, then add the eggs, salt and cheese. Cook over a low heat until they set.

Spoon the aubergine mixture on to the centre of the omelette and fold over the sides, then serve.

> Per serving: Net Carbs: 4.1g • Fibre: 0.9g • Protein: 15.4g
> Fat: 27.8g • Calories: 333

Herb Omelette

serves 2

4 eggs
1 tablespoon chopped chives
1 tablespoon finely chopped dill
2 tablespoons mascarpone
    cheese
30g/1oz butter
salt to taste

Combine all the ingredients together and beat until smooth and thoroughly combined.

Cook following the *Basic Omelette* instructions (see page 38).

> Per serving: Net Carbs: 1.5g • Fibre: 0g • Protein: 12.1g
> Fat: 28.9g • Calories: 317

Two-cheese Omelette

serves 2

30g/1oz unsalted butter
2 tablespoons finely chopped
   onion
4 eggs
2 tablespoons double cream
120g/4¹/₂oz soft cheese,
   mashed or chopped
60g/2¹/₂oz firm cheese, grated
1 tablespoon chopped parsley,
   to garnish

Heat the butter in a non-stick frying pan over a medium heat. Add the onion and cook until transparent.

Beat the eggs together with the cream and soft cheese. Cook following the *Basic Omelette* instructions (see page 38) until the eggs set.

Sprinkle the grated hard cheese over the eggs and cook for 1 minute. Slice the omelette in two and fold each semicircle in half. Flip over to melt the cheese and brown both sides. Serve hot and crisp. Garnish with parsley, if desired.

> Per serving: Net Carbs: 3.8g • Fibre: 0.3g • Protein: 23.5g
> Fat: 56.5g • Calories: 615

Prawn and Goat's Cheese Omelette

Butterfly the prawns by cutting three-quarters of the way through each prawn along the back vein. Remove the vein. Open the prawn to resemble a butterfly.

Heat the garlic oil in a non-stick frying pan or omelette pan and sear the prawns in the hot oil, which should take about 2 minutes on each side. Remove the prawns from the pan and drain on kitchen paper.

Beat the eggs together with the goat's cheese.

Wipe the oil from the pan and add the butter to the pan, then add the beaten egg mixture and cook following the *Basic Omelette* instructions (see page 38).

When the eggs are set, add the prawns and sun-dried tomatoes and fold over before serving.

Per serving: Net Carbs: 2.1g • Fibre: 0.3g • Protein: 14.5g
Fat: 54.8g • Calories: 550

serves 2

8 raw prawns, shelled
4 tablespoons garlic oil
4 eggs
60g/2½oz herbed goat's
   cheese, crumbled
30g/1oz unsalted butter
4 sun-dried tomato halves
   softened in olive oil,
   finely chopped

Scrambled Eggs

Break the eggs into a small bowl. Add the cream and beat well with a wire whisk.

Melt the butter in a non-stick frying pan, then add the eggs and cook on a low heat until the eggs set. Season with salt and pepper (you may add other seasonings if you like). When the eggs are set, scramble them with a fork, then slide them out of the pan.

Variations: Sprinkle grated cheese over the set eggs before scrambling or serve with thinly sliced smoked pancetta or streaky bacon.

serves 1

2 eggs
1 tablespoon double cream
15g/½oz unsalted butter
salt and freshly ground black
    pepper to taste

Per serving: Net Carbs: 1.6g • Fibre: 0g • Protein: 11.3g
           Fat: 29.3g • Calories: 318

Cheese-baked Eggs

Preheat the oven to 190°C/375°F/gas 5.

Fill a baking dish halfway up with boiling water. Divide the butter between 2 small ramekins, and carefully break an egg into each. Place 1 tablespoon of cream over each egg. Top with the cheese, divided evenly between the ramekins.

Place the ramekins in a roasting tin filled with enough boiling water to reach halfway up the sides and put in the oven. Bake for 10 minutes, add salt and pepper to taste, then serve immediately.

serves 1

10g/⅓oz unsalted butter
2 eggs, at room temperature
2 tablespoons double cream
2 tablespoons grated
    Parmesan cheese
salt and freshly ground black
    pepper to taste

Per serving: Net Carbs: 2.3g • Fibre: 0g • Protein: 16g
           Fat: 30g • Calories: 335

Scrambled Eggs (with bacon)

Eggs Florentine

serves 6

½ recipe Cheese Sauce
   (see page 157)
450g/1lb fresh or frozen spinach
6 eggs
salt

Preheat oven to 180°C/350°F/gas 4.

Prepare the *Cheese Sauce*. Wash the spinach leaves in cold water, place in a saucepan with a tightly fitting lid and cook over a low heat for 2 minutes. Drain well and chop finely.

Place the spinach in 1 or 2 shallow baking dishes then make a hollow for each egg in the spinach. Break one egg into each hollow and add a pinch of salt to taste. Pour the cheese sauce over the eggs and spinach and bake for 25 minutes.

> Per serving: Net Carbs: 2.2g • Fibre: 1.4g • Protein: 14.5g
> Fat: 19.4g • Calories: 244

Salmon Soufflé

serves 6

30g/1oz butter
3 tablespoons soy flour
1 teaspoon salt
250ml/8floz double cream,
   heated
250g/9oz salmon fillet,
   poached and flaked (see
   page 73), or canned, drained
and boned
salt and cayenne pepper
   to taste
3 eggs, separated
4 teaspoons fresh lemon juice

Preheat oven to 200°C/400°F/gas 6.

Prepare the soufflé dish by greasing the bottom and sides with half the butter. Place in the refrigerator until ready to use.

Melt the remaining butter in a saucepan over a low heat and stir in the flour and salt. Whisk vigorously for 1 full minute to cook it and avoid a floury taste. Add the heated cream and continue cooking, whisking constantly until thickened. Remove from the heat and cool, then add the salmon, salt and cayenne.

Beat the egg yolks and blend them carefully into the salmon mixture. Whisk the egg whites until stiff and fold them into the salmon mixture along with the lemon juice. Pour the mixture into the prepared soufflé dish.

Set the dish in a roasting tin filled with hot water and bake for about 35 minutes until firm. Serve immediately.

> Per serving: Net Carbs: 2.3g • Fibre: 0.5g • Protein: 13.6g
> Fat: 23g • Calories: 273

Starters, Soups and Salads

STARTERS

There's no need for you to go hungry on Atkins as you can enjoy a starter before lunch or dinner, as well as an afternoon snack. You can eat most of these starters when you are on Induction – but you need to wait until you move on to OWL before you can have the Toasted Nuts.

Toasted Nuts

serves 5

5g/¼oz butter
140g/5oz nuts of your choice
    (such as almonds, walnuts,
    pecans or pine nuts)
salt, granular sugar substitute
    or chilli powder, to flavour
    (optional)

Melt the butter in a non-stick frying pan. Stir in the nuts and sauté until browned. Place on kitchen paper to absorb the oil.
    If you like them salty, use salt to taste.
    If you like them sweet, use a sugar substitute to taste.
    If you like them spicy, use chilli powder to taste.

> Per serving: Toasted Almonds Net Carbs: 2g • Toasted Walnuts Net Carbs: 2g • Toasted Pecans Net Carbs: 1g • Toasted Pine Nuts Net Carbs: 2g

Marbled Tea Eggs

12 egg halves

6 eggs, at room temperature
2 tablespoons soy sauce
2 tablespoons salt
3 tablespoons black tea
1 tablespoon anise essence

Place the eggs in a saucepan, cover with cold water and bring to the boil. Reduce the heat and simmer for 10 minutes.
    Remove the eggs, leave to cool, then crack the shells in several places, but do not peel the eggs.
    Bring 1 litre/1¾ pints of water to the boil. Add the remaining ingredients and the eggs. Simmer for one hour, then cool the eggs in the liquid. Place the eggs, still in the liquid, in the refrigerator and leave overnight.
    To serve, shell the eggs and cut in half.

> Per egg half: Net Carbs: 0.6g • Fibre: 0.1g • Protein: 3.5g Fat: 2.7g • Calories: 42

Guacamole

Place the avocado, onion, tomato and cucumber in a food processor and process for 10 seconds. Season with the salt, jalapeño pepper and chilli flakes. Add the sour cream and parsley or coriander and process for 5 more seconds, then tip into a serving bowl and refrigerate until needed. Use as a dip with cucumber sticks.

> Per serving: Net Carbs: 2.2g • Fibre: 1.9g • Protein: 0.8g
> Fat: 4.2g • Calories: 54

serves 8

1 avocado, peeled and chopped
80g/3oz onion, peeled and
   chopped
1 tomato, chopped
$\frac{1}{3}$ cucumber, peeled and
   chopped
$\frac{1}{2}$ teaspoon salt
1 jalapeño pepper, finely
   chopped
$\frac{1}{8}$ teaspoon hot chilli flakes
1 tablespoon sour cream
1 tablespoon chopped parsley
   or coriander

Swedish Meatballs

Mix the cream and water together in a small bowl. Combine the beef, pork and veal in another bowl.

Mix the cream mixture, meats and onion together. Add the salt. Shape into small balls. Melt the butter in a medium frying pan over a medium heat, add the meatballs and brown. Then remove the balls to a dish and keep warm.

Make the *Cream Sauce* and pour over the meatballs. Garnish the meatballs with nutmeg and caraway seeds, if desired, and serve hot.

> Per serving: Net Carbs: 2.5g • Fibre: 0g • Protein: 10.6g
> Fat: 28.6g • Calories: 307

serves 8

60ml/2floz double cream
60ml/2floz water
110g/4oz minced beef
110g/4oz minced pork
110g/4oz minced veal
1 large onion, peeled and finely
   chopped
2 teaspoons salt
40g/$\frac{1}{2}$oz butter
1 recipe Cream Sauce (see
   page 156)
$\frac{1}{2}$ teaspoon grated nutmeg,
   to garnish
1 teaspoon caraway seeds,
   to garnish

Chicken Wings

hors d'oeuvres for 6

750g/1lb 11oz chicken wings
   (about 12)
250ml/8floz soy sauce
2 tablespoons granular sugar
   substitute
60ml/2floz white wine
2 cloves garlic, peeled and
   mashed
60ml/2floz sesame oil
1/2 teaspoon ground ginger

Rinse the chicken wings and pat dry with kitchen paper. Cut into pieces at the joints and discard the wing tips. Spread the wings in a shallow baking dish, but do not overlap them.

Combine the remaining ingredients and pour the sauce over the wings. Marinate overnight in the refrigerator.

Heat the oven to 170°C/325°F/gas 3 and bake the chicken wings in the marinade for 1^1/2 hours. Serve warm.

> Per serving: Net Carbs: 5.9g • Fibre: 0.5g • Protein: 28.4g
> Fat: 29.2g • Calories: 410

Fran's Special Pâté

20 slices

4 rashers bacon
450g/1lb chicken livers
2 tablespoons butter
600–700g/1lb 5oz–1lb 9oz
   skinless chicken breast
   fillets, pounded flat
2 tablespoons white wine
110g/4oz water chestnuts,
   drained
2 hard-boiled eggs
4 teaspoons salt
1 Boursin cheese, about
   90g/3^1/2oz
3 tablespoons basil
freshly ground black pepper

Preheat the oven to 140°C/275°F/gas 1.

Fry the bacon until crisp, then drain and reserve the fat.

Heat 2 tablespoons of the bacon fat in a frying pan and sauté the chicken livers for about 5 minutes over a medium heat, then remove from the pan and set aside.

Add the butter to the pan and melt over a medium heat, then add the chicken breasts and sauté for 3 minutes on each side. Add the wine and simmer for a further 3 minutes.

Place the cooked bacon, chicken livers, chicken breast, water chestnuts and eggs into a large bowl or food processor and chop finely. Add the salt, the rest of the bacon fat, the Boursin cheese, basil and pepper to the bowl and mix well.

Pack the mixture into a large buttered deep dish or loaf tin, cover with foil and place a heavy weight on top to keep the pâté from rising. Bake for 2 hours then turn the oven off and allow the pâté to cool in the oven. Unmould and cut into slices.

> Per slice: Net Carbs: 1.5g • Fibre: 0.3g • Protein: 12.3g
> Fat: 7.8g • Calories: 130

Devilled-salmon Eggs

12 egg halves

6 eggs
3 tablespoons mayonnaise
120g/4^1/$_2$oz boneless cooked
   flaked salmon, canned or
   smoked (plus extra for
   garnish if desired)
^{1}/$_2$ teaspoon fresh lemon juice
1 teaspoon Dijon mustard
1 teaspoon Worcestershire sauce
^{1}/$_2$ teaspoon salt
dash freshly ground black
   pepper
sprigs dill, to garnish (optional)

Place the eggs in a saucepan, cover with cold water and bring to the boil. Cover the pan, remove from the heat and leave to stand for 18 minutes, then run the eggs under cold water and remove the shells.

Slice the eggs in half lengthways and remove the yolks.

Mash the yolks and mayonnaise together until smooth, then add all the remaining ingredients, except for the dill, and mix well.

Spoon the mixture into the egg whites and garnish with additional pieces of salmon and sprigs of dill, if desired. Refrigerate for at least 30 minutes before serving.

> Per egg half: Net Carbs: 0.4g • Fibre: 0g • Protein: 5g
> Fat: 5.7g • Calories: 74

Sardine Snack

serves 3

1 x 90-g/3^1/$_2$-oz can skinless
   and boneless sardines,
   drained
^{3}/$_4$ teaspoon dried dill
3 hard-boiled eggs, mashed
^{1}/$_4$ teaspoon salt
180g/6oz soft cream cheese,
   softened
30g/1oz chopped onion
^{3}/$_4$ teaspoon fresh lemon juice
lettuce leaves

Blend all the ingredients in a blender or food processor until smooth. Serve, well chilled, on a bed of lettuce leaves.

> Per serving: Net Carbs: 2.5g • Fibre: 0.3g • Protein: 17.5g
> Fat: 29g • Calories: 343

Gazpacho

serves 6

1 small clove garlic, peeled and
   chopped
1 onion, peeled and chopped
4 sprigs parsley, chopped
30ml/1floz wine vinegar
45ml/1$^{1}/_{2}$ floz olive oil
$^{1}/_{4}$ teaspoon cayenne pepper
$^{1}/_{4}$ teaspoon salt
375ml/12floz Chicken Stock
   (see page 61)
4 large tomatoes, peeled
   and chopped
$^{1}/_{2}$ cucumber, peeled,
   deseeded and diced, plus
   extra for garnish

Place all the ingredients in a blender or food processor and blend until smooth. Chill overnight. Serve in chilled bowls and garnish with additional cucumber and cayenne pepper as desired.

Per serving: Net Carbs: 7.5g • Fibre: 2.3g • Protein: 7.7g
Fat: 10.4g • Calories: 158

Courgette Soup

serves 4

2 tablespoons olive oil
4 spring onions, chopped
1 teaspoon grated ginger root
1 clove garlic, peeled and
   chopped
900ml/1$^{1}/_{2}$ pints vegetable
   stock (see page 64)
250ml/8floz water
2 medium courgettes, thinly
   sliced
$^{1}/_{2}$ teaspoon salt
$^{1}/_{4}$ teaspoon freshly ground
   black pepper
1 medium avocado, stoned,
   peeled and chopped
1 tablespoon fresh lemon juice
1 tablespoon chopped red
   pepper, to garnish

Heat the oil in a large saucepan over a medium heat. Add two-thirds of the spring onions and cook for 3 minutes; stir in the ginger and garlic and cook, stirring, for 1 minute more.

Add the *Vegetable Stock*, water, courgettes, salt and pepper. Cover and cook for 10 minutes, until the courgettes are very soft. Cool slightly, then stir in the avocado.

Purée the soup in batches in a food processor or blender. Return to the pan to heat through. Stir in the lemon juice. Garnish with red pepper and the remaining spring onions, if desired.

Per serving: Net Carbs: 6.5g • Fibre: 4.5g • Protein: 4.5g
Fat: 14.7g • Calories: 180

Cauliflower Soup with Dill and Caraway

Melt the butter in a medium-sized saucepan. Add the leeks and cauliflower and sauté for 3 minutes. Stir in the *Chicken Stock* and stock cube and cook over a medium heat for $^1/_2$ hour.

Remove the soup from the heat and cool, then place in a blender or food processor and blend until smooth. Add the cream and blend for 10 seconds more.

Return the soup to the pan and stir in the dill and caraway seeds. Heat the soup but do not let it boil, then pour into individual bowls and top each serving with 1 tablespoon of mascarpone and 1 tablespoon of Parmesan. Garnish with sprigs of dill, if desired.

Per serving: Net Carbs: 9.4g • Fibre: 2g • Protein: 6.2g
Fat: 27g • Calories: 300

serves 6

30g/1oz unsalted butter
3 leeks (white part only), chopped
$^1/_2$ medium cauliflower, chopped
750ml/1$^1/_4$ pints Chicken Stock (see page 61)
1 chicken stock cube
250ml/8floz double cream
2 tablespoons finely chopped dill
1 teaspoon caraway seeds
salt to taste
6 tablespoons mascarpone cheese
6 tablespoons grated Parmesan cheese
sprigs dill, to garnish

Egg Dumpling Soup

Grease the bottom and sides of the top of a double boiler with the butter. Beat the egg, egg yolk, cream, salt and nutmeg together, then pour into the top of the double boiler.

Cook over hot (but not boiling) water for 45 minutes, or until set and firm.

Turn the dumpling mixture out on to greaseproof or parchment paper and cool, then slice into cubes. Add to clear hot *Chicken Stock* and serve immediately.

Per serving: Net Carbs: 4.8g • Fibre: 1.2g • Protein: 28.1g
Fat: 28.5g • Calories: 397

serves 4

15g/$^1/_2$oz butter, softened
1 egg plus 1 extra yolk
125ml/4floz double cream
pinch salt
pinch grated nutmeg
1 litre/1$^3/_4$ pints Chicken Stock (see page 61)

New England
Fish Chowder

serves 6

900g/2lb cod fillets
4 rashers bacon, diced
1 small onion, peeled and
    chopped
2 tablespoons chopped parsley
500ml/16floz Fish Stock
    (see page 64)
1 bay leaf
1 teaspoon salt
freshly ground black pepper to
    taste
500ml/16floz double cream

Cut the fish fillets into 2.5-cm/1-in cubes.

Place the bacon in a deep saucepan over a low heat and sauté until golden brown. Add the onion and sauté until transparent, then add the parsley and cook for 1 minute more.

Add the *Fish Stock*, bay leaf, salt and pepper, then cover and cook for a few minutes to combine the flavours. Add the fish and simmer for 10 minutes, then add the cream and warm until just heated through but do not let it boil. Serve immediately.

Per serving: Net Carbs: 4.3g • Fibre: 0.3g • Protein: 27.3g
Fat: 33g • Calories: 418

New England
Clam Chowder

serves 6

36 clams
4 rashers bacon, diced
1 small onion, chopped
2 tablespoons chopped parsley
500ml/16floz clam stock and
    Fish Stock (see page 64)
1 bay leaf
1 teaspoon salt
freshly ground black pepper to
    taste
500ml/16floz double cream

Wash the clams thoroughly. Place in a deep saucepan, cover with 10 to 15cm/4 to 6in of boiling water, cover with a lid and steam until the shells open (no longer than 5 minutes). Strain and reserve the clam stock and use with the *Fish Stock*.

Chop the clams coarsely, then follow the directions for *New England Fish Chowder* (see above), substituting the clams for the cod fillets.

Per serving: Net Carbs: 9.8g • Fibre: 0.4g • Protein: 36.8g
Fat: 41.2g • Calories: 561

SALADS

You can eat a very varied selection of salad vegetables each day, which means you can create a wide range of different salad dishes. During Induction you can have any of the salads given in the following pages except for the Tricolor Salad with Three Cheeses and Moulded Roquefort, as they contain nuts. If you want to prepare them but omit the nuts then you can have them during Induction, otherwise you need to wait until OWL.

Hot Beef Salad

serves 6

1 small round iceberg lettuce
1 small head Chinese leaves
1 large cucumber, thinly sliced
1 red onion, peeled and
    thinly sliced
1/2 small daikon radish,
    thinly sliced
2 small tomatoes, each cut into
    8 pieces
6 mint leaves
6 coriander leaves
60ml/2floz walnut oil
675g/1¹/₂ lb sirloin steak
1/2 teaspoon salt

Dressing:
2 cloves garlic, peeled and
    minced
60ml/2floz fresh lime juice
1–2 teaspoons granular sugar
    substitute
1 tablespoon Tamari soy sauce
1 teaspoon crushed red pepper
    flakes

Wash and dry the lettuce and Chinese leaves, tear into bite-sized pieces and tip into a serving bowl. Mix the cucumber, onion, radish, tomatoes, and the mint and coriander leaves together and pour over the lettuce. Toss well.

Heat the walnut oil in a non-stick frying pan over a medium heat. Add the steak, sprinkle with the salt and fry quickly until the meat is just rare. Remove from the pan and slice thinly.

Fan out the cooked meat on top of the salad. Mix the dressing ingredients together and pour over the salad.

> Per serving: Net Carbs: 5.5g • Fibre: 2.9g • Protein: 24g
> Fat: 23.4g • Calories: 333

Greek Salad

serves 4

1 large tomato, cubed
1/2 large green pepper,
    deseeded and cubed
1/2 large cucumber, peeled
    and cubed
80g/3oz stoned ripe olives
3 spring onions, sliced
2 tablespoons capers, drained
120g/4 1/2 oz feta cheese,
    crumbled
60ml/2floz olive oil
30ml/1floz wine vinegar
1/4 teaspoon cracked pepper
1/2 teaspoon dried oregano

Combine the tomato, green pepper, cucumber, olives, spring onions, capers and cheese in a salad bowl.

Mix the olive oil, vinegar, pepper and oregano together in a small bowl. Pour the dressing over the salad, toss and serve.

Per serving: Net Carbs: 4.4g • Fibre: 1.8g • Protein: 5.2g
Fat: 22.4g • Calories: 240

Moulded Roquefort

serves 8

1 tablespoon gelatine
180g/6oz Roquefort cheese
180g/6oz full fat soft cream
    cheese, softened
125ml/4floz whipping cream
4 spring onions, finely chopped
2 tablespoons pine kernels
4 black olives, stoned and
    chopped
salt to taste

Measure 60ml/2floz of cold water into a bowl, sprinkle the gelatine over and leave for 5 minutes to soften. Then add 60ml/2floz of hot water and stir until the gelatine has completely dissolved.

Push the Roquefort through a sieve. Add the cream cheese and cream to the Roquefort and mix well. Add the gelatine, spring onions, pine kernels, olives and salt to the cheese mixture and mix well.

Pour into a 750-ml/1 1/4-pint capacity ring mould that has been sprayed with oil or non-stick cooking spray and chill for about 2 hours until set.

Per serving: Net Carbs: 2.5g • Fibre: 0.4g • Protein: 8.3g
Fat: 21.1g • Calories: 230

Tricolor Salad with Three Cheeses

serves 8

1 recipe Mustard Vinaigrette
   (see page 84)
1 small head of radicchio
3 chicory heads
1 head Cos or romaine lettuce
90g/3¹/₂ oz Parmesan cheese
   shavings
150g/5oz Camembert, cut into
   8 wedges
120g/4¹/₂ oz herbed goat's
   cheese, cut into 8 wedges
40g/1¹/₂ oz pine kernels,
   toasted (or substitute
   Toasted Nuts, see page 52)

Preheat the oven to 230°C/450°F/gas 8.

Prepare the *Mustard Vinaigrette* and place in the refrigerator for 30 minutes.

Separate the leaves of the lettuces. Wash and dry them (make sure they are very dry), and tear into bite-size pieces. Place the leaves in a large salad bowl and toss in the Parmesan cheese.

Place the Camembert and goat's cheese wedges on a non-stick baking tray and melt in the oven for 1 minute.

Place the cheese wedges on top of the salad, top with the dressing and pine kernels or *Toasted Nuts* and serve immediately.

Per serving: Net Carbs: 5.3g • Fibre: 0.6g • Protein: 12.1g
Fat: 42.5g • Calories: 452

Fresh Tuna and Avocado Salad

Heat the grill to its highest temperature. Grill the tuna steaks for 5 minutes on each side. If necessary, baste with butter during cooking to prevent the tuna drying out.

Toss all the ingredients, except for the tuna, in a medium bowl until well combined, then drizzle with the *Lime Dill Dressing*. Divide between 6 plates.

Slice the fish into strips and place across the top of each plate of salad.

Per serving: Net Carbs: 2.3g • Fibre: 2.1g • Protein: 34.6g
Fat: 12.3g • Calories: 269

serves 6

675g/1¹/₂ lb fresh tuna steaks
butter, for basting
1 large avocado, stoned, peeled
   and cubed
2 celery sticks, chopped
6 radishes, sliced
1 tablespoon fresh lemon juice
1 tablespoon tarragon vinegar
¹/₂ small onion, peeled and
   chopped
¹/₄ teaspoon cayenne pepper
salt to taste
1 recipe Lime Dill Dressing (see
   page 87)

Alternative Potato Salad

Cut the swede into four pieces. Drop into a saucepan of boiling water and boil until tender, which should take about 30 minutes. Drain well and cool.

After the swede has cooled, finely chop it and place in a salad bowl. Sprinkle with the sugar substitute, if using, and the lemon juice. Add the spring onions, pickle, celery, salt, paprika and mayonnaise. Toss well, then fold in the eggs.

Chill before serving.

Per serving: Net Carbs: 3.1g • Fibre: 0.9g • Protein: 3.3g
Fat: 19.1g • Calories: 202

serves 8

1 medium swede, peeled
1 teaspoon granular sugar
   substitute (optional)
1 tablespoon fresh lemon juice
60g/2¹/₂ oz spring onions,
   finely chopped
1 medium dill pickle, chopped
120g/4¹/₄oz celery with leaves,
   finely chopped
1¹/₂ teaspoons salt
dash paprika
180g/6oz mayonnaise
4 hard-boiled eggs, chopped

Tossed Salad with Tomato Dressing

serves 8

2 heads lettuce (any variety)
2 tomatoes, peeled, chopped
   and deseeded
6 spring onions, finely chopped
1 tablespoon Dijon mustard
1 teaspoon salt
2 tablespoons olive oil
2 tablespoons tarragon vinegar
60ml/2floz vegetable oil
1 tablespoon mayonnaise

Wash the lettuce, dry thoroughly, tear into bite-size pieces and refrigerate.

To make the dressing, mash the tomatoes with the spring onions until they almost form a paste. Add the remaining ingredients, except for the lettuce, and beat with a whisk. Refrigerate until needed.

To serve the salad, place the lettuce in a large salad bowl, pour the dressing on top and toss well. Serve immediately.

Per serving: Net Carbs: 4.7g • Fibre: 2.1g • Protein: 2g
Fat: 12.2g • Calories: 138

Egg Salad

serves 4

8 hard-boiled eggs
125ml/4floz mayonnaise
1 tablespoon Dijon mustard
$^1/_2$ teaspoon salt
$^1/_4$ teaspoon freshly ground
   black pepper
30g/1oz finely chopped celery
   (optional)

Chop the eggs roughly, or push them through the large-holed side of a box grater.

In a large mixing bowl, mix the eggs with the mayonnaise, mustard, salt and pepper. Stir in the chopped celery, if using. Serve immediately.

Per serving: Net Carbs: 1.6g • Fibre: 0.2g • Protein: 11.2g
Fat: 32.7g • Calories: 355

Not Just Another Tossed Salad

Sauté the prawns in the garlic oil in a frying pan until they turn pink. Allow to cool, then refrigerate them while you prepare the salad.

Tear the spinach and lettuce leaves Into bite-size pieces then toss all the vegetables and bacon together in a bowl.

Make the dressing by beating the eggs, lemon juice, oil, cheese and salt together.

Top the lettuce salad with the prawns, then drizzle the dressing over the top and serve.

> Per serving: Net Carbs: 4.1g • Fibre: 2.9g • Protein: 24.5g
> Fat: 25g • Calories: 346

serves 8

900g/2lb large prawns, peeled
  and deveined
60ml/2floz garlic oil
225g/8oz fresh spinach,
  washed and dried
1 small round lettuce, washed
  and dried
80g/3oz black olives, stoned
  and sliced
60g/2¹/₂ oz celery, diced
5 spring onions, chopped
6 radishes, sliced
80g/3oz cauliflower florets,
  blanched and diced
1 avocado, stoned, peeled
  and diced
8 rashers crispy cooked bacon,
  crumbled
2 soft-boiled eggs (boiled for
  2 minutes), peeled and
  chopped
60ml/2floz fresh lemon juice
60ml/2floz groundnut oil
30g/1oz grated Parmesan
  cheese
salt to taste

Salad Niçoise

serves 12

2 teaspoons Dijon mustard
2 tablespoons wine vinegar
1$^{1}/_{2}$ teaspoons salt
2 cloves garlic, peeled and
    finely chopped
90ml/3floz olive oil
90ml/3floz groundnut or
    vegetable oil
freshly ground black pepper
    to taste
1 teaspoon chopped fresh
    thyme, or $^{1}/_{2}$ teaspoon dried
900g/2lb green beans
2 green peppers
4 celery sticks
280g/10oz cherry tomatoes
3 x 200-g/7-oz cans tuna,
    drained
1 x 60-g/2$^{1}/_{2}$ oz can anchovies,
    drained
10 stuffed green olives
10 black olives, stoned
1 large or 2 small red onions,
    peeled and very finely
    sliced
2 tablespoons chopped basil
5 tablespoons finely chopped
    parsley
40g/1$^{1}/_{2}$ oz spring onions, finely
    chopped
6 hard-boiled eggs, quartered

Combine the mustard, vinegar, salt, garlic, olive oil, groundnut or vegetable oil, pepper and thyme in a bowl to make the dressing. Beat until well blended, then set aside.

Pick over the beans and break into 3.5-cm/1$^{1}/_{2}$-in lengths. Place them in a saucepan and cook in salted water until crisp but tender. Run under cold water and drain in a colander, then set aside.

Remove the cores, seeds and white membranes from the green peppers. Cut the peppers into thin rounds and set aside.

Trim the celery stalks, cut crossways into thin slices and set aside.

In a large salad bowl make a more or less symmetrical pattern of the green beans, peppers, celery and tomatoes. Flake the tuna and add to the bowl. Arrange the anchovies on top and scatter the olives over the salad.

Scatter the onion slices over the salad and sprinkle with basil, parsley and spring onions. Pour over the dressing and top with the hard-boiled eggs.

Per serving: Net Carbs: 5.1g • Fibre: 2.5g • Protein: 20.2g
Fat: 22.2g • Calories: 308

Roquefort Dressing

Whisk together all the ingredients, except the cheese, until well combined. Refrigerate until needed, then stir in the cheese just before serving.

Per tablespoon serving: Net Carbs: 0.2g • Fibre: 0g
Protein: 0.7g • Fat: 10g • Calories: 92

serves 8

60ml/2floz tarragon vinegar
$1/4$ teaspoon salt
$1/4$ teaspoon freshly ground
   black pepper
90ml/3floz olive oil
2 tablespoons double cream
$1/2$ teaspoon fresh lemon juice
30g/1oz Roquefort cheese,
   crumbled

Lime Dill Dressing

Whisk together all the ingredients, except for the olive oil, in a small bowl. Slowly add the oil a little at a time, whisking continuously. Refrigerate for 30 minutes before using.

Per 2-tablespoon serving: Net Carbs: 0.5g • Fibre: 0g
Protein: 0g • Fat: 23g • Calories: 215

serves 10

1 teaspoon Dijon mustard
60ml/2floz fresh lime juice
$1/4$ teaspoon salt
1 clove garlic, peeled and finely
   chopped
1 tablespoon dill, finely chopped
pinch granular sugar substitute
250ml/8floz extra-virgin
   olive oil

Italian Dressing

Place all the ingredients in a screw-top jar and shake well. Refrigerate. Shake again before serving.

Per 2-tablespoon serving: Net Carbs: 0.4g • Fibre: 0g
Protein: 0g • Fat: 15g • Calories: 152

serves 7

125ml/4floz olive oil
60ml/2floz wine vinegar
1 clove garlic, peeled and chopped
$1/2$ teaspoon dried oregano
$1/2$ teaspoon dried basil
$1/2$ teaspoon salt
$1/4$ teaspoon freshly ground
   black pepper

House Dressing

Put all the ingredients in a screw-top jar and shake until well blended. Refrigerate until needed.

> Per 2-tablespoon serving: Net Carbs: 0.4g • Fibre: 0g
> Protein: 0.1g • Fat: 19g • Calories: 168

serves 5

2 tablespoons olive oil
60ml/2floz vegetable oil
2 tablespoons tarragon vinegar
1 teaspoon salt
1 teaspoon Dijon mustard
1/2 teaspoon crushed garlic
1 tablespoon mayonnaise
1/4 teaspoon granular sugar
   substitute

Thousand Island Dressing

Mix the spring onions, pickle and tomatoes together in a bowl. Add the rest of the ingredients and mix well. Refrigerate until needed.

> Per 2-tablespoon serving: Net Carbs: 1.4g • Fibre: 0.5g
> Protein: 1.4g • Fat: 10.7g • Calories: 104

serves 10

6 spring onions, chopped
1 large dill pickle, chopped
2 tomatoes, peeled, chopped
   and deseeded
1/2 teaspoon garlic powder
1 teaspoon salt
1 tablespoon olive oil
1 tablespoon tarragon vinegar
125ml/4floz mayonnaise

Curry Dressing

Place all the ingredients in a screw-top jar and shake well. Refrigerate until needed.

> Per 2-tablespoon serving: Net Carbs: 0.8g • Fibre: 0.1g
> Protein: 0.1g • Fat: 16g • Calories: 145

serves 7

60ml/2floz white wine vinegar
2 tablespoons olive oil
90ml/3floz sunflower oil
1 teaspoon fresh lemon juice
1 teaspoon curry powder
1/4 teaspoon garlic powder
1 teaspoon sesame seeds
1/2 teaspoon salt

Creamy Celery-seed Dressing

Place all the ingredients in a screw-top jar and shake well. Refrigerate until needed. Shake again before serving.

> Per a tablespoon serving. Net Carbs: 0.8g • Fibre: 0g
> Protein: 0.3g • Fat: 10g • Calories: 97

serves 10

90g/3½oz sour cream
110g/4oz mayonnaise
2 tablespoons passata or
   tomato purée
½ teaspoon Worcestershire
   sauce
1 teaspoon crushed celery
   seeds
½ teaspoon salt
¼ teaspoon freshly ground
   black pepper

Vinaigrette Cream Dressing

Mix the vinegar, salt and pepper together, then add the oil, olives, parsley, sour cream and chopped egg yolk.

Beat well with a fork and chill for several hours before serving.

> Per 2 tablespoon serving: Net Carbs: 0.2g • Fibre: 0g
> Protein: 0.2g • Fat: 11g • Calories: 96

serves 16

60ml/2floz tarragon vinegar
¾ teaspoon salt
¼ teaspoon cracked pepper
175ml/6floz olive oil
1 teaspoon green olives, stoned
   and finely chopped
1 teaspoon chopped parsley
2 tablespoons sour cream
1 yolk from a hard-boiled egg,
   finely chopped

Main Courses

Meat
Poultry
Fish and Seafood
Pasta
Vegetables
Sauces

MEAT

During Induction (and the following stages) you can eat any kind of meat – beef, pork, veal, lamb or beef – either grilled, roasted or pan-fried. You can also choose from a variety of delicious burgers, as well as Steak au Poivre, Stuffed Leg of Lamb, Luscious Lamb, Loin of Lamb with Horseradish Cream, Roast Veal, Veal Scalloppine, Veal Stew, Mother's Pot Roast, Spicy Spare Ribs and Calf's Liver in Red Wine.

In OWL you can extend your choice by including Steak Pizzaiola, Beef Stir-fry and Moussaka. You will need to wait until Pre-Maintenace to have the Dolma.

Steak au Poivre

serves 4

4 sirloin steaks, pounded to
　3-mm/^{1}/8-in thickness
freshly ground black pepper,
　to taste
90g/3^1/2 oz butter
2 teaspoons dried rosemary
　leaves, crumbled, or
　1 tablespoon fresh, finely
　chopped
2 teaspoons dried sage leaves,
　crumbled, or 1 tablespoon
　fresh, finely chopped
125ml/4floz cognac, warmed
185ml/6floz double cream
2 teaspoons Worcestershire
　sauce
2 tablespoons Dijon mustard

Cover both sides of the sirloin steaks with the ground black pepper, pressing it firmly into the steaks.

Melt the butter in a large frying pan and add the rosemary and sage.

Add the steaks and brown quickly on both sides. Pour the warm cognac over the steaks and ignite. When the flame goes out, remove the steaks from the frying pan and keep warm.

Add the cream, Worcestershire sauce and mustard to the pan juices. Stir well and simmer for 3 minutes. Pour over the steaks and serve immediately.

> Per serving: Net Carbs: 3g • Fibre: 0.6g • Protein: 47g
> Fat: 67g • Calories: 886

Moussaka

serves 6

1 medium aubergine
40g/1½ oz unsalted butter
3 egg yolks
300ml/10floz water
60ml/2floz double cream
50g/2oz grated Parmesan
  cheese
90ml/3floz olive oil
1 large onion, peeled and
  chopped
1 large green pepper, chopped
2 cloves garlic, peeled and
  finely chopped
450g/1lb minced lamb or
  225g/8oz minced lean beef
250ml/8floz prepared tomato
  sauce or passata
1½ teaspoons ground cumin
¼ teaspoon grated nutmeg
¼ teaspoon dried oregano, or
  1 teaspoon fresh, chopped
2 teaspoons salt

Peel and slice the aubergine and arrange the slices on a large plate. Place the plate in the sink (the juices will run out) and cover with another large plate, allowing the plate to press down on the aubergine. Leave to drain for 30 minutes, then press each slice with kitchen paper to dry it.

Preheat the oven to 180°C/350°F/gas 4.

To prepare the cream sauce, place the butter in the top of a double boiler over hot water. Add the egg yolks one at a time and beat constantly with a rotary or hand electric beater. Add 60ml/2floz of the water, the cream and the Parmesan cheese. Continue to beat until the sauce thickens, which should take about 10 minutes. Set aside.

Heat a third of the olive oil in a large frying pan. Add the onion and green pepper and sauté until light golden brown. Add the garlic and meat and cook until browned.

Add the tomato sauce, remaining water, cumin, nutmeg, oregano and salt and simmer for 15 minutes.

Heat the remaining olive oil and sauté the aubergine slices until lightly browned. Drain on kitchen paper then place half the aubergine slices in a well-oiled baking dish. Spread with half the meat mixture then place the remaining aubergine slices on top and cover with the rest of the meat. Cover the top with the cream sauce and bake for 30 minutes until bubbling and golden brown.

> Per serving: Net Carbs: 9.1g • Fibre: 3.4g • Protein: 19.7g
> Fat: 37.7g • Calories: 462

Stuffed Leg of Lamb

Preheat the oven to 150°C/300°F/gas 2.

Melt half the butter in a heavy frying pan. Add the minced meat, onion and garlic and brown lightly. Pour the wine into the pan slowly and cook for 2 minutes. Add the tomato sauce or passata, dill and parsley and cook over a medium heat for 10 minutes, or until the liquid has been absorbed. Remove from the heat, then sprinkle with Parmesan cheese, salt and pepper.

Wipe the lamb with damp kitchen paper and sprinkle with salt and pepper. Spread the minced meat mixture on to the lamb and roll up carefully with the minced meat inside. Use skewers to fasten the lamb securely or tie with string.

Melt the remaining butter in a medium-size roasting tin. Add the lamb and brown over a medium heat.

Bake for 2 hours or until the meat is tender. (If the tin gets dry, add 2 or 3 tablespoons water.)

serves 8

30g/1oz butter
450g/1lb minced veal or beef
30g/1oz onion, peeled and chopped
1 clove garlic, peeled and finely chopped
125ml/4floz white wine
250ml/8floz prepared tomato sauce or passata
1 tablespoon chopped dill
1 tablespoon chopped parsley
50g/2oz grated Parmesan cheese
salt and freshly ground black pepper to taste
1 leg of lamb, boned and flattened

> Per serving: Net Carbs: 2.7g • Fibre: 0.5g • Protein: 40g
> Fat: 21g • Calories: 467

Spicy Spare Ribs

Preheat the oven to 230°C/450°F/gas 8.

Place a single layer of ribs, meaty side down, in a shallow roasting tin. Roast for 30 minutes, then drain off the fat.

Combine the rest of the ingredients and sprinkle evenly over the ribs.

Turn the oven down to 180°C/350°F/gas 4. Roast the ribs, meaty side up, for a further 30 minutes to 1 hour for pork spare ribs. Beef ribs will take about 1 to 1^1/$_2$ hours.

serves 4

1.8 kg/4lb pork spare ribs, or beef ribs
1 tablespoon paprika
2 teaspoons chilli powder
^{3}/$_4$ teaspoon salt
^{1}/$_2$ teaspoon dry mustard
^{1}/$_4$ teaspoon garlic powder
^{1}/$_8$ teaspoon freshly ground black pepper

> Per serving: Net Carbs: 1g • Fibre: 1g • Protein: 61g
> Fat: 64g • Calories: 844

Luscious Lamb

serves 4

8 lamb chops
1/2 teaspoon garlic powder
30g/1oz butter
2 tablespoons Worcestershire
    sauce
2 tablespoons fresh lemon juice
2 tablespoons gin
1 teaspoon salt

Rub the lamb chops with a small amount of garlic powder and place in a dish.

Melt the butter in a small pan and add the Worcestershire sauce, lemon juice, gin and salt. Pour the liquid over the lamb chops and allow to marinate in the refrigerator for 30 minutes.

Remove the lamb from the marinade and grill or barbecue to desired doneness.

Meanwhile, boil the marinade in a small saucepan for 2 minutes. Top the lamb with the marinade before serving.

> Per serving: Net Carbs: 2.1g • Fibre: 0g • Protein: 41g
> Fat: 21g • Calories: 392

Veal Scaloppine

serves 4

675g/1 1/2 lb veal, cut in
    escalopes 5mm/1/4in thick
salt and freshly ground black
    pepper to taste
90g/3 1/2 oz butter
250ml/8floz Chicken Stock
    (see page 61)
60ml/2floz dry white wine
450g/1lb porcini mushrooms,
    sliced
2 tomatoes, peeled and chopped
1 clove garlic, peeled and
    finely chopped
25g/1oz Parmesan cheese,
    grated

Preheat the grill.

Pat the salt and pepper onto both sides of the veal.

In a frying pan melt 50g/2oz of the butter, then add the veal and fry until brown. Remove from the pan and keep warm.

Pour the *Chicken Stock* and wine into the pan. Simmer until the liquid reduces by half then pour into a jug and keep warm until needed.

Sauté the mushrooms in the remaining butter until brown. Add the tomatoes and garlic and simmer for 5 minutes.

Place the mushroom mixture in a baking dish, add the veal and cover with the wine sauce. Sprinkle with grated Parmesan cheese and grill until the cheese is brown and bubbly. Serve immediately.

> Per serving: Net Carbs: 2.6g • Fibre: 1.2g • Protein: 25g
> Fat: 12.5g • Calories: 237

Mother's Roast Beef

Rub the garlic powder and salt into the meat and place in the refrigerator for 30 minutes.

Place the onions and garlic in a food processor. Push the tomatoes through a sieve to rid them of seeds, then add the tomato pulp to the food processor. Purée together.

Place the meat in a large pot or casserole dish. Cover with the tomatoes and *Beef Stock*, then cover the pot and simmer for 1½ hours. Turn the meat and simmer for about 1 hour more or until fork-soft. Add water if needed. Remove the meat from the pot to a cutting board to cool, then slice.

Place the sauce in the refrigerator and remove any fat that rises to the top. Place the meat in the sauce, reheat and serve, garnished with parsley, if desired.

serves 6

½ teaspoon garlic powder
1 teaspoon salt
1.7kg/4lb top rump of beef
2 medium onions, peeled and
  sliced
2 cloves garlic, peeled
3 tomatoes, skinned and
  quartered
250ml/8floz Beef Stock (see
  page 60)
parsley, to garnish

Per serving: Net Carbs: 3.3g • Fibre: 1g • Protein: 56g
Fat: 37g • Calories: 582

Steak Pizzaiola

Combine the garlic oil with half the olive oil, the vinegar, pepper and 1 teaspoon of water. Place the steak in the mixture and marinate in the refrigerator for at least 2 hours.

Heat the remaining olive oil, and add the tomatoes, garlic, parsley, oregano, salt and pine kernels. Cook over a medium heat for 3 minutes. Remove from the heat, add the sugar substitute, if using, and keep warm.

Grill the steak to preferred doneness, slice and pour the sauce over the top of it. Serve immediately.

serves 6

30ml/1floz garlic oil
60ml/2floz olive oil
30ml/1floz tarragon vinegar
¼ teaspoon cracked black
  pepper
1.4kg/3lb sirloin steak
8 plum tomatoes, cut into strips
2 cloves garlic, peeled and
  crushed
1 tablespoon chopped parsley
1 teaspoon dried oregano, or
  1 tablespoon fresh, chopped
⅛ teaspoon salt
40g/1½ oz pine kernels
1 teaspoon granular sugar
  substitute (optional)

Per serving: Net Carbs: 4.6g • Fibre: 1.4g • Protein: 45g
Fat: 45g • Calories: 614

Beef Stir-fry

serves 4

675g/1½ lb beef fillet
90ml/3floz spicy sesame oil
60ml/2floz Tamari soy sauce
freshly ground black pepper to
    taste
225g/8oz shiitake mushrooms,
    sliced thinly
1 onion, peeled and thinly sliced
125g/4½ oz bamboo shoots,
    cut into thin strips
3 celery sticks, cut into thin
    strips
225g/8oz spinach, steamed,
    drained well and chopped
2 tablespoons sake
125ml/4floz Beef Stock
    (see page 60)

Cut the meat into thin strips and sauté in a large frying pan using half the sesame oil. Brown the meat on both sides. Sprinkle the meat with half the soy sauce and the pepper, then remove from the pan.

Put the mushrooms, onion, bamboo shoots and celery into the frying pan with the remaining oil and sauté for 3 minutes. Return the beef to the pan, add the spinach and toss everything together with the remaining soy sauce, sake and *Beef Stock*. Cook over a low heat for 3 minutes or to preferred doneness.

> Per serving: Net Carbs: 12.4g • Fibre: 4.6g • Protein: 36g
> Fat: 48g • Calories: 646

Roast Veal

serves 6

1 2–2.5kg/4½–5½ lb veal
    roast (leg, loin, rump,
    shoulder or breast) – ask
    the butcher to bone and tie
    the meat for you
1 clove garlic, peeled and cut
    into slivers
3 tablespoons olive oil
40g/1½ oz onion, chopped
2 celery sticks, finely chopped
4 anchovies (optional)
125ml/4floz white wine or
    Chicken Stock (see page 61)
225g/8oz thick-sliced bacon
    (streaky or back)

Preheat the oven to 170°C/325°F/gas 3.

Cut a few incisions in the veal and insert the garlic slivers.

Heat the oil in a roasting tin or a casserole dish and brown the veal. Add the onion, celery, anchovies, if using, and wine or *Chicken Stock* and arrange the bacon on top. Cover and cook in the oven for 30 minutes per 500g/1lb 2oz, basting occasionally.

Remove the veal from the pan and let it rest for 10 minutes. Remove the vegetables from the pan juices, skim off any excess fat, and pour the pan juices over the veal. Serve in slices, warm or cold, with *Vinaigrette Cream Dressing*, see page 89.

> Per serving: Net Carbs: 0.9g • Fibre: 0.5g • Protein: 66g
> Fat: 26.6g • Calories: 538

Dr Atkins' Fromage Burgers

serves 6

900g/2lb minced beef
1 tablespoon chopped chives
1 tablespoon chopped tarragon,
    or $^3/_4$ teaspoon dried
1 tablespoon chopped parsley
2 teaspoons salt
30g/1oz finely chopped spring
    onions
1 small tomato, finely chopped
1 egg, beaten
175g/6oz Cheddar cheese,
    coarsely grated
40g/1$^1/_2$ oz butter (optional)

Combine the beef, chives, tarragon, parsley, salt, spring onions, tomato and egg and mix well.

Shape the mixture into 12 equal-sized balls then flatten each ball to make a thin disc. Divide the grated cheese into 6 piles and press each pile of cheese together. Place 1 pile of the cheese in the centre of 6 of the meat discs. Place the second burger discs on top and press the edges together to seal them.

Dr Atkins cooked these on an outdoor barbecue. If one is not available, grill or sauté the burgers in butter in a non-stick frying pan for 5 minutes on each side.

Per serving: Net Carbs: 1.2g • Fibre: 0.3g • Protein: 37g
Fat: 38.5g • Calories: 506

Brit Burgers

serves 4

60g/2$^1/_2$ oz butter
60g/2$^1/_2$ oz chopped onion
560g/1$^1/_4$lb minced beef
$^1/_2$ teaspoon salt
$^1/_2$ teaspoon freshly ground
    black pepper
$^1/_2$ teaspoon chopped sage

Melt half the butter in a frying pan and sauté the onions until golden. Remove and set aside.

Combine the beef, salt, pepper and sage with the onions and mix well, then shape into burgers. In the same pan melt the remaining butter and sauté the burgers for 5 minutes on each side.

Per serving: Net Carbs: 1.1g • Fibre: 0.4g • Protein: 26.2g
Fat: 24g • Calories: 427

Veal Stew

3 rashers back bacon, diced
40g/1¹/₂ oz butter
1 tablespoon chopped onion
40g/1¹/₂ oz mushrooms, sliced
900g/2lb cubed stewing veal
125ml/4floz water or Chicken
    Stock (see page 61)
225g/8oz sour cream, plus extra
    for garnish
1 teaspoon salt
¹/₄ teaspoon paprika, plus extra
    for dusting

Preheat the oven to 120°C/250°F/gas 3/4.

Place the bacon, butter, onion and mushrooms in a frying pan and sauté slowly until the onion and bacon are lightly browned. Remove the mixture with a slotted spoon and place in an ovenproof serving dish.

Leave the bacon fat and butter in the frying pan, then add the veal. Brown the meat on all sides then remove, leaving the fat in the pan. Place the meat in the baking dish with the bacon mixture and mix well.

Add the water or *Chicken Stock*, sour cream, salt and paprika to the frying pan. Heat until just boiling then pour over the meat mixture. Cover the dish and bake for 1 hour, or until the veal is tender when pierced with a fork. If you wish, serve with a dollop of sour cream and dust with paprika.

> Per serving: Net Carbs: 4.2g • Fibre: 0.2g • Protein: 49g
> Fat: 29g • Calories: 480

Calf's Liver in Red Wine

serves 4

3 shallots or 1 small onion,
    peeled and finely chopped
125ml/4floz red wine
2 tablespoons fresh lemon juice
60ml/2floz olive oil
¹/₂ teaspoon dried oregano, or
    1¹/₂ teaspoons fresh, finely
    chopped
¹/₂ teaspoon salt
¹/₄ teaspoon freshly ground
    black pepper
450g/1lb calf's liver, sliced
60g/2¹/₂ oz butter

Combine the shallots, wine, lemon juice, oil, oregano, salt and pepper in a large bowl to make a marinade. Marinate the liver for 1 hour, then turn the meat and marinate for another hour.

Remove the liver from the marinade. Discard the marinade.

Melt the butter in a frying pan and sauté the liver for 5 minutes on each side.

> Per serving: Net Carbs: 7.3g • Fibre: 0.9g • Protein: 34g
> Fat: 41g • Calories: 572

POULTRY

During Induction (and any of the following stages) chicken, turkey, duck, goose and even quail and pheasant are all acceptable foods. You can therefore have a fantastic variety of meals during Induction, including Gourmet Poussins, Lemon-basted Roast Chicken, Austrian Paprika Chicken, Chicken Croquettes, Chicken Cacciatore and Ivan's Crispy Chicken.

You can vary your meals even more during OWL, when you can enjoy Spanish Summer Day Chicken, Chicken Stuffed with Goat's Cheese, Tandoori Chicken, Duck in Red Wine, Coq au Vin, Chicken Almandine, Joan's Chicken Mascarpone and Turkey Sausages. Wait until Pre-Maintenance to have Chicken Stir-fry.

Gourmet Poussins

serves 6

180g/6oz butter
185ml/6floz white port wine
2 tablespoons fresh tarragon
6 cloves garlic, peeled
1$\frac{1}{2}$ teaspoons salt
$\frac{3}{4}$ teaspoon freshly ground
   black pepper
2–3 tablespoons garlic powder
6 poussins, about 550g/1lb 4oz
   each

Preheat the oven to 200°C/400°F/gas 6.

Melt the butter in a saucepan. Add the wine and 1 tablespoon of the tarragon and heat thoroughly.

Place 1 clove garlic, $\frac{1}{2}$ teaspoon tarragon, $\frac{1}{4}$ teaspoon salt and $\frac{1}{8}$ teaspoon pepper in each poussin. Sprinkle the outside liberally with garlic powder and tie the legs together with string.

Place the poussins in a large shallow tin, or two smaller tins, without a rack. Pour the wine sauce over the poussins and roast for about 1 hour, or until well browned and the drumsticks twist easily. Baste frequently with sauce to keep the poussins moist.

> Per serving: Net Carbs: 3.6g • Fibre: 0.5g • Protein: 58g
> Fat: 77g • Calories: 1005

Chicken Cacciatore

serves 6

1 2.2kg/5lb chicken, jointed
    into 8 pieces
125ml/4floz olive oil
60g/2$^{1}/_{2}$oz butter
60g/2$^{1}/_{2}$oz chopped onion
225g/8oz shiitake mushrooms,
    sliced
3 cloves garlic, peeled
185ml/6floz dry white wine
2 bay leaves
1 teaspoon chopped basil
$^{1}/_{2}$ teaspoon freshly ground
    black pepper
80ml/2$^{1}/_{2}$floz prepared tomato
    sauce or passata
salt to taste

In a large frying pan, sauté the chicken in the olive oil until light golden brown – this should take about 20 minutes.

Melt the butter in a separate frying pan, then add the onion and mushrooms and sauté until golden. Add the garlic and cook for 4 more minutes.

Spoon the mushrooms, onions and garlic over the chicken and pour on the wine. Add the bay leaves, basil and pepper. Simmer for about 15 minutes, partially covered, then stir in the tomato sauce or passata and add salt to taste. Cook, uncovered, over a low heat for about 15 more minutes then serve.

> Per serving: Net Carbs: 7g • Fibre: 1.3g • Protein: 46g
> Fat: 52g • Calories: 708

Lemon-basted Roast Chicken

serves 4

4 chicken portions (legs or
    breasts with wings)
$^{1}/_{2}$ teaspoon dried oregano, or
    1$^{1}/_{2}$ teaspoons fresh, finely
    chopped
$^{1}/_{4}$ teaspoon garlic powder
60g/2$^{1}/_{2}$oz butter
salt and freshly ground black
    pepper to taste
90ml/3floz fresh lemon juice

Preheat the oven to 200°C/400°F/gas 6.

Sprinkle the chicken with the oregano and garlic powder. Melt the butter in a roasting tin or casserole dish, add the chicken and turn to coat. Sprinkle with salt and pepper.

Roast the chicken skin-side up, uncovered, for 30 minutes or until golden brown. Turn the pieces over and continue roasting until brown, about 30 more minutes. Squeeze the lemon juice over the chicken.

Cover and leave the chicken to rest in the turned-off oven for 15 minutes. Remove to a platter and serve.

> Per serving: Net Carbs: 2.2g • Fibre: 0.2g • Protein: 52g
> Fat: 25g • Calories: 461

Turkey Sausages

8 sausages

2 tablespoons garlic oil
1 small onion, peeled and
    finely chopped
1 clove garlic, peeled and
    finely chopped
450g/1lb minced turkey
3 tablespoons sour cream
110g/4oz breadcrumbs made
    from low carbohydrate
    bread
½ teaspoon finely chopped sage
½ teaspoon salt
1 tablespoon walnut oil

Heat the garlic oil in a non-stick frying pan. Add the onion and garlic and sauté until the onions are golden.

Mix all the other ingredients except the walnut oil together in a bowl. Add the onions and garlic and shape into 8 balls. Roll the balls into long sausages.

Heat the walnut oil in a frying pan and sauté the sausages until brown on both sides and cooked through.

Per sausage: Net Carbs: 6.1g • Fibre: 0.4g • Protein: 12g
Fat: 13.3g • Calories: 197

Tandoori Chicken

serves 4

1 x 2.2kg/5lb chicken, jointed
    into 8 pieces
4 cloves garlic
5-cm/2-in piece ginger root,
    peeled
2 bay leaves
2 teaspoons chilli powder
1 teaspoon salt
2 teaspoons turmeric
1 teaspoon ground coriander
2 teaspoons ground cumin
½ teaspoon ground cinnamon
½ teaspoon ground cloves
125ml/4floz olive oil
350g/12oz whole milk yogurt
90ml/3floz fresh lemon juice
fresh lemon wedges, to serve

Place the chicken in a covered glass baking dish large enough for the pieces to lie side by side.

Place the next 11 ingredients in a blender or food processor and blend to a paste.

Combine the paste with the yogurt and lemon juice.

Dip each piece of chicken into the mixture and coat it completely. Return the chicken to the baking dish and place in the refrigerator to marinate overnight.

Preheat the oven to 180°C/350°F/gas 4.

Wipe most of the marinade off the chicken with kitchen paper, then bake the chicken, covered, for 30 minutes in a large dish. Uncover the chicken, coat with a little more marinade and cook for a further 15 to 20 minutes until golden. Serve with lemon wedges.

Per serving: Net Carbs: 8.8g • Fibre: 2g • Protein: 76g
Fat: 68g • Calories: 969

Austrian Paprika Chicken

Preheat the oven to 180°C/350°F/gas 4.

Heat the butter and oil together in a frying pan. Brown the chicken carefully in the oil on all sides and add a pinch of salt. Remove the chicken from the pan.

Sauté the onions and garlic in the oil until the onions are golden. Add the paprika, *Chicken Stock* and sour cream stirring constantly until the mixture is smooth.

Place the chicken in a casserole dish and cover with the mixture, making sure the pan is well scraped of all drippings. Then bake, covered, for 1 hour.

> Per serving: Net Carbs: 7.4g • Fibre: 1.4g • Protein: 54g
> Fat: 42g • Calories: 647

serves 6

30g/1oz butter
30ml/1floz vegetable oil
1 x 2.2kg/5lb chicken, jointed
   into 8 pieces
pinch salt
4 small onions, peeled and
   quartered
1 clove garlic, peeled and finely
   chopped
2 tablespoons paprika
250ml/8floz Chicken Stock
   (see page 61)
230g/8oz sour cream

Chicken Croquettes

Preheat the oven to 190°C/375°F/gas 5.

Mix the chicken, egg whites, poultry seasoning and salt together well, then cool in the refrigerator for 30 minutes or until firm. Form into rough cylinders or croquettes 2.5cm/1in wide and 7.5cm/3in long. Heat the oil in a frying pan and cook for 4 to 5 minutes until crisp and cooked through.

> Per serving: Net Carbs: 0.5g • Fibre: 0g • Protein: 31g
> Fat: 13.9g • Calories: 248

serves 2

350g/12oz minced chicken
2 egg whites
1/4 teaspoon poultry seasoning
   (or pinch each of ground
   nutmeg and allspice)
pinch salt
vegetable oil, for deep frying

Duck in Red Wine

Preheat the oven to 180°C/350°F/gas 4.

Melt the butter or fat in a large frying pan. Add the pieces of duck and brown over a medium heat, then remove the duck with a slotted spoon to a casserole dish.

Add the garlic to the fat and cook for 1 minute.

Add the red wine, mushrooms, parsley, bay leaves, thyme and salt. Bring to the boil, stirring constantly, and cook until the sauce thickens.

Place the pickling onions and carrots into the casserole dish with the duck and pour over the sauce. Cover and bake for 1 hour.

Per serving: Net Carbs: 4.98 • Fibre: 1.3g • Protein: 31g
Fat: 22g • Calories: 440

serves 4

30g/1oz butter, or rendered
   duck or chicken fat
1 2.2–2.6kg/5lb–5lb 12oz
   duck, skin removed, jointed
   into 8 pieces
2 cloves garlic, peeled and
   finely chopped
500ml/16floz dry red wine
50g/2$^{1}/_{2}$oz mushrooms, thinly
   sliced
2 sprigs parsley, chopped
2 small bay leaves
1 teaspoon fresh thyme or
   $^{1}/_{4}$ teaspoon dried
1 teaspoon salt
8 small white pickling onions,
   peeled
2 carrots, peeled and quartered

Spanish Summer Day Chicken

serves 4

1 x 2.2 kg/5lb chicken, jointed
    into 8 pieces
60ml/2floz sunflower oil
2 cloves garlic, peeled
3 tablespoons fresh lemon juice
1 teaspoon grated orange zest
2 bay leaves
125ml/4floz vinegar
250ml/8floz white wine
250ml/8floz Chicken Stock (see
    page 61)
$\frac{1}{2}$ teaspoon freshly ground
    black pepper
salt to taste

Rinse the chicken and dry with kitchen paper.

Heat the oil in a frying pan and lightly brown the chicken over a medium heat. Transfer the chicken to a saucepan.

Combine the remaining ingredients and pour over the chicken. Simmer, covered, for 1 hour. Add more *Chicken Stock*, if necessary, to keep the chicken covered.

Serve warm or chilled.

> Per serving: Net Carbs: 3.1g • Fibre: 0.5g • Protein: 69g
> Fat: 61g • Calories: 891

Chicken Stuffed with Goat's Cheese

serves 4

60g/2$\frac{1}{2}$ oz goat's cheese,
    crumbled
20g/$\frac{3}{4}$oz finely chopped basil
1 tablespoon chopped sun-dried
    tomatoes in olive oil
$\frac{1}{4}$ small onion, peeled and
    finely chopped
$\frac{1}{2}$ teaspoon dried oregano, or
    1$\frac{1}{2}$ teaspoons fresh,
    finely chopped
$\frac{1}{2}$ teaspoon salt
4 skinless chicken breast fillets
60ml/2floz dry white wine

Preheat the oven to 180°C/350°F/gas 4. Oil a glass baking dish.

In a small bowl combine all the ingredients except the chicken and wine and blend well. Pound the chicken breasts until thin, then spread the mixture evenly on to the breasts and roll them up. Fasten with cocktail sticks.

Arrange the chicken in the baking dish so the rolled breasts do not touch each other. Pour the wine over the chicken rolls and bake for 45 minutes.

> Per serving: Net Carbs: 1.4g • Fibre: 0.3g • Protein: 33g
> Fat: 9.5g • Calories: 243

Chicken Stir-fry

serves 2

2 teaspoons sesame oil
2 tablespoons olive oil
2 teaspoons finely chopped
    ginger root
2 cloves garlic, peeled and
    finely chopped
4 skinless chicken breast fillets,
    cubed
4 large shiitake mushrooms,
    sliced thinly
2 spring onions, finely chopped
225g/8oz broccoli, coarsely
    chopped
1 tablespoon soy sauce
2 tablespoons rice wine vinegar

Heat the sesame oil and 2 teaspoons of the olive oil in a non-stick wok or frying pan. Do not allow the oil to smoke.

Add the ginger and garlic and stir-fry for 30 seconds. Add the chicken and mushrooms and stir-fry for 3 minutes more, then remove from the frying pan.

Heat the remaining olive oil in the wok or frying pan. Add the spring onions and broccoli and stir-fry for 1 minute. Return the chicken mixture to the wok and add the soy sauce and rice wine vinegar.

Remove the chicken and vegetables from the pan with a slotted spoon and place on a serving plate. Boil the sauce for 30 seconds then pour over the chicken.

> Per serving: Net Carbs: 17.3g • Fibre: 1.4g • Protein: 64g
> Fat: 27g • Calories: 571

Ivan's Crispy Chicken

serves 4

1 x 2.2kg/5lb chicken, jointed
    into 8 pieces
60ml/2floz garlic oil
60ml/2floz white wine
1 red onion, peeled and thinly
    sliced
salt to taste
30g/1oz Jarlsberg cheese,
    grated
30g/1oz mature Cheddar
    cheese, grated

Preheat the oven to 180°C/350°F/gas 4.

Rinse the chicken and dry with kitchen paper, then brush with the garlic oil. Place in a baking dish and sprinkle over the wine. Cover with the onions, add salt and bake, covered, for 30 minutes.

Uncover the pot, sprinkle with the cheeses and bake uncovered until the chicken, onions and cheeses are crisp, about 45 minutes.

> Per serving: Net Carbs: 2.8g • Fibre: 0.5g • Protein: 73g
> Fat: 80g • Calories: 1052

FISH AND SHELLFISH

You can have any fish or shellfish during Induction (and the following stages), which means that you once again have a huge selection of seafood from which to choose and create meals. As well as simply grilling, frying or baking fish or shellfish, while you are on Induction why not try Lime-seared Tuna, Curried Crab, Sole with Sour Cream, Fennel Red Mullet, Halibut Roll-ups or Tuna Bake.

In OWL the choice gets even larger, with exotic Prawn Stir-fry, Parmesan Prawns, Swordfish Topped with Goat's Cheese and Crab and Almond Pie. By Pre-Maintenance you can savour the delicious Seafood Ceviche.

Seafood Ceviche

serves 4

450g/1lb whitefish (or trout),
   cut into bite-size pieces
450g/1lb medium prawns,
   shelled and deveined
450g/1lb queen scallops
185ml/6floz fresh lime juice
185ml/6floz fresh lemon juice
1 teaspoon finely chopped garlic
6 slices root ginger, peeled
1 medium red onion, peeled and
   thinly sliced
2 tablespoons chopped
   coriander

Rinse and dry the fish and shellfish on kitchen paper.

Mix all the remaining ingredients together and place in a glass baking dish just large enough to hold the fish, prawns and scallops.

Add the fish, prawns and scallops to the baking dish and toss well. Refrigerate for 4 to 6 hours until the fish and shellfish are opaque and appear to have been cooked. This can be drained and kept in the refrigerator for one day. Serve cold.

> Per serving: Net Carbs: 14g • Fibre: 1g • Protein: 64g
> Fat: 9.5g • Calories: 406

Prawn Stir-fry

serves 2

1 tablespoon vegetable oil
450g/1lb raw prawns, shelled
and deveined
1 tablespoon sesame oil
2 spring onions, chopped
1 clove garlic, peeled and finely
chopped
50g/2oz bean sprouts
$^1/_4$ head cabbage, shredded
2 tablespoons soy sauce
1 tablespoon rice wine vinegar
dash of granular sugar
substitute
paprika, to garnish

Heat the vegetable oil in a frying pan, add the prawns and sauté until almost cooked through. Tip the prawns onto a plate and keep warm.

Heat the sesame oil, add the spring onions, garlic, bean sprouts and cabbage to the frying pan, with 60ml/2floz water, and cook for 8 minutes, partially covered, until tender.

Return the prawns to the frying pan. Add the soy sauce, rice wine vinegar and sugar substitute. Mix well and cook for 2 to 3 minutes. Sprinkle with paprika, if desired.

Per serving: Net Carbs: 9.3g • Fibre: 3.6g • Protein: 50g
Fat: 18g • Calories: 425

Parmesan Prawns

serves 2

30ml/1floz olive oil
80g/3oz finely chopped onion
2 cloves garlic, peeled and
finely chopped
900g/2lb raw prawns, shelled
and deveined
225g/8oz prepared tomato
sauce or passata
$^1/_4$ teaspoon dried oregano, or
$^3/_4$ teaspoon fresh, finely
chopped
1 tablespoon finely chopped
basil
salt and freshly ground black
pepper to taste
225g/8oz mozzarella cheese,
shredded
20g/1$^1/_2$ oz Parmesan cheese,
grated

Preheat the grill.

Heat 1 tablespoon of the oil in a frying pan. Sauté the onion until golden, add the garlic, and sauté for 1 minute. Add the prawns and sauté for 3 minutes, then remove from the pan and place in a baking dish.

Heat the remainder of the oil in the frying pan and add the tomato sauce or passata, oregano and basil. Simmer for 15 minutes. Add salt and pepper. Pour the sauce over the prawns and add the shredded mozzarella cheese on top. Top with Parmesan and grill until bubbling.

Per serving: Net Carbs: 9.2g • Fibre: 1.3g • Protein: 59g
Fat: 24g • Calories: 510

Swordfish Topped with Goat's Cheese

Preheat the oven to 180°C/350°F/gas 4.

Rinse the swordfish and dry on kitchen paper. Sprinkle both sides with the lemon juice and place in a covered glass baking dish.

Spread the garlic purée evenly over the fish. Top with the dill, tomato and mushrooms. Sprinkle the olive oil and sunflower seeds evenly across the top. Spread the sugar snap peas over the fish, then pour the wine over the top.

Cover and place the fish in the oven for 20 minutes. Uncover, add the goat's cheese and cook for 10 minutes more, basting frequently.

> Per serving: Net Carbs: 9.1g • Fibre: 2.5g • Protein: 44g
> Fat: 22.5g • Calories: 440

serves 6

1.2kg/2lb 11oz swordfish steak
3 tablespoons fresh lemon juice
3 teaspoons garlic purée
2 tablespoons chopped dill,
   or 2 teaspoons dried
1 medium tomato, thinly sliced
225g/8oz shiitake mushrooms,
   sliced
45ml/1½ floz olive oil
80g/3oz shelled sunflower
   seeds
225g/8oz sugar snap peas,
   trimmed
60ml/2floz dry white wine
90g/3½ oz herbed goat's
   cheese, crumbled

Sole with Sour Cream

Preheat the oven to 180°C/350°F/gas 4.

Rinse and dry the fish on kitchen paper. Oil a baking dish just large enough to hold the fish fillets. Rub the fillets with the lemon juice, salt and pepper, then place in the dish.

Sprinkle the fish with tarragon. Cover with the sour cream and bake for 20 minutes, or until the fish flakes easily. Remove from the oven and sprinkle with the chives and parsley.

> Per serving: Net Carbs: 5.9g • Fibre: 0.1g • Protein: 41.5g
> Fat: 15g • Calories: 342

serves 6

1.4kg/3lb sole fillets
   (or plaice)
fresh lemon juice
salt and freshly ground black
   pepper
1 teaspoon dried tarragon, or
   1 tablespoon fresh, finely
   chopped
450g/1lb sour cream
½ tablespoon chopped chives
½ tablespoon chopped parsley

Fennel Red Mullet

serves 4

4 fillets of red mullet or
 snapper, about 675g/1¹/₂ l b
60g/2¹/₂ oz butter, softened
1 teaspoon fennel seeds,
 roughly crushed
¹/₂ teaspoon fresh lemon juice
1 teaspoon chopped tarragon
1 clove garlic, peeled and finely
 chopped
salt and freshly ground black
 pepper to taste
1 small fennel bulb, finely sliced

Preheat the oven to 200°C/400°F/gas 4.

Rinse the fish and dry on kitchen paper.

Combine half the butter, the fennel seeds, lemon juice, tarragon, garlic, salt and pepper. Spread the mixture on the fish fillets. Roll up the fillets and fasten with cocktail sticks to secure them.

Melt the rest of the butter in a frying pan and sauté the sliced fennel until tender, then add the fish and sauté until tender. Place the fish in a baking dish. Top with the fennel, cover and bake for 20 minutes, until the fish is cooked.

> Per serving: Net Carbs: 2.9g • Fibre: 2g • Protein: 46g
> Fat: 18g • Calories: 374

Halibut Roll-ups

serves 4

900g/2lb halibut fillets
salt
3 rashers streaky bacon, diced
125g/4¹/₂ oz shiitake
 mushrooms, sliced
30g/1oz diced celery
20g/³/₄oz diced onion
1 clove garlic, peeled and finely
 chopped
1 tablespoon chopped parsley
50g/2oz unsalted butter, melted
125ml/4floz dry white wine
20g/³/₄oz Parmesan cheese,
 grated
paprika to taste

Preheat the oven to 180°C/350°F/gas 4.

Rinse the fish and dry on kitchen paper. Sprinkle the fish with salt and allow to stand for about 10 minutes.

In a frying pan, sauté the bacon, mushrooms, celery and onion until the vegetables are soft and the bacon is crisp. Add the garlic and cook for 2 minutes, then add the parsley and blend well. Spread the mixture over the fillets, roll up, and fasten with cocktail sticks.

Place one third of the melted butter in the bottom of a glass baking dish and add the fish. Pour the remaining butter over the fish, and add the wine. Sprinkle the fish with the Parmesan cheese and paprika and bake for 30 minutes.

> Per serving: Net Carbs: 5.1g • Fibre: 0.9g • Protein: 39g
> Fat: 47g • Calories: 626

Lime-seared Tuna

Rinse the fish and dry on kitchen paper.

Mix the lime zest, salt, coriander, pepper and ginger together in a small bowl. Add 1 tablespoon of the olive oil and mix well to form a paste. Spread the paste on both sides of the tuna steaks.

Heat 1 tablespoon of olive oil in a large frying pan over a high heat. Sear the steaks for 2 to 3 minutes on each side for rare doneness. If you prefer your fish well done, increase the cooking time by 2 minutes per side.

While the fish is cooking, toss the rocket with the remaining olive oil and the vinegar. Add salt and pepper.

To serve, cut the tuna into 0.5-cm/^{1}/$_4$-in slices and lay over the rocket salad.

serves 4

2 tablespoons grated lime zest
2 teaspoons coarse salt
4 teaspoons roughly ground
   coriander seeds
1^1/$_2$ teaspoons freshly ground
   black pepper
1^1/$_2$ teaspoons ground ginger
4 tablespoons olive oil
4 (2.5cm/1-inch thick) tuna
   steaks (about 675g/1^1/$_2$lb)
280g/11oz rocket leaves
1 teaspoon red wine vinegar
salt and freshly ground black
   pepper

Per serving: Net Carbs: 1g • Fibre: 0.5g • Protein: 42g
Fat: 18g • Calories: 345

Tuna Bake

Preheat the oven to 180°C/350°F/gas 4.

Drain the tuna and flake it into a small bowl. Add the onion and capers to the fish.

In another bowl combine the mayonnaise, eggs, parsley, cream and salt and stir until smooth.

Add half the cream sauce to the fish and mix. Place the fish mixture in a buttered loaf tin or baking dish and bake for 30 minutes. To serve, slice the tuna bake and spoon the remaining cream sauce over the slices.

serves 4

500g/1lb 2oz canned tuna,
   drained
10g/^{1}/$_3$oz finely chopped onion
2 teaspoons capers
225g/8oz mayonnaise
2 eggs, lightly beaten
2 tablespoons finely chopped
   parsley
125ml/4floz double cream
^{1}/$_2$ teaspoon salt

Per serving: Net Carbs: 1.5g • Fibre: 0.1g • Protein: 40g
Fat: 65g • Calories: 767

Curried Crab

serves 4

2 tablespoons vegetable oil
120g/4^{1}/$_2$ oz chopped onion
2 tablespoons curry powder
185ml/6floz double cream
450g/1lb crabmeat, flaked and
    picked over
2 tablespoons chopped parsley
^{1}/$_4$ teaspoon crushed red
    pepper flakes
2 tablespoons fresh lemon juice
^{1}/$_2$ teaspoon salt
^{1}/$_2$ teaspoon freshly ground
    black pepper
60g/2^{1}/$_2$ oz Parmesan cheese,
    grated
30g/1oz butter
1 lemon, cut into wedges

Preheat the grill.

Heat the vegetable oil in a frying pan and sauté the onion until soft. Add the curry powder and cook, stirring constantly, for 1 minute. Then add the cream and cook until most of the liquid has been soaked up.

Stir in the crabmeat, parsley and red pepper flakes, and sauté for 2 minutes. Add the lemon juice, salt and pepper and sauté for 1 minute more.

Divide the crab mixture between 4 buttered scallop shells or small ramekins, sprinkle each serving with Parmesan, and dot the tops with butter. Place under the grill for 2 to 3 minutes, or until the cheese has melted. Serve with lemon wedges.

> Per serving: Net Carbs: 6.1g • Fibre: 2.1g • Protein: 32g
> Fat: 33g • Calories: 436

Crab and Almond Pie

serves 8

40g/1^{1}/$_2$ oz chopped toasted
    almonds (see Toasted Nuts,
    page 52)
2 eggs plus 2 extra egg yolks
2 teaspoons Dijon mustard
2 teaspoons salt
2 tablespoons chopped chives
225g/8oz fontina cheese,
    grated
115g/4oz frozen crabmeat,
    defrosted, or canned and
    drained
375ml/12floz double cream

Preheat the oven to 150°C/300°F/gas 2.

Place the toasted almonds on the bottom of a 23-cm/9-in shallow pie dish or ceramic quiche mould.

Put the eggs and extra yolks in a bowl and beat well. Add the mustard, salt, chives, cheese and crabmeat and mix well.

Pour the cream into a non-stick pan and scald it by bringing it right up to boiling point (but do not let it boil).

Add the cream to the crab mixture and pour into the pie dish. Bake for 1 hour.

> Per serving: Net Carbs: 2.6g • Fibre: 0g • Protein: 13.9g
> Fat: 27g • Calories: 324

Cannelloni

serves 4

1 recipe Pasta Crêpes (see page 140)
60g/2½ oz butter
3 chicken livers
1 chicken breast fillet
5 thin slices prosciutto ham
¼ teaspoon dried marjoram, or ¾ teaspoon fresh, finely chopped
75g/3oz Parmesan cheese, grated
1 recipe Cream Sauce (see page 156)

Preheat the oven to 120°C/250°F/gas ½.

Prepare 12 *Pasta Crêpes* and set aside.

Heat the butter in a frying pan, add the chicken livers and chicken breast and sauté until brown on both sides. Leave to cool, then process the livers, chicken breast and prosciutto in a food processor. Mix in the marjoram and 50g/2oz of the Parmesan cheese. Add 150ml/5floz of the *Cream Sauce* and mix.

Place 2 tablespoons of the chicken mixture in the centre of each crêpe and roll up the crêpe. Repeat for all the crêpes.

Butter a baking dish and place the crêpes seam-side down. Cover with the remaining sauce and Parmesan cheese and bake for 45 minutes.

> Per serving: Net Carbs: 5.2g • Fibre: 1g • Protein: 31g
> Fat: 36g • Calories: 480

Manicotti

serves 6

1 recipe Pasta Crêpes (see above)
375ml/12floz prepared tomato sauce or passata
450g/1lb ricotta cheese
180g/6oz mozzarella cheese
2 tablespoons chopped parsley
½ teaspoon chopped oregano
½ teaspoon salt
2 eggs
5 tablespoons grated Parmesan cheese

Preheat the oven to 150°C/300°F/gas 2.

Prepare 12 *Pasta Crêpes* and set aside. Cover the bottom of a large baking dish with a thin layer of tomato sauce or passata.

In a bowl mix the ricotta and mozzarella cheeses, parsley, oregano, salt, eggs and 2 tablespoons of the Parmesan cheese. Place about 3 full tablespoons of the ricotta mixture in the centre of a crêpe. Roll the crêpe around the stuffing, then place in a baking dish, seam-side down. Repeat with each crêpe, placing them side by side in an ovenproof dish. Pour the remaining sauce over the crêpes, sprinkle the remaining Parmesan cheese on top and bake for 20 minutes.

> Per serving: Net Carbs: 9.5g • Fibre: 1.9g • Protein: 24.5g
> Fat: 24.5g • Calories: 370

Baked Spinach

Preheat the oven to 180°C/350°F/gas 4.

Heat the olive oil and butter in a frying pan, then add the onion, garlic and prosciutto. Fry slowly until the onion is light brown, then add the onion mixture to the spinach and place in a baking dish.

Beat the eggs with the cream and add the pepper. Pour the mixture over the spinach and sprinkle with Parmesan cheese.

Bake for 30 minutes, or until set.

Per serving: Net Carbs: 2.1g • Fibre: 0.9g • Protein: 11.7g
Fat: 17.8g • Calories: 217

Serves 4

1 tablespoon olive oil
1 tablespoon butter
30g/1oz finely chopped onion
1 clove garlic, peeled and finely
    chopped
2 slices prosciutto, diced
140g/5oz cooked spinach, well
    drained and chopped
5 eggs
45ml/1¹⁄₂ floz double cream
pinch of freshly ground black
    pepper
20g/³⁄₄oz Parmesan cheese,
    grated

Chinese Mangetout

Heat the oil in a heavy frying pan. Add the onion, garlic, salt and water chestnuts and sauté until the onion is golden. Add the mangetout, soy sauce and *Chicken Stock*. Cover and cook for 5 minutes, then uncover and cook for 3 more minutes.

Per serving: Net Carbs: 6.8g • Fibre: 2.4g • Protein: 4.5g
Fat: 8.1g • Calories: 122

Serves 4

2 tablespoons vegetable oil
1 onion, peeled and finely
    chopped
1 clove garlic, peeled and finely
    chopped
¹⁄₂ teaspoon salt
40g/1¹⁄₂ oz water chestnuts,
    sliced
225g/8oz mangetout
1 tablespoon Tamari soy sauce
60ml/2floz Chicken Stock
    (see page 61)

Stuffed Aubergine

Preheat the oven to 180°C/350°F/gas 4.

Wash the aubergines but do not peel them. Parboil the whole aubergines in salted boiling water for 5 minutes. Remove from the water and cut in half lengthways. Spoon out the centre pulp carefully and chop, leaving about a 5-mm/$\frac{1}{4}$-in shell.

Melt the butter in a saucepan. Add the onion and garlic and sauté for 3 minutes. Add the meat and aubergine pulp and cook, stirring continuously. Brown lightly, then add the tomato sauce or passata, cumin, parsley, salt and pepper. Cook over a low heat until all the liquid has been absorbed.

Place the aubergine shells in a lightly oiled roasting tin or large casserole dish and stuff with the meat mixture.

Beat the egg, water and lemon juice together and pour over the aubergines. Sprinkle with Parmesan cheese and bake for 20 minutes until lightly browned.

Per serving: Net Carbs: 12.5g • Fibre: 7.5g • Protein: 19.3g
Fat: 16.2g • Calories: 294

Serves 8

4 aubergines
30g/1oz butter
40g/1$\frac{1}{2}$ oz chopped onion
1 clove garlic, peeled and finely
   chopped
450g/1lb minced beef or lamb
250ml/8floz prepared tomato
   sauce or passata
1 teaspoon ground cumin
1 teaspoon chopped parsley
1 teaspoon salt
freshly ground black pepper
   to taste
1 egg
1 tablespoon water
1 tablespoon fresh lemon juice
30g/1oz Parmesan cheese,
   grated

Green Beans Almandine

serves 4

450g/1lb fresh or frozen
   stringless green beans
60g/2½ oz butter
225g/8oz shiitake mushrooms,
   sliced
½ teaspoon salt
30g/1oz sliced almonds

Top and tail the beans, if needed. Simmer in a small amount of water for 6 to 7 minutes.

Melt the butter in a frying pan and sauté the mushrooms until brown. Add the salt and almonds.

Add the beans to the frying pan and toss well. Simmer for 4 minutes and add more salt if needed. Serve hot.

> Per serving: Net Carbs: 9.4g • Fibre: 3.8g • Protein: 3.4g
> Fat 19g • Calories: 230

Cauliflower Cheese

serves 6

30g/1oz butter
½ onion, peeled and finely
   chopped
4 cloves garlic, peeled and
   finely chopped
225g/8oz cauliflower, chopped
2 eggs, beaten
110g/4oz Parmesan cheese,
   grated
5 rashers streaky bacon, cooked
   until crisp then crumbled

Preheat the oven to 180°C/350°F/gas 4.

Heat the butter in a frying pan. Add the onion and garlic and sauté until the onion turns golden. Add the cauliflower and continue to sauté for 1 minute more. Transfer to a bowl and add the eggs, Parmesan cheese and crumbled bacon. Mix well, then spoon into a buttered baking dish and bake for 1 hour or until brown.

> Per serving: Net Carbs: 5.2g • Fibre: 1.4g • Protein: 11.7g
> Fat: 14.2g • Calories: 191

Pesto Sauce

serves 6

1 clove garlic, peeled and
  crushed
60g/2½ oz fresh basil
20g/²/₃oz fresh parsley
30g/1oz Parmesan cheese,
  grated
¼ teaspoon salt
⅛ teaspoon freshly ground
  black pepper
60ml/2floz olive oil

In a food processor fitted with a steel blade, pulse the garlic until coarsely chopped. Add the basil, parsley, Parmesan cheese, salt and pepper; process until the herbs are finely chopped. While the processor is running, add the olive oil and process until just blended.

Per 2-tablespoon serving: Net Carbs: 0.5g • Fibre: 0.5g
Protein: 2.4g • Fat: 11g • Calories: 108

Tartare Sauce

serves 7

160ml/5floz mayonnaise
1 tablespoon tarragon vinegar
1 teaspoon finely chopped onion
1 teaspoon capers, drained
1 teaspoon finely chopped
  cornichons
1 teaspoon finely chopped olives
1 teaspoon finely chopped
  parsley

Combine all the ingredients together and mix well.

Store in a covered jar in the refrigerator. This will keep for several weeks.

Per 2-tablespoon serving: Net Carbs: 0.1g • Fibre: 0g
Protein: 0g • Fat: 18g • Calories: 164

Horseradish Cream

serves 10

125ml/4floz double cream
2 tablespoons grated
  horseradish
2 teaspoons Dijon mustard
1 teaspoon salt

Whip the cream until stiff.

Mix together the horseradish, mustard and salt, then carefully fold into the whipped cream.

Per 2-tablespoon serving: Net Carbs: 0.7g • Fibre: 0.1g
Protein: 0.3g • Fat: 4g • Calories: 39

Hot Barbecue Sauce

serves 10

30g/1oz butter
1 medium onion, peeled and
    chopped
1 clove garlic, peeled and finely
    chopped
60ml/2floz prepared tomato
    sauce or passata
2 tablespoons wine vinegar
Tabasco sauce to taste
2 tablespoons granular sugar
    substitute
1 teaspoon salt
1 teaspoon dry mustard
60ml/2floz water

Melt the butter in a saucepan and sauté the onion and garlic until golden. Add the remaining ingredients, bring to the boil and simmer for 15 minutes. Leave to cool, then store in a covered jar and refrigerate.

Per 2-tablespoon serving: Net Carbs: 3.2g • Fibre: 0.3g
Protein: 0.3g • Fat: 3g • Calories: 43

Fresh Lemon Sauce

serves 6

1 small clove garlic, peeled
$^1/_2$ teaspoon salt
125ml/4floz olive oil
60ml/2floz fresh lemon juice
2 tablespoons chopped onion
2 teaspoons sugar substitute
    (optional)
$^1/_2$ teaspoon dried thyme, or
    $1^1/_2$ teaspoons fresh, finely
    chopped
$^1/_2$ teaspoon grated lemon zest

Mash the garlic clove in a bowl. Add the salt, then mix in the oil and add the remaining ingredients. Chill to blend the flavours.

Per 2-tablespoon serving: Net Carbs: 2.2g • Fibre: 0.2g
Protein: 0.1g • Fat: 19g • Calories: 177

Mustard Sauce

Mix the ingredients together well and refrigerate.

> Per 2-tablespoon serving: Net Carbs: 2.2g • Fibre: 0.1g
> Protein: 1.2g • Fat: 4.4g • Calories: 54

serves 10

60ml/2floz Dijon mustard
230g/8oz sour cream
2 tablespoons chopped chives
1 teaspoon granular sugar
  substitute
salt and freshly ground black
  pepper to taste

Bolognese Sauce

Place the pork chops and the olive oil in a large heavy-based pan and cook until the chops are well-browned on both sides. Add the minced beef and brown, slowly breaking the mince up into small pieces.

Meanwhile, place the sausages in another heavy frying pan without any oil. Prick them with a fork and cook until well browned on all sides. Drain well, discard the fat and slice into 1-cm/^{1}/$_2$-in pieces. Add the sausage pieces to the pork chop mixture.

Add the tomato sauce or passata, water, garlic and salt to the meat mixture. Bring to a slow boil and allow to simmer for 3 hours, stirring occasionally. Add the oregano and thyme for the last 30 minutes.

Remove the pork chops from the sauce, chop up the meat and return to the sauce. Add sugar substitute to taste before serving.

Note: while this recipe is suitable for a crowd, if you are not going to use it within two days, you can freeze it in individual portions for up to one month.

> Per serving: Net Carbs: 4.9g • Fibre: 1g • Protein: 6.5g
> Fat: 8.9g • Calories: 138

serves 24

2 boneless pork chops
2 tablespoons olive oil
450g/1lb minced beef
450g/1lb mild or hot Italian
  sausages
1^1/$_2$ litres/2^1/$_2$ pints prepared
  tomato sauce or passata
750ml/1^1/$_4$ pints water
3 large cloves garlic, peeled and
  finely chopped
1 teaspoon salt
1 teaspoon dried oregano, or
  1 tablespoon fresh, finely
  chopped
1 teaspoon dried thyme, or
  1 tablespoon fresh, finely
  chopped
2–4 teaspoons granular sugar
  substitute, to taste

Puddings and Cakes

Puddings
Cakes
Biscuits
Drinks

PUDDINGS

Unlike most other weight-loss programmes, puddings are perfectly acceptable on Atkins as long as they are not sweetened with sugar and don't include bleached white flour. Fortunately, advances in sweeteners and the use of soy and nut flours allow for a variety of sweet delights. Your choices are fairly limited in Induction, when you will not be eating nuts or fruit of any kind, but you are allowed Confetti Mould. By the time you are in OWL, you can savour Frozen Blood Orange Mousse, Baked Cheesecake and Crêpes with Strawberry Coulis. In Pre-Maintenance you can enjoy Poached Peaches, Strawberry Parfait, Pineapple Cheesecake and Blueberry Crème Anglaise. In Lifetime Maintenance you can also have Coconut Panna Cotta, Almond Cheesecake, Lemon Pie and Chocolate Rum Pie.

Even ice cream is acceptable when you're doing Atkins, although like any treat, it should be consumed in moderation and only on occasion. Unfortunately, none of the ice cream recipes that follow are acceptable for Induction and only a few – including Vanilla, Butter Pecan, Coconut Macadamia and Coffee – are suitable for OWL. But when you get to Pre-Maintenance, it gets even better: you may add Chocolate, Chunky Chocolate Fudge, Raspberry Rapture and Maple Walnut Ice Cream, among other delights. And your reward for reaching Lifetime Maintenance includes Mocha Hazelnut Ice Cream, Raspberry Sorbet and Cantaloupe Granita.

Preparing these creamy delights is easy. All you need are these recipes and an ice cream maker. This may sound expensive but it need not be. Hand-churned ice cream makers are very low in price, and using them is easy. The preparation time is a little longer because the custard must be refrigerated for two hours before you can churn it. The electric machines start at about £30. The most economical require some available freezer space, as the custard is churned in a container you pre-freeze in your freezer. The entire process takes about half an hour once the prepared custard is cooled or chilled. You will rejoice at the way these ice cream makers make the pudding while you eat your main course.

Also available are electric ice cream makers with integral freezer units. These machines are more expensive, but offer the convenience of making ice cream at a moment's notice and the capability of making several batches of ice cream on the trot. Both types of machine make delicious ice creams from these recipes.

Ice Cream Custard

Heat the cream in a heavy-based saucepan over a low heat. Whisk in one egg yolk at a time. Add the vanilla pod scrapings and whisk until the custard begins to thicken. Remove from the heat and cool.

Beat one tablespoon of the sugar substitute at a time into the cooled custard.

Pour the mixture into an ice cream maker and churn according to the manufacturer's instructions. At this point the custard is ready to have recipe ingredients added that make it ice cream (see recipes that follow).

The custard can also be refrigerated as it is and used as a delicious, rich dessert, or you could whisk in a tablespoon of brandy or brandy flavouring and serve it over berries.

serves 6

500ml/16floz double cream
4 egg yolks
1/2 vanilla pod, slit open and
   scraped
5 tablespoons granular sugar
   substitute

Per serving: Net Carbs: 10.1g • Fibre: 0g • Protein: 3.8g
Fat: 34g • Calories: 361

Chocolate Ice Cream

Prepare the *Ice Cream Custard*.

Whisk in the cocoa powder and beat until smooth. Remove from the heat and whisk in the sugar substitute and dessert mix powder if using. Cool to room temperature, then place the custard in an ice cream maker and churn according to the manufacturer's instructions.

serves 8

1 recipe Ice Cream Custard (see
   above)
50g/2oz cocoa powder
2 tablespoons granular sugar
   substitute
2 tablespoons sugar-free
   chocolate dessert mix
   powder (optional)

Per serving: Net Carbs: 13.1g • Fibre: 2.2g • Protein: 4.2g
Fat: 27g • Calories: 302

Chunky Chocolate Fudge Ice Cream

serves 9

1 recipe Chocolate Ice Cream
(see page 165)
½ recipe Chocolate Fudge
(see page 218)

Prepare the *Chocolate Ice Cream* and *Chocolate Fudge* recipes.

Cut the fudge into 5-mm/¼-in squares and add to the ice cream maker just before the ice cream is ready.

> Per serving: Net Carbs: 15g • Fibre: 2.1g • Protein: 4.5g
> Fat: 27.5g • Calories: 318

Maple Walnut Ice Cream

serves 8

1 recipe Ice Cream Custard
(see page 165)
1 tablespoon maple or caramel
flavouring
30g/1oz unsalted butter
120g/4½ oz walnut halves
4 teaspoons granular sugar
substitute

Prepare the *Ice Cream Custard* and whisk in the maple or caramel flavouring.

Melt the butter in a small frying pan, then add the nuts and sauté for 1 minute. Sprinkle with the sugar substitute and mix well. Add the nuts to the custard and cool to room temperature. Place in an ice cream maker and churn according to the manufacturer's instructions.

> Per serving: Net Carbs: 11.9g • Fibre: 1g • Protein: 5.2g
> Fat: 39g • Calories: 409

Butter Pecan Ice Cream

serves 8

1 recipe Ice Cream Custard
(see page 165)
30g/1oz unsalted butter
110g/4oz pecan halves,
coarsely chopped
1 tablespoon granular sugar
substitute
1 teaspoon butterscotch
flavouring (optional)

Prepare the *Ice Cream Custard* and allow to cool.

Melt the butter in a small frying pan and add the nuts. Sauté for 1 minute, then sprinkle with the sugar substitute. Remove from the heat and mix well, coating the nuts.

Whisk the butterscotch flavouring, if using, and the nuts into the cooling custard mixture, then cool to room temperature.

Place in an ice cream maker and churn according to the manufacturer's instructions.

> Per serving: Net Carbs: 9.8g • Fibre: 1.2g • Protein: 4g
> Fat: 38g • Calories: 391

Coffee Ice Cream

serves 8

1 recipe Ice Cream Custard
(see page 165)
250ml/8floz very strong
decaffeinated coffee
1 tablespoon coffee flavouring
or liqueur

Prepare the *Ice Cream Custard*.

Brew the coffee using 500ml/16floz of water and 4 tablespoons of decaffeinated ground coffee. When brewed, simmer over a low heat until it reduces by half. Remove from the heat, whisk in the coffee flavouring or liqueur and allow to cool.

Whisk the cooled coffee mixture into the *Ice Cream Custard* and cool to room temperature. Place in an ice cream maker and churn according to the manufacturer's instructions.

> Per serving: Net Carbs: 8.7g • Fibre: 0g • Protein: 2.9g
> Fat: 25g • Calories: 279

Cantaloupe Granita

Purée the melon in a food processor fitted with a steel blade.

In a small saucepan bring the water, lime zest, lime juice and sugar substitute to the boil. Stir in the cantaloupe,

Pour into a 33-cm/13-inch by 3.5-cm/9-inch cake tin. Place in the freezer and scrape often with a fork to break up the layers of ice as they form.

serves 6

1 medium cantaloupe melon, peeled, deseeded and chopped
250ml/8floz water
1 teaspoon grated lime zest
60ml/2floz fresh lime juice
50g/2oz granular sugar substitute

Per serving: Net Carbs: 17g • Fibre: 0g • Protein: 1g
Fat: 0g • Calories: 70

Frozen Blood Orange Mousse

Stir the gelatine into the juice and leave for 5 minutes to soften.

Heat a third of the cream and the sugar substitute in a small saucepan over a medium heat until it has dissolved and is just hot. Add the gelatine mixture and stir until dissolved. Place the pan over an ice bath and gently whisk until it starts to thicken, which should take 2 to 4 minutes, then remove from the bath.

Using an electric whisk, whip the remaining cream to just stiff peaks, adding the rum gradually towards the end. Turn down the speed to medium and add the gelatine mixture in three additions, blending until smooth.

Spoon into four custard or soufflé cups. Cover with clingfilm and freeze for a minimum of 1 hour for a soft frozen texture or up to 3 days ahead. Leave the frozen mousse to stand at room temperature for 15 minutes before serving

serves 4

1 1/2 teaspoons granular gelatine
125ml/4floz unsweetened blood orange or ruby red grapefruit juice
250ml/8floz double cream
180g/6oz granular sugar substitute
2 tablespoons rum

Per serving. Net Carbs: 6.6g • Fibre: 0g • Protein: 2g
Fat: 22g • Calories: 244

Raspberry Sorbet

serves 8

250ml/8floz double cream
2 egg yolks
1 teaspoon lemon essence
6 tablespoons granular sugar
    substitute
120g/4^{1}/2 oz raspberries
1 teaspoon raspberry flavouring
125ml/4floz framboise (red
    raspberry liqueur)

Heat the cream in a saucepan over a low heat, then whisk in the egg yolks one at a time. Add the lemon essence and half the sugar substitute. Whisk until the mixture begins to thicken, then remove from the heat.

Rinse and dry the raspberries, place in a bowl and sprinkle with the rest of the sugar substitute. Add the raspberry flavouring and framboise and mix well. Whisk the raspberry mixture into the cream mixture and cool to room temperature.

Place the mixture in an ice cream maker and churn according to the manufacturer's instructions.

> Per serving: Net Carbs: 16.5g • Fibre: 1g • Protein: 1.7g
> Fat: 13g • Calories: 227

Coconut Panna Cotta

serves 6

500ml/16floz double cream
7^{1}/2 tablespoons granular sugar
    substitute
2 teaspoons granulated gelatine
3 tablespoons water
250ml/8floz plain whole milk
    yogurt
1^{1}/2 teaspoons coconut extract
few grains salt
1 teaspoon butter
40g/1^{1}/2 oz unsweetened
    coconut shards

Heat the cream and 6 tablespoons of the sugar substitute in a medium saucepan over a medium heat, and bring to a simmer, stirring to dissolve the sweetener. Sprinkle the gelatine over the water in a cup and leave to stand for 5 minutes.

Take the cream off the heat, stir in the gelatine and cool until it is just warm. Whisk in the yogurt, coconut extract and salt. Set the mixture over an ice bath and stirring, chill the mixture to a batter consistency. Pour through a strainer into six custard cups, cover with clingfilm and refrigerate until cold.

Meanwhile, heat the oven to 150°C/325°F/Gas 2. Melt the butter in a baking tin in the oven, add the coconut and toss to coat. Sprinkle with the rest of the sugar substitute, toss again, spread out and bake for 4 to 5 minutes, then cool. Turn out each panna cotta and top with a tablespoon of coconut shards.

> Per serving: Net Carbs: 17.7g • Fibre: 0.8g • Protein: 4g
> Fat: 35g • Calories: 367

Pastry Case

In a bowl beat the flour, butter, cream cheese, sour cream and sugar substitute, if using, until just combined. Shape into a disc and chill for 20 minutes.

Roll out the dough between two pieces of greaseproof paper to form a 30-cm/12-inch circle. Loosen the greaseproof paper, replace with new paper and turn over the dough. Continue to roll until the dough is 3mm/$\frac{1}{8}$in thick, replacing the greaseproof paper as needed.

Pick up the paper and invert the dough on to a pie dish. Peel off the paper and patch any tears. Crimp the edges and prick the bottom with a fork. Chill for 30 minutes in the freezer.

Meanwhile, preheat the oven to 220°C/425°F/gas 7.

Bake the pastry case for 18 minutes, lightly covered with foil, then remove from the oven and cool on a wire rack.

serves 8

120g/4$\frac{1}{2}$ oz soy flour
60g/2$\frac{1}{2}$ oz butter, softened
80g/3oz cream cheese, softened
1 tablespoon sour cream
6 teaspoons granular sugar
   substitute (optional)

> Per serving: Net Carbs: 2.2g • Fibre: 1.7g • Protein: 4.4g
> Fat: 13.5g • Calories: 152

Chocolate Rum Pie

In a pan over a medium heat melt the chocolate with a third of the cream, the water, cocoa powder and sugar substitute, whisking often to mix well. Remove from the heat and leave to cool to room temperature.

In a medium bowl, beat the remaining cream until soft peaks form. Stir in the chocolate mixture, rum and vanilla essence and mix well. Pour into the *Pastry Case* and chill for 3 hours, or until set.

serves 8

75g/3oz unsweetened chocolate
375ml/12floz double cream
60ml/2floz water
2 tablespoons unsweetened
   cocoa powder
300g/11oz granular sugar
   substitute
1$\frac{1}{2}$ tablespoons rum
1 teaspoon vanilla essence
1 pre-baked Pastry Case (see
   above)

> Per serving: Net Carbs: 31.6g • Fibre: 4.3g • Protein: 6.8g
> Fat: 22g • Calories: 355

Lemon Pie

In a saucepan over a medium heat combine the egg yolks, 160g/5^1/$_2$oz sugar substitute, the lemon zest, lemon juice and butter. Stir constantly for 5 to 7 minutes until the mixture is thick enough to coat the back of a spoon. Remove from the heat and strain through a fine sieve placed over a large bowl. Cover with clingfilm and refrigerate for 1 hour or until cool.

In a small heatproof bowl sprinkle the gelatine over the water. Leave to soften for 5 minutes, then heat until melted.

Meanwhile, beat the cream and the remaining 3 tablespoons of sugar substitute until soft peaks form, then slowly mix in the gelatine until well combined.

In three additions, fold the cream into the lemon mixture. Pour into the baked *Pastry Case* and chill for 3 hours or until set.

serves 12

6 large egg yolks, lightly beaten
160g/5^1/$_2$ oz plus 3 tablespoons granular
   sugar substitute
1 tablespoon grated lemon zest
175ml/6floz fresh lemon juice
6oz/180g unsalted butter
1^1/$_2$ teaspoons gelatine
1^1/$_2$ tablespoons water
375ml/12floz double cream
1 pre-baked Pastry Case (see page 177)

> Per serving: Net Carbs: 31.7g • Fibre: 2.9g • Protein: 12.6g
> Fat: 77g • Calories: 858

Strawberry Parfait

Sprinkle the strawberries lightly with ^{1}/$_8$ of a teaspoon of sugar substitute.

Mix the yogurt, remaining sugar substitute and almond or coconut essence together in bowl.

Spoon one-third of the yogurt mixture into the bottom of a tall glass. Top with half of the strawberries. Cover with most of the remaining yogurt, reserving about 2 tablespoons. Add the remaining strawberries, drizzle the remaining yogurt over the top and sprinkle with the almonds.

serves 1

60g/2^1/$_2$ oz ripe strawberries,
   sliced
2 teaspoons granular sugar
   substitute
125ml/4floz plain whole milk
   yogurt
^{1}/$_8$ teaspoon almond or coconut
   essence
1 tablespoon lightly toasted
   sliced natural almonds,
   lightly crushed

> Per serving: Net Carbs: 11g • Fibre: 3g • Protein: 6.5g
> Fat: 9g • Calories: 160

Crêpes with Strawberry Coulis

serves 5

125ml/4floz double cream
3 tablespoons water
1½ tablespoons granular sugar
    substitute
1 egg
1 egg white
2 tablespoons unsalted butter,
    melted
3 tablespoons soy flour
2 tablespoons wholewheat
    flour

Strawberry Coulis:
125g/4½ oz sliced strawberries
3 tablespoons water
1 tablespoon granular sugar
    substitute

125ml/4floz double cream,
    whipped to soft peaks

In a blender, mix the first six ingredients until smooth, then add the flours, blending until smooth. Transfer to a bowl and leave to stand for 10 minutes.

To make the coulis, clean the blender and purée the strawberries, water and sugar substitute until smooth.

Spray a 15-cm/6-inch non-stick frying pan with oil and heat over a medium-low heat. Spoon 2 tablespoons of batter into the frying pan and immediately tilt to coat the bottom. Cook until the bottom of the crêpe is evenly browned and the top is dry and set, which should take 40 to 60 seconds. Loosen around the edge and then under the crêpe with a small spatula and turn out onto a plate. Repeat to make nine more crêpes (stacking onto the first), spraying the pan each time. Cover the crêpes loosely with foil to keep warm.

To serve, fold two warm crêpes in half with the browned side facing out and arrange slightly overlapping. Spoon 2 tablespoons of the sauce over the top and add a dollop of cream in the centre.

Per serving: Net Carbs: 10.5g • Fibre: 1.6g • Protein: 46g
Fat: 24g • Calories: 268

Baked Cheesecake

serves 12

450g/1lb soft cream cheese, at
   room temperature
3 eggs
250ml/8floz crème fraîche or
   sour cream
8 tablespoons granular sugar
   substitute
scraped seeds from ½ vanilla
   pod

Preheat the oven to 180°C/350°F/gas 4.

Place all the ingredients in a blender or food processor and blend for 15 minutes. Pour the mixture into a 23-cm/9-in springform tin, then enclose the bottom and sides of the tin in a single piece of aluminium foil to prevent leaking.

Place the springform tin in a roasting tin of hot water in the oven. If the water evaporates, add more hot water as needed. Bake for 1 hour, then turn off the oven and leave in the oven for 1 hour before serving.

> Per serving: Net Carbs: 8.5g • Fibre: 0g • Protein: 5g
> Fat: 17.4g • Calories: 211

Pineapple Cheesecake

serves 4 to 6

225g/8oz cream cheese, at
   room temperature
2 eggs
175ml/6floz double cream
8 teaspoons granular sugar
   substitute
1 tablespoon fresh lime juice
¼ teaspoon freshly grated
   lime zest

Topping:
6 tablespoons unsweetened
   crushed pineapple in juice,
   drained

Preheat the oven to 160°C/325°F/Gas 3. Place six soufflé or custard cups in a large roasting tin.

Process all the ingredients except for the topping in a food processor and mix until smooth.

Pour the batter into the cups. Add boiling water to the roasting tin to come halfway up the sides of the cups, cover the tin with foil and bake for 30 minutes. Turn the oven off and leave the cups to stand for 20 minutes. Remove from the oven, uncover and cool completely. Cover with clingfilm and chill.

To serve, turn out of the cups and top each cheesecake with a tablespoon of the pineapple. Leave the cheesecakes to stand at room temperature for 15 minutes before serving.

> Per serving: Net Carbs: 7.3g • Fibre: 0.2g • Protein: 8.1g
> Fat: 33.5g • Calories: 356

Blueberry Crème Anglaise

Heat the cream in a saucepan to the point where bubbles start appearing around the edges.

Meanwhile, beat the egg yolks with the sugar substitute, cinnamon and nutmeg until thick and lemon-coloured.

Slowly beat half of the hot cream into the egg yolks. Then add the yolk mixture to the rest of the cream in the saucepan and cook over a medium heat, stirring constantly, until thickened to a thin batter consistency. Immediately pour the sauce into a bowl and cool completely, then refrigerate in an airtight container until cold.

To serve, share the blueberries equally between six cocktail glasses and pour the Crème Anglaise over the top.

serves 6

375ml/12floz double cream
3 egg yolks
50g/2oz granular sugar
    substitute
1/8 teaspoon ground cinnamon
1/8 teaspoon freshly ground
    nutmeg
350g/12oz fresh blueberries

Per serving: Net Carbs: 14g • Fibre: 1g • Protein: 2.8g
Fat: 24.5g • Calories: 270

Confetti Mould

Prepare the first three packets of jelly separately, using 375ml/12floz of water for each.

Refrigerate each jelly in a separate shallow dish until thoroughly firm, then dice each into tiny cubes.

Mix all three packets of the lemon jelly with 685ml/ 1 pint 3 fl oz of water and allow to thicken. When the mixture is very thick, but not firm, add the cream and allow to thicken again. Fold in all the diced jelly cubes and the vanilla essence then chill, in a decorative mould, until thoroughly firm.

serves 8

1 x 11.5g packet sugar-free
    strawberry jelly crystals
1 x 11.5g packet sugar-free lime
    jelly crystals
1 x 11.5g packet sugar-free
    orange jelly crystals
3 x 11.5g packets sugar-free
    lemon jelly crystals
250ml/8floz double cream
1 teaspoon vanilla essence

Per serving: Net Carbs: 0.9g • Fibre: 0g • Protein: 0.7g
Fat: 11.6g • Calories: 110

Poached Peaches

10 peach halves

5 ripe summer peaches, stoned
   and peeled, cut into halves
3 tablespoons water
1 tablespoon granular sugar
   substitute
1 teaspoon almond essence

Place the peaches and water in a small saucepan. Simmer, covered, for 20 minutes.

Add the sugar substitute and almond essence to the liquid in the pan and swirl to dissolve. If preferred, substitute raspberry flavouring for almond. Serve hot or cold.

> Per peach: Net Carbs: 10.8g • Fibre: 1.9g • Protein: 0.8g
> Fat: 1g • Calories: 58

Almond Cheesecake

serves 8

60g/2^1/2oz sliced almonds
50g/2oz plus 2 tablespoons
   granular sugar substitute
450g/1lb cream cheese,
   softened
80g/3oz unsweetened
   chocolate, melted and
   cooled
3 eggs
120ml/4floz double cream
^{3}/4 teaspoon almond essence
^{3}/4 teaspoon vanilla essence

Preheat the oven to 160°C/325°F/gas 3.

Butter eight 180-g/6-oz ramekins or custard cups.

In a food processor process the almonds with 2 tablespoons of the sugar substitute until finely ground. Coat the prepared ramekins with the almond crumbs, then place the ramekins in a roasting tin.

Beat the cream cheese until soft and smooth then add the chocolate and beat until incorporated. Add the remaining sugar substitute, mixing until well incorporated, then add the eggs, one at a time, beating until combined. Add the cream, almond and vanilla essences and beat until it is very smooth.

Pour the mixture into the prepared ramekins, then pour enough boiling water into the roasting tin to come halfway up the sides of the dishes. Bake for 20 minutes until puffed and the middle is just set. Remove from the oven and cool in a water bath for 10 minutes, then place on a wire rack to cool to room temperature. Refrigerate until well chilled and serve cold.

> Per serving: Net Carbs: 20.3g • Fibre: 2g • Protein: 10.2g
> Fat: 40g • Calories: 438

CAKES AND BISCUITS

Although you cannot have any of these cakes and biscuits during Induction, you can eat all of them during OWL. A real treat to look forward to.

Spice Cake

serves 9

6 eggs
60g/5½ oz soy flour
110g/4oz granular sugar
  substitute
1½ teaspoons ground ginger
½ teaspoon ground cinnamon
¼ teaspoon ground allspice
⅛ teaspoon ground cloves
120g/4½ oz butter, melted and
  cooled
60ml/2floz water

Preheat the oven to 180°C/350°F/gas 4.

Grease a 23-cm/9-inch square baking tin.

In a large bowl, beat the eggs for 5 minutes, until they form a ribbon when the beater is lifted from the bowl.

Meanwhile, in another bowl whisk the soy flour, sugar substitute, ginger, cinnamon, allspice and cloves together. Stir in the butter and water and mix well.

Stir one-third of the eggs into the spice mixture to lighten and combine. In two additions, fold the remaining eggs into the spice mixture then pour the cake mix into the prepared tin. Bake for 20 minutes, until a metal skewer inserted into the centre comes out clean. Serve either warm or at room temperature, cut into squares.

> Per serving: Net Carbs: 10.3g • Fibre: 1.9g • Protein: 8g
> Fat: 15.6g • Calories: 218

Coffee Cream Layer Cake

Preheat the oven to 140°C/275°F/gas 1.

Butter three 23-cm (9-inch) round cake tins.

Whisk the egg whites until they form soft peaks. Add 1 tablespoon of sugar substitute and beat until stiff. Divide the whites between the three tins. Bake for 45 minutes, then leave in the oven to cool.

Combine half the cream and the instant decaffeinated coffee granules in the top of a double boiler. Stir with a wire whisk until the granules dissolve.

Dissolve the gelatine in the cold water. Add the gelatine to the coffee mixture and heat just to boiling point, stirring constantly with a whisk. Remove from the heat and whisk in the egg yolks, 1 yolk at a time. Add the butter and beat well until melted. Add the flavourings and remaining sugar substitute, then put in a freezer to cool.

Whip the remaining cream until stiff.

When the coffee mixture is cool, fold it into the whipped cream and refrigerate until the meringue layers have cooked and cooled down.

Pile the cream between the layers of meringue as you would ice a layer cake. Top with the coffee cream, making sure you cover the sides. Sprinkle the nuts on the top and sides and refrigerate the cake until you are ready to serve.

> Per serving: Net Carbs: 6.5g • Fibre: 0.5g • Protein: 5.2g
> Fat: 30g • Calories: 313

serves 10

5 egg whites, at room temperature
4 tablespoons granular sugar substitute
500ml/16floz double cream
1½ teaspoons instant decaffeinated coffee granules
1½ teaspoons gelatine
1 tablespoon cold water
4 egg yolks, at room temperature
50g/2oz butter, at room temperature
1 teaspoon coffee flavouring
1 teaspoon chocolate flavouring
80g/3oz chopped walnuts

Peanut Butter Cookies

40 cookies

125g/4$^{1}/_{2}$ oz chunky, sugar-free
   peanut butter
185ml/6floz double cream
75g/3oz chopped pecans
2 teaspoons vanilla essence
2$^{1}/_{2}$ tablespoons granular sugar
   substitute
2 tablespoons soy flour
1 teaspoon baking powder

Preheat the oven to 190°C/375°F/gas 5.

Spray a baking tray with oil.

Mix all the ingredients together in a bowl and blend well.

Place teaspoonfuls of the cookie mixture onto the tray and bake for about 10 minutes or until lightly browned.

> Per cookie: Net Carbs: 1.6g • Fibre: 0.4g • Protein: 1g
> Fat: 4.2g • Calories: 48

Pecan Orange Macaroons

30 macaroons

90g/3$^{1}/_{2}$ oz unsweetened flaked
   coconut
40g/1$^{1}/_{2}$ oz pecans, lightly
   toasted and finely chopped
2 tablespoons double cream
$^{1}/_{4}$ teaspoon pure orange
   extract
2 large egg whites, at room
   temperature
$^{1}/_{4}$ teaspoon cream of tartar
110g/4oz granular sugar
   substitute

Preheat the oven to 180°C/350°F/gas 4.

Mix the coconut, pecans, cream and orange extract together in a bowl.

Beat the egg whites until thick and foamy. Add the cream of tartar and the sugar substitute gradually, beating until stiff peaks form. Gradually fold in the coconut mixture.

Line two baking trays with parchment paper and drop slightly rounded teaspoonfuls (walnut size) onto the sheets. Bake for 10 to 12 minutes until the tops are lightly browned and the bottom is golden. Cool on a wire rack.

> Per macaroon: Net Carbs: 3.5g • Fibre: 0.5g • Protein: 0.5g
> Fat: 2.4g • Calories: 31

DRINKS

You can have Spiced Iced Decaf Coffee and Iced Chamomile Tea during Induction, Mocha Coffee and Hot Chocolate during OWL, and Thick Raspberry Shake in Lifetime Maintenance.

Iced Chamomile Tea

serves 1

4 chamomile tea bags
1.4 litres/2¼ pints water
3 teaspoons granular sugar substitute
2 tablespoons fresh lemon juice

Brew the tea bags in the boiling water for 5 minutes, then discard the tea bags and chill the tea for 1 hour.

Dissolve the sugar substitute in the cold tea, add the lemon juice, stir and serve over ice.

Per serving: Net Carbs: 5.1g • Fibre: 0.1g • Protein: 0.2g
Fat: 0g • Calories: 19

Thick Raspberry Shake

serves 2

2 scoops Vanilla Ice Cream (page 169) or Raspberry Rapture Ice Cream (page 168)
250ml/8floz diet ginger ale
45ml/1½ floz double cream
1–2 teaspoons raspberry flavouring

Place all the ingredients in a blender and blend for 1 minute at medium speed, then pour into a tall glass.

Per serving: Net Carbs: 16.4g • Fibre: 0g • Protein: 1.5g
Fat: 9.9g • Calories: 158

Hot Chocolate

serves 1

80ml/2¹/₂ floz double cream
160ml/5¹/₂ floz water
2 teaspoons granular sugar
   substitute
1 teaspoon unsweetened cocoa
¹/₂ teaspoon vanilla essence
whipped cream

Place all the ingredients in a saucepan and heat to boiling point, stirring constantly, but do not boil.

Serve in a mug, with a dollop of whipped cream on top, if desired.

> Per serving: Net Carbs: 8.9g • Fibre: 0.6g • Protein: 2.2g
> Fat: 30g • Calories: 312

Mocha Coffee

serves 1

1 recipe Hot Chocolate (above)
¹/₂ teaspoon instant coffee
   granules
¹/₂ teaspoon brandy essence
1 cinnamon stick

Make the *Hot Chocolate*, then add the coffee and brandy essence.

Serve in a mug with a cinnamon stick.

> Per serving: Net Carbs: 9.1g • Fibre: 0.6g • Protein: 2.2g
> Fat: 30g • Calories: 319

Spiced Iced Decaf Coffee

serves 4

2 tablespoons decaffeinated
   instant coffee granules
750ml/1¹/₄ pints boiling water
5 whole allspice
5 whole cloves
dash cinnamon
8 ice cubes
4 teaspoons double cream

Combine all the ingredients except for the ice cubes and cream in a 1-litre/ 1³/₄-pint container. Cover and refrigerate for 1 hour or more.

When you are ready to serve the drink, strain it, and pour over ice cubes into four tall glasses. Top each glass with 1 teaspoon of cream.

> Per serving: Net Carbs: 1.5g • Fibre: 0.5g • Protein: 0.5g
> Fat: 19g • Calories: 27

Entertaining

ENTERTAINING

When you are controlling your carb intake, you can still easily entertain friends. During Induction you are allowed all the recipes in this section except for Crunchy Seafood Salad, Gnocchi, Ginger and Apricot Pork Tenderloin, Chocolate Brownies and Chocolate Fudge, all of which you can introduce during OWL. You have to wait until Pre-Maintenance before you can have either Almond Stuffing or Earl Grey Pots de Crème.

Sour Cream Clam Dip

serves 8

250g/9oz sour cream
1 x 200-g/7oz can chopped
    clams, drained, reserving
    1 tablespoon juice
4 tablespoons mayonnaise
1 tablespoon grated onion
1 teaspoon celery seeds
1 tablespoon fresh lemon juice
1 tablespoon Worcestershire
    sauce
salt and freshly ground black
    pepper to taste

Mix all the ingredients together well and refrigerate for at least 1 hour before eating. Serve with vegetables or low carb crudités.

> Per serving: Net Carbs: 4.1g • Fibre: 0g • Protein: 7.5g
> Fat: 11.3g • Calories: 153

Klara's Aubergine Dip

serves 6

1 medium aubergine
1 medium onion, peeled and
    thinly sliced
1 tablespoon extra-virgin
    olive oil
1 teaspoon balsamic vinegar
1/4 teaspoon salt
freshly ground black pepper to
    taste

Preheat the oven to 140°C/275°F/gas 1.

Bake the aubergine for 1 hour until soft. Leave to cool then peel. Mash the aubergine until smooth and combine with the remaining ingredients. Chill, then serve with low carb crackers.

> Per serving: Net Carbs: 4.2g • Fibre: 2.2g • Protein: 1g
> Fat: 2.4g • Calories: 47

Cold Avocado Soup

Place the avocado, lime juice, salt, pepper and nutmeg in a blender and add 125ml/4floz of the *Chicken Stock*. Blend for 30 seconds at high speed, then pour into a large bowl

Whisk in the remaining stock and chill until icy cold.

Serve In soup bowls garnished with a spoonful of whipped cream and a sprinkle of nutmeg.

> Per serving: Net Carbs: 2.3g • Fibre: 1.7g • Protein: 1.2g
> Fat: 9.2g • Calories: 97

serves 6

1 avocado (about 500g/1lb 2oz), peeled, stoned and finely chopped
45ml/1½ floz fresh lime juice
½ teaspoon salt
pinch freshly ground black pepper
pinch nutmeg
750ml/1¼ pints Chicken Stock (see page 61)
60ml/2floz double cream, whipped, to top
nutmeg, to top

Japanese Egg Custard

Preheat the oven to 150°C/300°F/gas 2.

Combine the chicken or prawns, water chestnuts, mushrooms, spring onions and sherry in a bowl. Mix well, then divide the mixture evenly between six ramekins.

Beat the eggs, salt and *Beef Stock* together. Pour into the ramekins and cover with the spinach or lettuce leaves.

Place in a large roasting tin and pour in enough boiling water to come halfway up the sides of the ramekins. Cover the tin with foil and bake for 30 minutes or until the mixture is set. Serve in the ramekins.

> Per serving: Net Carbs: 3.7g • Fibre: 1g • Protein: 13g
> Fat: 5.4g • Calories: 126

serves 6

140g/5oz cooked chicken, finely chopped, or raw prawns, peeled and finely chopped
3 water chestnuts, finely chopped
6 mushrooms, finely chopped
2 spring onions, chopped
1 tablespoon sherry
4 eggs, beaten
1 teaspoon salt
750ml/1¼ pints Beef Stock (see page 60)
12 spinach or lettuce leaves

Crunchy Seafood Salad

serves 6

1 x 180-g/6-oz can tuna
1 x 180-g/6-oz can crabmeat
1 x 180-g/6-oz can prawns, or
    fresh prawns, cooked and
    peeled
1 large head lettuce
120g/4$^{1}/_{2}$oz celery, finely
    chopped
80g/3oz spring onions, chopped
$^{1}/_{2}$ medium ripe avocado,
    peeled, stoned and chopped
50g/2oz walnuts, chopped
50g/2oz roasted unsalted
    soybeans
50g/2oz sunflower seeds
2 hard-boiled eggs, diced
1 tomato, cut in wedges

Drain the three cans of seafood and discard the bony tissue from the crab. Mix them together in a bowl and refrigerate.

Combine the remaining ingredients except for the tomato in a large salad bowl and toss well. Add the seafood and toss well again.

Add the salad dressing of your choice (see pages 84 to 89). Toss the salad again before serving, and decorate with tomato wedges.

Per serving: Net Carbs: 6.5g • Fibre: 5g • Protein: 27.5g
Fat: 16g • Calories: 290

Chicken Salad

serves 2

280g/10oz cooked chicken,
    skinned and diced
60g/2$^{1}/_{2}$oz marinated artichoke
    hearts, drained
20 green olives, stoned and
    sliced
30g/1oz finely chopped onion
15g/$^{1}/_{2}$oz unsalted butter,
    melted
2 tablespoons crème fraîche or
    sour cream
2 tablespoons mayonnaise
salt to taste

Toss the first five ingredients together.

Mix the crème fraîche and mayonnaise together, then add to the chicken mixture. Mix well and season with salt. Refrigerate until needed.

Per serving: Net Carbs: 7.1g • Fibre: 1.6g • Protein: 42.3g
Fat: 33.8g • Calories: 501

Pork Loin with Mustard

serves 6

6 x 1-cm/^{1}/$_2$-in slices of
  boneless pork loin
salt and freshly ground black
  pepper to taste
1 tablespoon olive oil
30g/1oz shallots, peeled and
  chopped
60ml/2floz dry white wine
185ml/6floz Chicken Stock
  (see page 61)
2 teaspoons granular sugar
  substitute
1 tablespoon Dijon mustard

Season the pork well with salt and pepper.

Heat the oil in a large frying pan over a medium heat but do not allow it to smoke. Fry the pork until cooked and brown, then transfer to a plate and cover to keep warm. Lower the heat, add the shallots to the pan and cook for about 3 minutes.

Pour in the wine and simmer until the liquid has reduced by half. Add the *Chicken Stock* and sugar substitute and whisk the mixture as it boils until the liquid is reduced by half. Add the pork and simmer for about 2 minutes until it is warm and has absorbed some of the sauce. Remove the pork to a serving plate then whisk the mustard into the sauce, adjust the seasoning, and spoon the remaining sauce over the pork.

> Per serving: Net Carbs: 2.3g • Fibre: 0g • Protein: 24g
> Fat: 15.5g • Calories: 255

Ginger and Apricot Pork Tenderloin

serves 4

2 whole pork tenderloins, about
  675g/1^1/$_2$ lb in total
500ml/16floz Chicken Stock
  (see page 61)
3 tablespoons grated ginger
  root
2 tablespoons no-sugar-added
  apricot jam or no-sugar-
  added marmalade
2 tablespoons soy sauce
2 cloves garlic, peeled and
  finely chopped

Combine all the ingredients in a large bowl and marinate in the refrigerator for at least 2, and up to 6, hours.

Preheat the oven to 200°C/400°F/gas 6.

Place the pork in a roasting tin, discarding the marinade, and roast for 20 minutes or until a meat thermometer registers 80°C/160°F. When cooked, leave the pork to stand for 10 minutes before slicing, for easier carving.

> Per serving: Net Carbs: 3g • Fibre: 0.5g • Protein: 36.5g
> Fat: 6g • Calories: 218

Roast Turkey

Preheat the oven to 200°C/400°F/gas 6.

Remove the giblets from the cavity of the turkey then run it under cold water to rinse it. Dry the turkey well with kitchen paper, then rub with the cut side of the garlic inside and out. Place sliced orange and lemon in the cavity and use the *Almond Stuffing* (below) to stuff the neck, not the cavity.

Tie the legs together. Bend the wing tips under the body and tuck the loose neck skin under the turkey to encase the stuffing. Place the turkey, breast-side up, in a covered stainless-steel roasting tin. Place the bacon rashers over the breast.

Bake for 20 minutes then turn the heat down to 180°C/350°F/gas 4 and cook for 3 hours. To check if it is cooked through, pierce the thickest part of the thigh to make sure the juices are running clear, without any blood. Garnish with sprigs of bay and rosemary, if desired.

> Per serving: Net Carbs: 0.2g • Fibre: 0g • Protein: 87g
> Fat: 15g • Calories: 650

serves 10

1 x 5.4kg/12lb turkey
1 large clove garlic, peeled and
   halved
1 orange, sliced
1 lemon, sliced
6 rashers of streaky bacon
sprigs of bay and rosemary, to
   garnish

Almond Stuffing

Melt the butter in a large frying pan, then add the onion and fry until light brown. Add the ham, parsley, thyme and pepper and mix well. Combine the mixture with the breadcrumbs, eggs, wine and almonds.

Use to stuff chicken, turkey, veal roast, or anything that needs a stuffing.

> Per serving: Net Carbs: 15.8g • Fibre: 3.5g • Protein: 16.3g
> Fat: 32.3g • Calories: 444

serves 6

120g/4¹/₂ oz butter
80g/3oz finely chopped onion
225g/8oz smoked ham,
   finely chopped
1 tablespoon chopped parsley
1 tablespoon chopped thyme
¹/₂ teaspoon freshly ground
   black pepper
250ml/8floz low carbohydrate
   breadcrumbs
2 eggs
60ml/2floz dry red wine
90g/3¹/₂oz blanched almonds,
   chopped finely

Tarragon Lobster Tails

Preheat the grill.

Remove the soft part of the lobster tail with scissors. Hit the hard shell slightly with a mallet or cleaver to make it lie flat.

Melt the butter in a saucepan, then add the ginger, tarragon, mustard and salt. Spoon generously over the tails, reserving a little for basting, and leave to stand for 20 minutes.

Grill the lobster tails about 10cm/4in from the heat for 10 to 15 minutes with the meaty side upwards, basting frequently.

serves 2

4 lobster tails, thawed if frozen
60g/2¹/₂ oz butter
1 tablespoon chopped ginger
    root (or 1 teaspoon ground)
1 teaspoon chopped tarragon
    (or ¹/₂ teaspoon dried)
¹/₂ teaspoon dry mustard
salt to taste

> Per serving: Net Carbs: 4g • Fibre: 0.2g • Protein: 50g
> Fat: 38g • Calories: 570

Fresh Spring Salmon Mousse

Place the salmon fillets in a saucepan and cover with water. Cover the pan and simmer the fish for 7 to 10 minutes, until cooked. Remove the fish from the pan, allow to cool, then remove the skin and bones.

Soften the gelatine in the cold water. Heat in a saucepan until completely dissolved, then cool.

Mix the sour cream and mayonnaise together. Add the gelatine and chill until slightly thickened.

Flake the salmon and add the onion powder, capers, dill, cucumber and salt. Mix well with the sour cream mixture.

Pour into a 1.25-litre/2-pint capacity mould and refrigerate until firm. Unmould and serve.

serves 8

675g/1¹/₂ lb fresh salmon
2 tablespoons gelatine
375ml/12floz cold water
140g/5oz sour cream
225g/8oz mayonnaise
¹/₂ teaspoon onion powder
1 tablespoon capers, drained
2 teaspoons chopped dill
120g/4¹/₂ oz cucumber, peeled,
    deseeded and chopped
1 teaspoon salt

> Per serving: Net Carbs: 1.7g • Fibre: 0.1g • Protein: 24g
> Fat: 28g • Calories: 368

Gnocchi

serves 8

450g/1lb ricotta cheese,
    pressed of liquid
225g/8oz full fat soft cream
    cheese or Boursin cheese
3 eggs, beaten
15g/^{1}/2 oz soy flour
dash of salt, cayenne pepper
    and nutmeg
225g/8oz unsalted butter,
    melted
50g/2oz Parmesan cheese,
    grated

Push the ricotta cheese and soft cheese through a fine sieve. (The easiest and fastest way is with your hands.)

Beat the eggs into the mixture with an electric or rotary beater. Blend in the soy flour and seasonings, then refrigerate for about 1 hour.

Bring a large pot of water to the boil. Lower the heat to just simmering and drop the cheese mixture into the water by teaspoonfuls. (They will drop and then rise to the top.)

Allow the gnocchi to poach (simmer on top of the water) for about 20 minutes. Remove carefully with a slotted spoon and allow to drain on kitchen paper.

Put half the butter in a large baking dish then place the drained gnocchi on top. Cover with the remaining melted butter and grated Parmesan cheese.

Gnocchi may be served immediately, kept warm in a low oven or refrigerated and reheated.

> Per serving: Net Carbs: 4.2g • Fibre: 0g • Protein: 14g
> Fat: 44g • Calories: 460

Asparagus with Goat's Cheese

serves 4

450g/1lb asparagus
45ml/1¹/₂ floz extra-virgin
    olive oil
30ml/1floz white wine
60g/2¹/₂ oz goat's cheese
2 sun-dried tomatoes in olive
    oil, finely chopped

Preheat the oven to 180°C/350°F/gas 4.

Wash and trim the asparagus, then place in a glass baking dish.

Mix the olive oil and wine together and sprinkle over the asparagus. Dot with the goat's cheese and sun-dried tomatoes. Cover and bake for 15 minutes or until the vegetables are tender.

> Per serving: Net Carbs: 3.1g • Fibre: 2.5g • Protein: 5.2g
> Fat: 13.5g • Calories: 162

Ricotta-stuffed Courgettes

serves 4

2 courgettes
90g/3¹/₂ oz ricotta cheese
1 teaspoon chopped parsley
1 teaspoon dried basil, or
    1 tablespoon fresh, chopped
¹/₂ teaspoon dried oregano, or
    1¹/₂ teaspoons fresh,
    chopped
1 egg white, whisked stiffly
250ml/8floz prepared tomato
    sauce or passata

Preheat the oven to 150°C/300°F/gas 2.

Cut the courgettes into halves lengthways and scoop out the pulp, leaving a 1-cm/¹/₂in shell.

Combine the ricotta, parsley, basil and oregano and mix well. Fold in the egg white.

Stuff the mixture into the halved courgettes. Place in a baking dish and pour the tomato sauce or passata over the top.

Bake for 10 minutes, then lower the oven temperature to 120°C/250°F/gas ³/₄ and cook for a further 30 minutes. Baste frequently so they don't burn.

> Per serving: Net Carbs: 6.3g • Fibre: 2.2g • Protein: 5.5g
> Fat: 3.2g • Calories: 78

Lemon–Lime Mousse

serves 8

120g/4$\frac{1}{2}$oz butter
9 egg yolks
90ml/3floz fresh lemon juice
90ml/3floz fresh lime juice
3 tablespoons granular sugar
    substitute
2 teaspoons grated lemon zest
4 egg whites
1 teaspoon vanilla essence
375ml/12floz double cream

Melt the butter in a saucepan over a low heat. Beat in the egg yolks, one at a time, with a wire whisk. Remove from the heat, then add the lemon and lime juice, 2$\frac{1}{2}$ tablespoons of the sugar substitute and the lemon zest. Beat well, then cool.

Whisk the egg whites with the remaining sugar substitute and vanilla essence, then fold into the chilled mixture.

Whip the cream and fold into the mixture.

Refrigerate for at least 2 hours before serving.

> Per serving: Net Carbs: 7.2g • Fibre: 0.1g • Protein: 6g
> Fat: 38.2g • Calories: 393

Earl Grey Pots de Crème

serves 4

250ml/8floz double cream
60ml/2floz water
2 Earl Grey tea bags
3 egg yolks
75ml/2$\frac{1}{2}$floz sour cream
50g/2oz granular sugar
    substitute

Preheat the oven to 160°C/325°F/gas 3.

In a saucepan over a medium heat bring the cream and water to a simmer. Add the tea bags, cover the pan and leave to stand for 10 minutes. Squeeze out the tea bags and discard.

Whisk the egg yolks, sour cream and sugar substitute into the warm cream mixture until combined.

Pour the mixture through a strainer into four ramekins and place them in a large roasting tin. Carefully pour boiling water into the tin until the water comes halfway up the sides of the ramekins, then put the tin in the oven. Cover the entire tin with foil and bake for 33 to 35 minutes, until the custards are set but slightly wobbly in the centre. Leave to stand in the covered tin at room temperature for 15 minutes.

Remove the cups from the tin, cover with clingfilm (make sure it does not touch the custard) and refrigerate until cold.

> Per serving: Net Carbs: 15.1g • Fibre: 0g • Protein: 3.3g
> Fat: 28g • Calories: 297

Chocolate Brownies

30 squares

120g/4$\frac{1}{2}$ oz butter, at room temperature
2 eggs
3 tablespoons cocoa
2 tablespoons water
2 teaspoons chocolate flavouring
2 tablespoons soy flour
5 tablespoons granular sugar substitute
80g/3oz walnuts, coarsely chopped
45ml/1$\frac{1}{2}$ floz crème de cacao liqueur

Preheat the oven to 180°C/350°F/gas 4.

Grease a 20-cm/8-in cake tin or shallow 1.5-litre/2$\frac{1}{2}$-pint baking dish.

Cream the butter with an electric hand mixer. Add the eggs one at a time, beating well. Beat in the cocoa, water and flavouring. Add the soy flour and sugar substitute. Mix well and fold in the walnuts.

Turn the batter into a prepared tin and smooth the top. Bake for 15 minutes but do not overcook. Remove from the oven and sprinkle the crème de cacao over the top. Cool, then cut into at least 30 squares.

> Per square: Net Carbs: 2.5g • Fibre: 0.4g • Protein: 1g
> Fat: 6.3g • Calories: 72

Chocolate Fudge

15 squares

1 x 47-g/2-oz packet sugar-free chocolate instant pudding/dessert mix
125ml/4floz double cream
2$\frac{1}{2}$ tablespoons granular sugar substitute
1 tablespoon crème de cacao liqueur
50g/2oz chunky, sugar-free peanut butter

Mix all the ingredients together except for the peanut butter. Place in a saucepan over a low heat, melt, then add the peanut butter. Heat until the peanut butter melts and stir until well blended.

Lightly spray a small baking dish with oil and spoon the fudge mixture into the dish. Refrigerate until firm, then slice into at least 15 squares.

> Per square: Net Carbs: 5.9g • Fibre: 0.2g • Protein: 1g
> Fat: 4.5g • Calories: 67

Nutritional Supplementation

Can everyone get adequate nutrients from dietary sources? Unfortunately, the answer is probably not. Refined carbohydrates, including sugar and bleached flour, which form the basis of the typical British diet, provide very few nutrients. When you follow Atkins, you eat nutrient-dense foods, but it is still wise to supplement meals with vitamins, minerals, antioxidants and essential fatty acids. This is due both to the increasing depletion of nutrients in our soil and the parallel increasing toll on our bodies as a result of environmental toxins. Anyone, whether on the Atkins Nutritional Approach™ or on any other dietary programme, simply cannot be sure that he or she is getting adequate amounts of many nutrients from food sources. The consumption of supplementary vitamins and minerals is therefore essential to ensure optimal nutrition, which will help improve health and reduce the risk of disease.

Atkins Nutritionals makes two supplements that are specifically formulated to meet the nutrient needs of individuals following a controlled carbohydrate nutritional approach. They also contain natural substances that can help manage your appetite and metabolize fat. Atkins™ supplements contain only high-quality ingredients with no artificial ingredients, flavours, colours, hydrogenated oils, corn, wheat, salt, sugar, starch or gluten.

Atkins Basic 3™ is formulated with more than 24 nutrients to provide essential vitamins and minerals as well as antioxidants known to help neutralize the damaging effects of excess free radicals.

Atkins Essential Omegas™ contains omega-3 and omega-6 fatty acids from borage, fish and flaxseed oils to help maintain a healthy heart and circulation, as well as proper metabolic function, healthy joints and good immune system function.

For more information on Atkins supplements go to www.atkins.com/uk

Index